For [illegible]

Kushty Bok!

[illegible]

August 2017.

The Road to
CARAMEE

L. E. Hartley

authorHOUSE®

AuthorHouse™ UK
1663 Liberty Drive
Bloomington, IN 47403 USA
www.authorhouse.co.uk
Phone: 0800.197.4150

Images are property of the author
Illustrations by Colm Kenny

Published by AuthorHouse 02/18/2017

ISBN: 978-1-5246-7771-8 (sc)
ISBN: 978-1-5246-7772-5 (hc)
ISBN: 978-1-5246-7773-2 (e)

Print information available on the last page.

This book is printed on acid-free paper.

Contents

Dedication

To those who travelled the roads
before us, and the few who continued
to live the life after us.
Special thanks to the memory of
Aimi Becket Richardson and Tim Higgins for
the gift of our grandsons Jed and Erik.

Foreword

Twelfth Night approaches and the specially commissioned play is ready for performance. Still no title has been decided. Arguments amongst the cast haven't helped Will come to a final decision. In exasperation he presents it with the working title, and adds the subtitle 'Or What You Will.'

Four centuries later, on the eve of publication, I'm being bombarded by alternative titles for this long-awaited book. Originally written twenty-five years ago, I had no hesitation in calling it 'The Road To Caramee.' Except possibly the spelling of the place name, more correctly 'Cahirmee'.

Now family members, who feel quite rightly that it is their story too, have other ideas.

Should we cash-in on the 'Big Fat Gypsy' craze by including that in the title?

What about 'Sullivan's Travels'?

Or 'A Gypsy Horse's Tale/ tail/ trail/ trial'?

Stop! Should I just throw in the Shakespeare cop-out?

So, if anyone reading this thinks they have a better title, feel free to let me know. Meantime, the little-changed manuscript can go to print with its original title.

Be lucky,

L.E. Hartley,

February, 2017

Introduction

Ireland in the early 1980s was a very different place. Different to the Ireland of today. Different to anywhere else.

When the actual counterparts of the fictional characters depicted here arrived with a young family and an old dog, they left a Britain made intolerable by the changing laws introduced by the Old Iron Lady.

Having played their parts in the Free Festival movement, including the instigation of the infamous 'Convoy', they had already been horse-drawn for several years before taking The Boat. Living under canvas symbolized a kind of freedom. Ireland offered a decade-long extension of the chosen lifestyle.

Roadside verges, the Long Acre, stretched the length and breadth of the country. Overgrown hedgerows provided abundant firing. Water was rarely refused. In the days before Charity Shops became the norm, people were happy to pass on their unwanted clothes by the bag-full.

The seasons rolled by under the wheels of various horse-drawn vehicles. The Fairs were the meeting places of traditional travellers along with an ever-increasing band of 'New Agers'. Halcyon days we thought would last a lifetime.

Rocking and Pounding signalled the End for most.

Rocking? The practice of closing off every roadside camp with massive boulders.

Pounding? The snatching of horses from the remaining verges, usually during the night. The Pound they would be taken to was often far from the camp, in another part of the country. Gardai would accompany the impounders, so that even if they were heard and seen, there was no way of stopping them. The next day would begin the heartbreaking task of first of all finding where the horses had been taken to, tracking them down with the help of friends who had motors. Reclaiming them from amongst the tragic collection herded together in concrete yards. This involved presenting 'official' documents signed by Justices of the Peace, and the further expense of paying considerable sums of money for their release.

So, let Sullivan tell the story of just one year. Close to the time when the song prophesied "Your travelling days will soon be over..." but still filled with an optimism inspired by the freedom of the Open Road.

TIPPERARY CO. COUNCIL
NO CAMPING
OR
OVERNIGHT

Chapter One

"Sullivan John
down the road
you've gone,
Far away from
your native
home.
You've gone with
the tinker's
daughter,
Down the road
for to roam."

The woman's voice was anything but melodious as she chanted out the words to the song in time to my hoofbeats, but it was a voice that reassured me of my place in her life, and I was always happy to hear it close by. Until I heard that voice, I never understood the bond that other horses formed with people. No one had ever spoken to me the way she did, communicated with me in the way that only other horses had previously.

The first time I heard that voice was at the end of a long day in a ramshackle horse-box of sorts. I had been driven round the country all day. Through towns and villages, along lakeshore and between hills. I was cramped and uncomfortable and longing to just be out of this situation. Every time we stopped, I looked around hoping to see a lush meadow waiting for me. A cool stream to quench my road-dusty thirsty. Most of the stops were in traffic. Lights, junctions. Others were at camps like the one I left, or farmyard entrances.

But the last stop of that weary day was the one that changed my life. It would be a long time before I'd ever see the inside of a horse-box again.

The brake-lights of the old van twinkled, and the dilapidated contraption it was towing juddered to a halt.

I tentatively poked my nose out through the gap in the fence-wire and baler-twine that crisscrossed the top of the box, and shifted my weight.

Driver talking to the woman at the fire.

She lifts the black iron disc, with its mouth-watering-fresh bread onto the grass and hangs her kettle over the flames.

Stands, a good hand taller than the man stepping out of the van.

'Would you buy a good horse, Ma'am?'

'We've too many horses already. I'll sell you one!'

'What have you?' He has to know.

So they talk on for a while.

I struggle to turn my neck and see where I might be. It's a quiet lane, trees and bushes along both sides. Two curious-looking vehicles parked up on the narrow verge. A half-grown girl taking the bread from the fire-iron and spreading it with some other delicious smelling food before handing it to a pair of much younger girls.

I'd been inside this cramped space for most of the day; my hunger was genuine.

'Hey!' I called out to the girl. 'Give me some, please!'

'He's talking to you, Blue,' said the woman. 'Sounds like he wants a taste, too!'

The girl came over and shared her bit of bread with me. I thanked her most sincerely, then called to the woman, 'Is there more?'

She obligingly started to break another slice, the one from the bottom of the stack. Its smoky flavour was the best thing I'd ever tasted up to that time. I whickered my appreciation as the woman and I looked steadily into each other's eyes. Even the driver seemed to understand what I was saying:

'You've a friend for life now,' he told her.

'You like my burnt bread?' she asked me, and I licked her hands all over and rubbed them with my lips for another taste of the floury dough.

'Shall we get him out of the box?' she asks the driver, at which the two younger men climb down from the Hi-ace and start to untie the ropes and strings and wires that are holding the door on.

The clattering and jolting put the fear in me again as I think of having to step backwards as the floor tips; and the drop onto the road that always takes the skin off my knees, as the men lash me about the face with their whippy sticks. And there they are, in the hedgerow, tearing branches from a young ash-plant.

'Help me!' I give the woman my most pleading look. It sounds like a note of barely concealed panic in my throat as the men start waving the branches right in front of my face.

I throw my head back before remembering that I have it stuck through the entanglement over the top of the box. I'm stuck fast, and being lashed about the ears doesn't help me think of a way out.

'Wait! Wait!' The woman puts my plea into a language they seem to understand

'For godsakes! You're only frightening him. Just let him be quiet for a minute! I'll see him in the box.'

She stepped up off the road, tipping the trailer slightly. My feet start to slip, but it's more skittishness than real danger. I'm looking over my shoulder as she gently rests a hand on my back and walks steadily towards my head.

'Pass me a knife!' she calls to the girl, and talks quietly to me, rubbing behind my ears to ease my head away from the baler twine cutting into the top of my neck. A moment later the pain is gone and my head is free, but I'm still in the box, and the men with their sticks are still in front of me.

The woman is berating the driver about the state of the box: he's making some excuse about only having borrowed it.

When she talks to me, her voice overrides my fears; 'Come on, now. Brave boy! You can do it. That's right, give me your head down here, and...'

pushing me firmly on the shoulder with one hand as she holds my nose down with the other, 'Go BACK!'

I really want to trust her, want to believe I can do it. A short step back, another. Then the box starts to tip, my head rears up and hits off one of the bars over the middle of the open 'roof'. The branch is in my face immediately and the panic takes over again as my first foot slides back into the nothingness above the road. The woman is still beside me, shouting 'No! Stop!' to the man waving the branch, and 'Go on! Good boy!' to me.

Both back feet hit the road and she keeps the steady pressure on my shoulder to persuade me backwards. My front feet tremble and wobble uncontrollably as the rickety old trailer tips and rattles about me. Really there's no choice: my back feet have found firm ground, front feet make the cat-leap necessary to join them.

'Good boy, brave boy!' she murmurs in my ear as she pats my forehead with her floury hands. I rub my face against her shoulder and shake a cloud of dust from my coat to express my relief at being on solid ground.

The woman takes me by the forelock and saying 'Walk on!' leads me onto the verge behind the larger of the two parked vehicles. The grass is long and sweet and all I can think to do is pack as much as I can into my empty belly as she runs her hands over me, talking all the while to the little man who brought me here.

He's telling her how he paid 'twenty-eight hundred pounds' for my mother, and how she and I won the prize at Ballinasloe the year before last for 'Best Mare & Foal' at the show.

I don't remember that, but I was very young then!

And how I was 'cut' as a yearling because I was left running in the field with the mares and fillies. Ah, yes, I remember that day well enough! Being taken from the field and stood against the barn wall, calling all the time to my mother and the others. But they just ignored my calls, or worse... jeered at me, while the men held me with strong ropes about the neck and legs. A sort of numbness crept over my whole body then, and all my muscles relaxed at once so that I had no power to fight or run, but could only lean against the wall to stop myself from falling over.

Next thing I knew the men were all walking back to the road, and behind me a couple of lurchers were squabbling over two big lumps of steaming hot meat.

Some time later I was turned back into the field, a dull ache between my hind legs as the feeling came back into muscles.

I hobbled straight over to tell my mother, but she was busy suckling her new foal and just lashed a kick at me. The other mares and fillies were no more sympathetic. The two geldings who shared our field came over to me then and talked to me in a way they never had before. I'd never bothered with them, much preferring the company of the fillies, but now it was as if they understood what had happened to me. They were commiserating and at the same time offering me membership of a different 'club'.

The pain gradually subsided, and by the end of the week I was running around the same as before. But the mares and foals didn't let me forget. I'd lost all status within their herd; the mares no longer treating me as a foal, the fillies soon tiring of my attentions. The games we used to play had become somehow pointless now.

The seasons had rolled on since that day: through the cold dark hungry months when I had to suffer the bites and kicks of the mares for every mouthful of hay that was put over the wall.

They were all in foal, most were still suckling too: I had to content myself with whatever was left spread in the mud when they'd finished. The gnawing hunger was never really satisfied till the days started to get longer and the new grass showed around the edges of the field.

Changing Hands.

The woman is running her fingers around the corners of my mouth and asking the man if I've ever been 'tacked'. She disappears inside the vehicle beside us and comes back carrying a big leather object, saying 'I'll just see how he takes the collar.'

With a hand under my chin she lifts my head from the sweet grass. Still chewing on a mouthful, I'm introduced to the collar. She lets me have a good look at it, turning it every which way and then holding it in front of our faces so that I can see her framed by it. Next she puts her head right through the hole in the middle and the collar is on her shoulders.

This is all new to me, obviously.

She says 'Think you can handle that?' and looking me steadily in the eye, slips the collar off her own head and slides it up my face. I let it past my eyes; it feels slightly tight as it goes over my ears, but then it's on my neck.

'Good Boy!' she tells me as she twists it the right way up.

'Fits him perfect,' she says to the man.

When I put my head down for another mouthful of grass the collar slips down and bumps my ears, so she turns it again and takes it off me.

'Try the rest of the harness.' Suggests the little man, but 'No, its okay, so long as the collar fits, the rest will all adjust.'

The woman is looking at my feet. Picking them up, one at a time, and digging into my hooves with a bent piece of metal. Shifting the mud and bits of stone that lodge themselves around my soles. No-one has ever done this to me before. It feels strange at first, standing on three legs, the slight tickle as she runs the metal up the middle of my hoof. As she lowers each one back onto the road it feels good to be rid of all the muck.

'His feet are well over-grown.' She tells the man.

'Aye, that's because he was never shod.'

Leaving me to the grass, the woman picks up the collar. The little man follows her back to the fire. Their voices are indistinct now, blending with the sounds of hedgerow birds and the hum of bees. The edge is gone off my hunger when I look up again at the call of another horse.

I hear his metallic clip clop as the woman leads him along the road. A chain about his neck, a long coil of rope looped over the woman's shoulder.

They stop at the fire and I suppress the urge to call to them. The horse is uneasy, jibing about the road as the three men look him over. He's a bay pony cob, maybe a hand shorter than me, lighter all round.

Next time I lift my nose from the grass it's to watch the woman walking him round the back of the box I arrived in. The men start waving the sticks and the pony jumps nimbly aboard. The woman recovers the chain from around his neck and climbs down onto the road. The two young men are tying the door back on as the woman and the driver stand beside the van in earnest discussion. With a slap of their hands they part company; he hops up behind the wheel and starts the engine. A puff of black smoke as they rev off down the lane.

The woman comes over to me, still carrying the chain. She unties the leather belt from her waist and fastens it around my neck. Then she clips the chain onto the buckle.

'Well, mi-laddo,' she says to me, 'Looks like you're my horse now. Think I'll call you Sullivan. You can call me Liz.' And she gives a little laugh as she leads me onto the road. 'Come with me, Sullivan; we'll go find you some nice grass, and

I'll introduce you to Frankie. He'll tell you all about living with us and what you'll be expected to learn.'

I like the sound and the smell of this woman and I follow her quietly, trustingly down the lane away from the camp. At the crossroad we turn left and then I hear for the first time the call of the horse on the wide verge, away down the lane. He's obviously heard me on the road, looked up from his grazing to give me a sort of 'Who goes there?' call.

I answer him in my friendliest voice. Of course I'm on the defensive. This is his territory, I'm the stranger here. I feel very vulnerable and unsure of myself away from the familiar company of my own herd. As we walk closer I realise from his stance, his call, his smell, that this horse is a full stallion. I've met his kind before. As a tiny foal I was badly kicked by the horse who was left in our field for a few days. He bullied and seemed to fight with all the mares, savagely driving all of us foals away, rearing and screaming at our mothers. As a yearling, I still hadn't forgotten. I ran away and avoided him when he visited the mares again.

Now I was expected to meet with this massive white horse, already lashing out with his front hooves and half rearing on the end of his chain at our approach.

In reality, he was little over a hand taller than me, but as he crashed his great hairy iron-shod feet on the road and gave voice to his stallion-scream he had me rooted to the spot in blind fear.

'Don't mind him, Sullivan,' the woman told me, 'he's just showing off!'

Sensing that at any moment I might turn and run, she led me onto the verge and tied the rope attached to my chain around a road-sign. Patting my neck, saying 'Good boy. Stand up, now!' she left me there and walked on down the road to where the stallion was prancing and calling. Realising that he couldn't reach me, I felt brave enough to take a look at him.

His white body had only one black mark, a large almost-circle on his right flank. Over his ears a black mask fell down both sides of his face, covering his eyes, which were both bright blue. The broad white stripe down his nose was overhung with a long black forelock.

The woman strode right up to him, her hands outstretched, as if she were offering him something. He gave a dismissive snort as my scent told him I wasn't a mare, or even another stallion.

'Easy now, Frankie,' I heard the woman saying. 'This is Sullivan, and he's going to be travelling with us, so you just be nice to him, okay?'

Frankie tossed his great head back, mane flying from his powerful neck and gave a call that left me in no doubt who was Boss around here.

I spoke softly to the woman as she walked back towards me, seeking her reassurance, but she just walked right past me, back to her camp. She soon reappeared carrying two buckets of water. Leaving the first one beside the road sign she carried the other on to where Frankie was tied. He dipped his nose into the water, splashed it around. When he lifted his head, his luxuriant moustache was dripping wet.

This was the first time I'd ever been offered water in a bucket. I was used to wading into the river to get a drink. Sensing my uncertainty the woman came back to me and lifted the bucket to my nose. My thirst overcame my fear of putting my face into the tight space and I drank about half the bucket of water. It had an unfamiliar, earthy taste; the same taste was in the grass here, even in the air. I realised then that I must be in a different part of the country. I could no longer taste the salty air of my birthplace.

'There you go, Sullivan,' the woman was saying to me as she put the half-empty bucket back on the ground 'You'll be alright now?'

I watched her walk down the road till she turned at the crossroads. Frankie had turned his attention back to his grazing, so I just did the same.

Having discovered that the rounded corners of the road sign I was tied to were just the right height for scratching my back, I was giving myself a leisurely rub when two sounds simultaneously broke the quiet of the lane.

One was Frankie's high-pitched whinny, the other the distant clip of shod-hooves at a steady trot. Soon afterwards the other horse came into view. He was moving steadily along the straight road towards the camp and as he passed the crossroads I saw that he was pulling a two wheeled vehicle loaded up with dead wood. A man and a boy were sitting on the ledges on either side. They slowed up and looked down the lane to where Frankie and I were tied.

The horse called out 'Hey, who's the new boy?' and Frankie called back, something like, 'Nobody of any importance!'

There was a hedge alongside the camp but we could see the people moving about, separating the horse from the cart, taking off his harness. It wasn't long before he was coming to join us. A half-grown boy was walking at his head, just behind followed the woman and the man who had been driving the cart.

The horse was a stocky piebald cob, shorter in the leg than me, but every bit as heavy in the body. He was a stallion too, but not much older than me. I knew at once that he would be friendlier than Frankie. He bounced right up to me on the verge and with his face in my face started to ask me everything about myself. He totally overwhelmed me with all his questions, so that I found myself involuntarily opening and closing my mouth, clapping my lips together, but unable to utter a sound.

'Hey, stop that "foaling"! You're bigger than me! C'mon, let's see what you're made of!' and he grabbed my mane in his teeth and pulled me off balance before the boy realised what was happening and shouted to him, 'BUMPER! Easy! Stop that!' and slapped him on the nose.

I recovered myself and tried to keep the panic out of my voice as I said, 'That's not fair, I'm tied up here! You're stronger than me! I don't want to fight anyway!'

Bumper just laughed at me. He was covered in sweat from his work, but still bursting with energy. He wanted to rough and tumble with me but I was just not used to his boisterous play, and I told him so.

'Ah, you'll soon get used to it!' he assured me, as the boy led him away and let him go down the lane beyond where Frankie was tied.

The man was looking me over next. Picking up my foot the way the woman had done, he was pressing my sole with his thumbs. As he lowered my foot he squeezed the bones in my leg right up to my knee. Working his way around me he was talking to the woman.

I heard him ask her, 'So how much did you have to give him to swap?'

She replied 'Two hundred.'

He dropped my foot abruptly and yelled at her 'WHAT? For an unworked gelding!'

'Oh, come on!' she snapped back, 'he's twice the horse! You didn't have to drive that other thing! Going out of his mind every time he heard a tractor!'

'So what makes you think this one's gonna be any better?'

They argued on for a while, the boy rejoining them.

'What do you think, Tom?' the woman asked him.

'Yeah, he looks alright,' his noncommittal reply.

The man asked 'When's he coming back for his two hundred quid, then?'

'In a couple of weeks...'

More heated words about where did she intend to get the money from and then he stormed off back to the camp.

The woman asked the boy 'Did he sell "Springbok"?'

'Yeah, I think so. Yerman's coming over to see us later; we left the horse down at his place. He's got a little pony he was trying to deal-on. I don't think Ben wants it though. He just wants to sell Springbok for cash.'

Turning her attention back to me, putting an arm around my neck so that my head rested over her shoulder she stroked both hands down by mane.

She asked the boy: 'Would you have bought him?'

'That's not for me to say, Liz. I don't have any money to buy anything. For that matter, neither do you! I suppose Ben's just miffed because he sees he'll end up paying, and the money he's hoping to get for Springbok is his dealing money. You should have at least discussed it with him before you went ahead and agreed to the deal.'

'H'mm, you're right of course.' She admitted. Then she whispered in my ear, 'You're going to get me into a whole lot of trouble, lovely boy. I can tell!'

Meeting Bumper.

As Liz and Tom headed back to the camp, the horse Bumper came trotting down the lane. He exchanged words with Frankie and came straight towards me. I stretched up to my full height and gave a half-hearted little kick with my front leg just to say, 'Hold on! Back off! Don't come bouncing all over me!'

My defensiveness only amused him and he trotted right up beside me and sunk his teeth into my rump. I squealed from the pain and indignation, but he just hung on as I tried to side-step away. Bumper paid no heed to my yelping and only ducked nimbly away when I tried to kick him off me. Dodging my hooves, he was straight back in again: biting my neck and mocking my feeble attempts to defend myself. I tried to lift both front feet off the ground the way I'd seen other horses rear-up, but I'd forgotten about the chain, and the belt around my neck pulled me up short and I toppled over sideways in a most ungainly fashion. This amused Bumper more than ever and he stood in the road laughing at me as I struggled back to my feet. Then, as if to show me how it's done, he lifted both front feet high over his head, his chunky back legs throwing sparks off the road as he pranced towards me. I could only edge backwards in awe of his performance until my tail collided with the road-sign post and I stood transfixed as the iron-shod hooves clanked together so close to my face that I could feel the air they displaced. He could easily have kicked my head as I stood there, but he didn't. He just landed lightly on the grass beside me saying, 'That the sort of thing?'

He said it without malice, slightly mocking, just letting me know his position in this group. I was not about to argue. I just wanted to make friends. I still had a lot to learn, hoping that Bumper and maybe even Frankie would help me. My humble attitude was the right approach.

'Alright then,' said Bumper, as I nervously itched my tail against the post. 'You want to groom?'

'You mean it? No biting?'

'No hurting,' he promised, and came alongside of me and started to take gentle little nips at the base of my mane. I tentatively started to do the same for him, and in no time we were involved in a mutual grooming session. As we responded to each other's requests to scratch the spots we couldn't reach, Bumper told me all about himself.

My own life up to this time had been almost totally uneventful. The only company I had known were the geldings, mares and foals I shared a field with. The rest of the world was still a mystery to me.

But Bumper, he'd been taken away from his mother very soon after his birth. He couldn't remember her at all. He'd been fed milk from a bucket along with a herd of calves. The farmer who brought him up moved him around with the calves for about half a year, then as the days got shorter and the nights colder, the calves were taken away and he was put into a field with a flock of sheep. There was a puck-goat and a couple of donkeys in the field too. Bumper had to share feed with all these others through his first winter, so he knew all about being hungry too.

During his second summer the farmer moved him about the parish from one field to another till he knew his way around, and if the grazing got a bit sparse where he was, he'd think nothing of jumping the ditch or breaking through the fence and heading off down the road in search of new grass. He felt no herd-affinity with the other animals. He was a loner. When the farmer found him wandering the lanes, he'd just be driven back into one of the fields. There was no real contact with people until the end of that second summer.

As he recounted his story we were joined by another animal. Much smaller than us, with a shaggy grey coat. Two long horns between her ears.

'This is Birch. She's a nanny-goat,' said Bumper as she strolled up and started to rub herself against his leg.

'...and who's your new friend?' she asked in a high pitched voice as she looked me coolly in the eye. Ignoring her question, he continued with his story. Of how one day Liz and Ben had driven the bay pony into his farmyard, with Birch tied in the cart. She'd come to visit the puck. They'd left her for a few days, then caught her and took her away again. On that second visit the farmer and Ben had leaned on the gate watching Bumper as they talked. For the next week, Ben had visited the farm every day. At first Bumper had just run away from him. They were in a twenty-acre field and there was no way that one man could catch an unhandled colt. But each day he would come and just quietly follow the horse around, watching him canter away, calling to him with curious clucking sounds and low whistling that excited the horse's curiosity.

On the fourth day the man had climbed the gate into the field and walked straight to where the horse was standing. Bumper took off, but didn't go far. Looking over his shoulder, he saw the man standing perfectly still. As they stood looking at each other, the man slowly knelt down. Then he lowered his head to the ground and folded his hands behind his neck. The horse was totally intrigued by this, tilting his head to try for a different perspective on this strange sight. Curiosity overcame caution as he walked back to the place he'd been standing, where the man now crouched motionless. Bumper still couldn't figure out what was happening.

He asked the man, 'What's this game? Are you alright?' because as he drew closer he could hear whimpering noises that sounded like some hurt little animal. As the horse gently nuzzled the man's shoulder, Ben turned his head sideways and said quietly, 'You'll be coming home with me tomorrow.'

Bumper was startled to hear a man's voice so close, speaking directly at him, but he didn't run away. When the hand touched his chest for the first time a shiver rippled through him, but still he felt no fear. The man slowly straightened up into a kneeling position and reached a hand to the horse's nose. Bumper took in all the strange new scents. As well as the man himself, he could smell other horses, dogs, the nanny-goat, other people, wood smoke.

A whole other world that he just wanted to be a part of. Ben's other hand was offering an apple. Bumper snatched at the fruit, breaking it in half and stepping back to enjoy the juicy taste. As he was chomping the apple, the man was slowly standing up, taking a bite from the apple too. Now they were eye to eye and the man no longer posed any threat to the horse. He took another bite from the apple and then offered the core on his outstretched hand. Bumper couldn't resist it.

The man turned and walked away. Still slobbering over the core, the horse trotted after him, calling for more.

As he climbed the gate the man said 'I'll see you tomorrow, then!'

The next morning, Ben arrived at the farm carrying a rope over his shoulder. Bumper hadn't forgotten the sweet apple and when the man gave a high pitched call he sauntered over to the gate to see if he'd brought some more. Stopping at arms length; waiting for the man to make the next move. Sure enough, there was the apple. Unsuspectingly taking a bite as the rope was slipped around his neck. Realising what was happening, the horse's flight-instinct caused him to tug at the rope. But the man held firm; the rope tightened around his neck and the pain and difficulty in breathing made him stop at once.

'Stand up!' the man commanded him, and as he stopped struggling and relaxed, the rope no longer cut into his neck, he breathed easy again. The man fed him another apple, talking to him all the while. By the time they were out of the field and the man was closing the gate, Bumper was ignoring the rope and trying to bite through the cloth to get at the apples in the man's coat pocket.

As they walked down the lane past the house, the farmer opened the door and called out, 'You caught him, then?'

'Sure, why wouldn't I?'replied the man, and they walked on, out to the main road, then down the maze of lanes, most of them familiar territory, till they reached the woodland. Through another gate then, and along a forest track where Bumper had never been before.

Other horses calling at his approach.

A wood fire surrounded by people who came to greet him and the man with excited chatter, and hugs. Dogs sniffing around his feet.

The goat Birch, calling, 'Well, hello again!'

The man handing the rope to a boy and saying,

'Here he is, son. Are you still going to call him Bumper?'

'Have you thought of a better name?'

'No, he's just bumped me all the way here, he's the "bumperiest" horse I ever met!'

'Okay, then, Bumper he is.' And the boy led him away to meet the other horses. At that time there was the woman's bay pony, Frankie, and a stroppy yearling colt called Springbok.

Bumper had soon learned to pull the two wheeled cart, then a four-wheeled vehicle, a canvas-covered wagon, had been built for him. When the spring grass was on the verges they'd set off from the winter camp and travelled along from one patch of grass to the next till they'd reached here.

I asked 'Where's Springbok now?' and Bumper told me they'd gone out earlier in the day with him tied on the back of the cart, as usual, but they'd left him in a field with other horses. He asked me if I knew where "Brownie" was, but I had no idea.

A New Pony Joins the Herd.

Bumper had wandered off down the lane and I was packing my belly with the lush vegetation when the tranquillity was shattered by Frankie's stallion-cry. He must have caught the scent of the mare. I lifted my head, long grass dangling out the sides of my mouth as I stood silent, swivelling my ears for a clue of what had alerted him. Then I heard her deep-voiced reply drifting over the still hedgerows that muffled the clip-clop of her hooves.

She was being driven along the straight road, the way Bumper had approached the camp. As she passed the crossroads we saw the two men sitting up on a brightly painted flat-cart. A tiny foal hurried alongside her.

Frankie was rearing and screaming at the end of his chain. Then prancing up and down the road whickering loudly at the mare, calling for her attention. She was a well-marked piebald cob, her foal an almost-exact miniature replica. She ignored all of us, stopping as the man 'Whoa'd' her at the camp.

A nondescript little pony who had been following the cart turned at the crossroads and cantered down the lane to where we were grazing. He was a child's pony, under 13 hands. His coat a speckled dun, the only distinguishing mark a faint white star on his forehead. His mane had been completely hogged so that his ears looked too big, sticking out of his bald head. His sparse tail only added to his mulish look.

Frankie was still carrying on his performance for the benefit of the disinterested mare. Bumper had gone back to stripping leaves. The pony stopped abruptly in the road right beside me. Then, without bothering to say anything, just started eating the grass along the edge of the verge. I got the impression this pony was well-used to the company of other horses. His attitude was 'I'm here now. I'm with you.' He didn't actually make contact straight away, but somehow there was no ignoring him. I wished he'd go and eat somewhere else, leave me in peace but he took no notice of my polite request, just carried on as if all the grass belonged to him and I should be grateful he was willing to share it with me.

When I saw Ben walking down the lane with one of the men, I hoped they were coming to collect the pony. The girl I'd seen at the camp was with them. As she got closer I saw that she had another piece of the delicious bread and I called out to her, 'Is that for me?' but I was disappointed when she offered it to the pony. He snatched it greedily and turned his back on her as he gobbled it down.

The man was singing the praises of the pony, saying how quiet he was. How he'd been a child's pony in a riding school. How he was safe for any child; and so on. The girl was patting him and talking to him as he sniffed her hands for more bread. Next she was helped up onto the pony's back. He just stood there.

'See if you can trot him on,' said her father, and the girl gave the pony a dig in the ribs with her heels. Nothing happened. She tried again, saying 'Giddup!' but still the pony wouldn't budge. The man grabbed one of the pony's ears and jerked him forward. The girl almost lost her balance with nothing to hold on to, but she gripped with her knees and stayed on as the man led the pony a few paces up the lane away from me. Then, as soon as the man let go, the pony spun round and jog-trotted back to where he was before. Ben put out a hand to stop him, and helped his daughter dismount.

'Do you like him, Bluebird?' he asked her.

'I don't know,' she said. 'He's alright, I suppose.'

She was obviously not over-enamoured of him.

'It's a pity about his mane,' she added. 'And his tail.'

'They'll grow back.' The man assured her.

They talked on as Ben went through his ritual of looking at the pony's feet, feeling his legs, checking his teeth. Then there was the slapping of hands and the man was counting notes off a roll and handing them to Ben, who quickly bundled the money into his shirt-pocket. The man said 'Just tie him up till we're gone, then he'll stay with your horses.'

So the girl untied another chain from a fence-post across the road and slipped it around the pony's neck. She'd just finished tying the rope-end to a tree stump further down the lane as the men were turning the mare at the camp to drive back the way they'd come.

Frankie hadn't given up on the hope that she was coming to visit him and he renewed his calling as she trotted past the crossroads again. The pony, seeing he was being left behind, ran to the end of his tether. He yelled out his indignation, but everyone just ignored him. After a while he settled down and Bumper sauntered over to where he was tied. I watched for a while as they reared and snapped at each other in boisterous play, then I went back to my grazing.

The sun was setting behind the trees when the man and woman from the camp walked down the lane again. He was calling 'Whoop-whoop-whoop' in a high pitched voice which attracted the attention of Frankie and Bumper, who both answered with throaty grunts. When they reached me they parted company; Ben walked on down the lane, stopping briefly to feed Frankie an apple before carrying on to where Bumper was grazing the hedge.

Liz came up to me and offered me an apple too. I tried to take it but she held on so that I had to sink my teeth in and just take a bite. As I was crunching it up I didn't notice her slip the plastic tube into the corner of my mouth. The first thing I knew was a really foul-tasting paste hit the back of my tongue. It was cold and slimy and most of it had slid down by throat before I could spit it out. I lost most of my chewed up apple, though.

'I'm sorry,' she said to me as she offered me the rest of the fruit. I took it in an attempt to get the bad taste out of my mouth.

'I'm sure this stuff tastes disgusting,' she commiserated, 'but you'll feel better without that burden of worms, I promise.' And she stroked my nose, letting me lick her hand. She even picked up the chewed apple I'd spat out and tried to persuade me to eat it again, but I shied away from the smell of it.

By this time, Ben was walking back up the lane, leading Bumper by his halter. Liz took a hold of the horse, handing the plastic tube to Ben. He crossed the road to where the pony was tied and administered a dose to him. He obviously found it really distasteful too, tossing back his head and gagging as he shouted his disgust. Ben untied the chain from the pony's neck and Liz clipped it onto Bumper's halter.

'Do you think he'll be alright?' she asked, 'He won't wander off?'

'I shouldn't think so. He's used to being with other horses, he'll probably just stick around.'

And he did.

Chapter Two

First-time in Harness

The boy, Tom and his sister were the first people we saw the next morning. They were both carrying a bucket of water in each hand. I guzzled mine down in one gulp as soon as the girl set the bucket on the ground. She was carrying the other one across the road to Bumper, who was lying down on the verge with his front legs stretched out before him, the way a dog might lie. He didn't bother to get up at her approach. She put the bucket under his nose and he took a sip.

'Y'alright, Bumps?' she asked, and he said he was.

The raging thirst at me was only part-satisfied, so I called to the girl, at the same time kicking the empty bucket onto the road so that she'd see I wanted more.

'You had enough?' she asked Bumper, then she brought his water back across the road and I drank most of it in another mighty gulp.

They gathered up the empty buckets and headed back for the camp. A plume of blue smoke was rising between the wagons. The smell of the burning wood mingled with the new smell that permeated everything here, the water, the grass, the very air.

The sharp pains that had been attacking my gut all night seemed to have eased off, leaving only the salty aftertaste on the back of my tongue that the two buckets of water barely washed away.

The sun was halfway up the sky when Liz came to visit me.

'How you feeling now, lovely boy?' she asked.

She picked up a stick and started to poke about in my droppings.

'Ugh, don't suppose you've ever been wormed in your life, have you? Oh, well you'll be better off without having to feed this lot!' And tossing the stick into the hedge she untied the rope from the road sign and coiled rope and chain around her arm as she walked towards me.

'Ready to start your new life?' she asked me. 'Where do you want to begin?'

I fancied another mutual grooming session with Bumper, but that was not to be allowed.

'Come on!' she ordered, and taking hold of the leather belt round my neck, she steered me around and led me back down the lane towards the crossroad. I tried to tell her about the itch on my neck, but she just said 'Later! First you're going to try on some harness.'

I was ignoring her, still intent on some mutual-grooming; maybe if I wasn't allowed to go to Bumper, she'd be willing to give me a bit of a scratch? I rubbed my nose against her back.

'What do you want?' she asked and just to show her, I gave a little nip on the top of her arm. I never expected anything like her response. She was supposed to give me a bite, or maybe a scratch on my shoulder. Instead she spun round and dealt me a hard punch on the end of my nose.

'Don't you ever bite me again!' she yelled, and carried on berating me as I cowered back away from her anger; fear and bewilderment overtaking me as my lip smarted inside from being smashed against my teeth. I mumbled I was sorry, I didn't know, begged her not to be angry. Liz caught the sadness, the misunderstanding in my voice, and in my eye.

The gentleness came back into her voice as she pulled the layers of clothing off her shoulder and showed me the reddening mark on her arm where my teeth had bitten into her flesh.

'Look what you done!' she said to me. 'I'm not another horse! You mustn't do that, okay?'

So much to learn.

'Good boy,' she said, softly stroking my nose and rolling back my lip to see if she'd done me any damage.

'Guess that makes us just about even. Now. Shall we start again?'

We were standing in the road.

'Walk on!' she said, and I followed her obediently back to the camp.

So this was the harness. I'd seen Bumper and the mare pulling their carts, the leather straps over their backs and heads. As she took each separate piece from the rack beside the wagon Liz showed it to me, let me sniff it, look at it from all angles.

First came the collar.

'Let's see if you're as good today,' she said as she slid it along my nose. Over the ears, turn it right way up.

'Looks like we finally got the horse to fit that English collar,' said Ben, who was standing by the fire with a china mug in his hand.

'Great, eh?' agreed Liz. 'The rest of Brownie's straps should adjust up to fit him, what do you think?'

'Try them and see.'

'This is the straddle,' she told me, 'and here's its girth strap, tugs, belly band, meter-strap, braker-straps…' she gave a different name to each bit of buckled-on leather as she spread it between her hands.

Then added, 'All you really need to know is… it goes on your back, okay?' and smoothing the hair along my spine she gently lowered the tangle of straps over my back. Struggling to unfasten buckles that had obviously not been adjusted for quite some time, she lengthened the straps one by one, pulling the harness into position as I stood patiently in the road.

'Now this is the crupper,' I heard her saying from somewhere directly behind me. 'You have to lift your tail for this one.'

At the touch of her hand under my dock, the first instinct was to clamp my tail down hard. But she just scratched the top of my tail till I started to relax and saying, 'Come on Sullivan, it won't hurt!' she slid the hard roll of leather under my tail, and as I clamped down again she deftly buckled it onto the meter-strap. I felt it pull up tight as she moved the straddle forward and fastened the girth.

'Good boy,' she patted the side of my neck, 'you're looking very handsome!'

'Now, the hard bit!' said Ben, as she took the last piece of harness from the rack.

'That meant to be a joke?' she asked him, and holding the jangling collection of leather and metal up for my appraisal, said 'This is the winkers, Sullivan. And this is actually a very soft bit...' Showing me the bright silver bar with long cross pieces at each end '…at least the way you'll be wearing it. So don't mind him. Look, it goes over your face like this.'

She held it in front of her own face as I looked on in amazement.

'First though, you have to open your mouth. That's it, good boy.' Her fingers were in the corners of my mouth and as my teeth parted, the silver bar pushed over my tongue and for the first time in my life I had a bit in my mouth. It pulled hard against my cheeks as Liz reached up to get the leather part over my ears. I started to protest but she at once undid the side buckles and lengthened the straps so that the cross pieces rested against the corners of my mouth without pressure.

'There. That better?' she asked me.

Better than what? I wondered, as she fiddled with the loops of the bit, attaching the longest of the straps, which she told me were called the reins.

'There you go. This is the last of it,' she said as she untied the rope holding two strips of curved metal around another collar which had been sitting on the axle of the wagon.

'These hames have fitted every collar we've had for the last three years, so presumably they'll fit this one too.' And she reached her arms around my collar. Holding the metal on one side as she passed the rope through the loop at the top, she pulled it up tight.

A heavy-duty strap with a short length of chain at the end was sewn onto a big ring on each of the metal strips she called the hames. These were the traces, now being crossed over my rump to stop them trailing along the road.

'I still think you're expecting too much of him,' Ben was saying.

'Look at him,' replied Liz, waving her arms in my direction. 'Look how quiet he is! He'll be grand!'

'Hum. Sitting up half the night reading Rarey doesn't make you a horse trainer! But go ahead! You'll find out!' he called after us as Liz led me away from the wagons to where two long straight poles stood against the hedge.

'Now don't mind him at all,' she said to me, 'you'll be fine.'

The girl came and stood beside my head, holding the reins under my chin as Liz struggled to lift the two poles out to the road. I saw that they were fixed together and held apart by two shorter cross pieces at one end.

'This is a sort of travois,' she told me as she let me sniff the wood.

'It should help you get used to the feel of shafts.' I had no idea what was happening but stood quietly while the two of them brought the long poles one each side of me and fed the ends through the tugs of my straddle. Liz used some short bits of rope to attach the traces to the cross-bar of the travois.

Finally she buckled the belly-band. Gathering up the reins which were held along my back by metal hoops on the hames and the straddle, Liz went to stand just alongside my tail. She was in the middle of the road. Her daughter was still standing at my head, between me and the verge. Taking a deep breath, Liz said 'Walk on, Sullivan!'

I felt trapped amongst all this leather and metal and wood, afraid to put a foot forward. 'Easy, boy!' said Blue, taking hold of the cheek strap of my winkers. 'You can do it. Walk on!'

'Walk on!' repeated Liz, this time giving my rump the gentlest of slaps with the reins. The shake of the reins was amplified by the bit and set up a rattle in my mouth which made me want to flee this whole situation. I started forward, jerking and jibbing as all the straps tightened at once and the poles scraped along the road as though they were chasing me.

'Easy! Easy!' called Liz, pulling on the reins so that the bit stopped jangling and held firmly at the corners of my mouth; the pain just enough to take my mind from all my other fears. I stood still. The bit relaxed, the reins eased off.

'Okay Blue?' she called to the girl. 'Take two?'

Again the reins slapped my rump and I heard the command 'Walk on!'

Determined not to be afraid and to avoid the pull of the bit, I started to walk steadily forward. The collar pressed against my shoulder and I felt the slack of the traces tighten and the wooden poles bumped against my sides as they joggled along the uneven surface of the road.

Liz was calling to me all the time, 'Brave boy Sullivan! Good boy!' and the girl walking along beside my head was saying much the same. I was feeling very proud of myself as we walked past the camp and I heard Ben's voice saying 'Good. Go easy on him!' and I was starting to get used to the feel of the harness as we walked past the crossroads and the other horses called out their encouragement. The strangest part was the winkers, only being able to see the stretch of road directly in front, all sideways vision cut off by a big square of curved leather that covered each eye. I kept wanting to turn my head this way and that to try and see sideways, but each time a sharp pain at the edge of my mouth brought my face back in line.

I heard the silly new pony come racing down the lane as we passed the junction and Ben shouting from the camp. 'Catch that animal, Girl! Tie him up!' and Blue had to leave my side to go chasing down the lane and grab him by the halter to stop him following us. While she let Bumper off his tether and used it to tie her pony, we carried on walking down the quiet road. It stretched on straight before us as far as I could see. I thought I was doing really well. So did Liz. She kept on congratulating me, as we walked steadily along. All was peace and tranquillity. I heard birds in the hedgerows change their song at our approach. A hive of wild bees in a hollow tree went about their buzzing business. Then a strange shudder started to shake the road.

'What's that?' I asked Liz, but she just ignored me saying 'Easy now, good boy.'

But it didn't stop. It just grew stronger. Soon I could hear a distant rumble too. By this time the road was quaking under my feet as though it would break up at any moment. At last Liz noticed it too.

'Oh, no!' I heard her moan.

I jerked my head from side to side, looking for an escape, but there was a thick thorn hedge to one side and nothing but a flat expanse of brown desert on the other. And the great rumbling monster was moving inexorably closer down the long straight road. It rolled towards us on huge wheels that spread across the entire width of the tarmac. It loomed enormous in my tunnel vision, belching puffs of stinking gas from up-pipes on either side of its great yellow body.

I was completely overtaken by panic. Liz was frightened too, as she rushed to my head and tried to stop me rearing by grabbing the cheek strap. Too late. She caught the neck strap but my front feet were already off the ground and as I backed away the leather snapped and the winkers twisted around my face, momentarily blinding me altogether. I gave a mighty shake and as my feet hit the road again the winkers fell forward and dangled from my mouth. I spat out the bit. Now I could see even more clearly the full magnitude of the horrific creature shaking the earth as it rumbled and roared towards us. I reared again and felt the poles dig in to the road behind me. As I stepped back my hind legs hit off the cross-bar and the end of one of the poles poked hard into my neck. I jibbed to one side, my leg going over the pole as the tug-strap holding it snapped. I knew I was getting hopelessly entangled in breaking harness. Liz was trying to catch my nose, but I was thrashing about in blind panic. The short strap holding the bottom of the hames was the next thing to snap. I jerked forward as the hames separated from the collar and shot along my back. They hit against the straddle, as the reins brought the two sets of rings sharply into collision.

I instinctively reared again and the stitching on the girth-strap gave out. Straddle and hames slid along my back and down over my rump, stopped by the belly-band and the one remaining tug still attached to the pole. This all seemed to be happening at once. I had no time to think of anything except 'Fight or flight' as the adrenalin raced through me.

'Flight! Flight!' screamed every confused and terrified nerve.

Then, as suddenly as it had started, it was over. With a cough and a splutter, the monster fell silent. The road stopped shaking. The air was still heavy with the stench of its exhaust fumes, the massive yellow bulk still occupied the whole road in front of us, but somehow the threat was gone.

Liz took a piece of wood from her pocket and tapped it on the road. A steel blade opened out and she cut quickly through the ropes holding the traces to the cross-bar of the travois. The dangling hames and the straddle slid down my hind legs. She lifted the winker-set over by head and said 'Walk on, Sullivan.' It wasn't easy. I was still astride one of the poles and the other was digging me in the neck. The crupper was still clamped hard under my tail, as the rest of the harness hung around my back legs.

'Oh, just walk on, will you?' she snapped impatiently, and slapped my rump with the flat of her hand. I stepped forward, gingerly trying to disentangle myself from wood and leather. As the harness hit the road behind me I lifted my tail to let the weight of the straddle pull away the crupper.

Then I was standing in the road, wearing only the fine new English collar, the rest of the straps a jumbled mess of metal and leather in a heap on the road. Liz was talking to a man who had stepped down from inside the monster. Asking him if he could spare a few minutes to help her get this stuff off the road.

He was saying 'Aye, no bother, take your time there,' and as they gathered up the harness and dragged the poles into the hedge I had time to see the yellow 'monster' at close quarters. By now of course I realised it was just another vehicle. By far the largest, noisiest one I'd ever encountered, but now, with its engine switched off, no more of a threat than any other.

Liz tied one of the reins around my neck to lead me back to the camp. As we passed the crossroads the other horses jeered me and I felt really stupid walking along with just the collar that slid up my neck and hit off my ears every time I hung my head. We got much the same reception from the people at the camp. They'd seen the whole carry-on. A slow hand-clap from Ben as Liz pulled the collar unceremoniously over my head, and put it on the harness rack. Then she replaced the rein with her belt and the chain.

'So much for that!' she said, and turning to Ben. 'Alright, you smug bastard! You were right. As usual! So what do I do now?'

'Looks like you'll be spending the rest of the day sewing harness.' He grinned.

'I know that,' she snapped. 'But what about him?'

'Well, if those guys are going to be working on the bog today, you'd do well to tie him down there so he gets used to them.'

So I spent the first half of the day with my chain attached to a running line tied between two bushes in the hedgerow, right beside where

I'd trashed the harness. The big yellow bog-tractor, and another one pulling a huge box-trailer, rumbled past me and turned at the crossroads away from the camp and the other horses. At first they slowed down as I panicked on the end of my chain, but after they'd driven back and forth a few times I took less notice of them, and they of me.

In the afternoon Liz moved me along to the junction and tied me on the other side of the road so that I had to get used to them passing me on the corner. They were even noisier and smellier as they negotiated the bend, but there was good grass on the verge, and by the end of the day I was no longer the least bit afraid of their earth-shaking passing.

Shortly after the vehicles rumbled off down the straight road for the last time, the boy Tom brought me a fresh bucket of water, and another apple. I'd been sipping water all afternoon, but the apple tasted good.

'Fancy a bit of a race?' he asked me, as he slipped a halter over my ears.

It was soft and light compared to the winkers; it didn't restrict my vision at all. It carried no bit. Tom tied a length of rope to the ring on the side of the halter, looped it over my neck and tied it on the other side. He upended the empty water bucket alongside of me, and using it as a step, leapt nimbly up onto my back. I'd seen other horses with people sitting astride them, but this was the first time for me. I gave a little buck to try to dislodge him, but he clung on with his knees and grabbed a handful of hair at the base of my mane.

Still determined to get this weight of my back, I bolted to the end of my tether. The chain jerked me back and in my frustration I tossed my head sideways to try and break free. The chain was supple and much too strong for me to break, but the leather belt had a weak spot where the buckle fed through a hole, and it snapped. I was thrown off balance by the force of by own momentum, but the boy stayed on my back, exerting pressure on the bridge of my nose by pulling on the rope attached to the sides of the halter. He leaned forward, and his voice close to my ear said 'Giddup, then!' as I found my balance again and took off at a canter down the lane to where Bumper and Frankie were tied, and the new pony was grazing free with them. They all looked up at my approach, the two horses with expressions of having seen it all before, the pony giving a joyful shout of 'Yeah! Let's DO it!' as he pranced into the road right in front of me. Tom pulled on one side of the halter, calling 'Whoa, Boy' whilst trying to steer me round the pony. I sidestepped onto the verge and spun right around to look back at the other horses down the lane. They were just ignoring me, but the pony obviously enjoyed this game. He came right up beside me and as soon as I started to trot back down the lane, he was there with me like a shadow. When I broke into a canter he matched my pace. Turning at the crossroads, he was almost under my feet. We were back at the camp and I already felt easy under the boy's weight.

'Come on Blue!' he called to his sister as he pulled back on my nose to stop me. 'Get up on the pony!'

She and Liz stopped what they were doing and, after tying a rope to his halter too, Liz gave the girl a leg-up onto the pony's back. We trotted down the lane till we were out of sight of the camp, our riders laughing and joking together. Then Tom pulled me around and said 'Race you back' before his sister even realised he was doing it. The little pony knew though, and without waiting for any command from the girl he had spun round in the road and was passing us at a canter. Tom gave me a dig in the ribs with his heels and whooped in my ears, but I didn't need any encouragement. Soon I was alongside the pony and we were cantering side by side back to the camp. Tom reined me in as Liz stepped into the road and patted me on the neck.

'That's enough for now' she told the boy 'You were supposed to be moving him for me, remember? Still, he rides well enough doesn't he?'

'Hmm, he was a bit skittish at first though. Er,... he bust your belt.'

'Oh thanks a lot, Tom! That's all I need! Will you look at the blisters on my hands from sewing harness all day!'

He ducked as she aimed a slap at his head and I heard his voice, 'C'mon then, Sullivan, let's get outta here.'

Blue had untied the rope from her pony's halter and he followed us back to the crossroads where Tom dismounted and retrieved my chain. He wrapped the shortened belt around his own waist and clipping the chain onto my halter, led me down the lane past the other horses and tied my rope to a fencepost alongside a bucket of water. The pony went and took a drink, then he stayed close by me for the rest of the evening. Since everyone here had a name, I decided to call him "Shadow".

Moving Camp.

The sun dispersed the bog-mist, promising another scorching day. There seemed to be more activity at the camp this morning. Lots of shouting and moving things around. Ben and Tom came walking down the lane, but instead of bringing us fresh water they stopped at Frankie and Bumper, untied them and led them back up to the camp.

I called out 'Hey, what's happening?' as the pony trotted off after them, leaving me still tethered. Bumper called back something but I didn't really hear him over the excited yells of the pony running around them. Back at the camp, the two horses were having their harness put on. I saw them being backed into the shafts of the wagons, first Bumper, whose wagon was facing in the direction they were intending to move. The canvas top swayed and tilted precariously as it bounced off the verge and onto the road. Bumper walked steadily forward, pulling the wagon a short way down the road past where Ben was holding

Frankie. As soon as the way was clear, the big horse started to move his wagon forward. From where I was watching it seemed as though he would walk onto the smouldering remains of the breakfast fire, but at the last minute he turned onto the road. The wagon lurched after him as the front wheels hit the road and the whole vehicle spun around in its own length to end up facing the way it was meant to be going. The two wheeled cart still stood on the verge with its shafts pointing at the sky, and various boxes and water churns standing alongside. I heard some more shouting, then Bumper started to walk his wagon along the road, closely followed by Frankie with the bigger wagon. The Shadow pony was prancing excitedly up and down, calling and generally making a nuisance of himself. Everyone did their best to ignore him.

At the crossroads they turned left and came down the lane towards me. I was a little alarmed at the sight of the wagons lumbering in my direction, and tried to back into the hedge. There was none of the engine noise or fumes that I had come to associate with vehicles moving along the road. Very little vibration, just the slow walking beat of the horses iron-shod hooves on the tarmac.

It was a fascinating spectacle. As they drew level with me Liz hopped down from the front ledge of Bumper's wagon and came over to me.

'What do you think of that, then?' she asked me as I gazed at the passing entourage in total amazement. She was tying the short length of rope to the sides of my halter again. Like Tom, she upended my water bucket alongside me and threw a leg over my back. She pulled herself into an upright position saying 'Easy boy, stand up!' as she leaned forward to unclip the chain from my halter. She seemed about twice the weight of Tom, and I wasn't sure if I wanted to carry her for any distance, but I was keen to follow the other horses. She slackened the pressure on the nose-band and said 'Go on then!' giving me a little dig with her heels. I needed no telling. I was off down the road at a fast trot. Liz was obviously not such a good rider as her son. She didn't instantly relax and move with me the way he did. I could feel her gripping hard with her knees as she joggled and bounced out of time to my trot. She managed to stay on my back somehow, and we soon caught up with the others. The Shadow was cantering along the verge and calling to me to do the same but I was quite content to walk alongside Bumper as he pulled the wagon steadily down the lane.

'How far is this new camp?' Liz called to Tom, who was sitting up on the ledge of the wagon, reins in hand.

'Its only about a quarter of a mile,' he replied. 'Just around the next bend!'

So we plodded along until we came to a place where the lane widened. There was an unmetalled track leading off to the right, a huge old oak tree standing at the junction. We turned off the road there, Bumper not seeming to mind the rattling and clattering as his wagon bounced over the uneven surface. He carried on down the track for a short distance till we were stopped by a fence of barbed-wire, overgrown with creeping plants. Tom pulled him round and the short little wagon turned to face back out towards the road. Ben had stopped Frankie almost as soon as the wheels of the big wagon were on the track.

'I'm not taking this one any further' he called to Tom. 'Are you parking down there?'

'Yeah, why not?'

'You could get stuck if it rains.'

'Its not going to rain, Ben! Look at the sky!' And he threw his arms up at the clear blue expanse.

'We could be here a while, now...' said his father.

'All the more reason we need a big camp. Anyway Bumper could pull this wagon out of a bog-hole if he had to.'

The boy had already started to loosen the straps.

'Let's hope it doesn't come to that!' said Ben.

He lifted one of the wagon shafts and said to his horse, 'Walk on, Frankie!'

The big horse obediently took a couple of steps forward, sliding the tugs from the shafts.

'Stand up!' commanded Ben, lowering the shaft to the ground. Frankie gave a mighty shake which rattled all the buckles on his harness, then stood patiently waiting to be untacked.

Liz had meantime jumped off my back and was stroking my face and talking quietly to me. Tom walked past leading Bumper, still in his harness, and handed Liz a chain and rope. She wrapped the chain around my neck and tied the end of the rope to a clump of bushes alongside this wide track which was to be the new camp. Tom leapt nimbly up onto Bumper's back and settled himself behind the straddle. Without ever pulling on the bit he coiled the long driving reins a few times around his elbow, then he gave Bumper a sharp dig in the ribs with his heels and at his command the horse went trotting briskly back along the road the way we'd come. Shadow went cantering along with them.

Liz and Blue were collecting water buckets out of the wagons. They disappeared off down the lane and returned a short time later, each carrying a bucket full to the brim. These they gave to me and to Frankie, who was tied on the wide verge across the road from the end of the track.

I was just taking in my new surroundings, and enjoying the fresh grass when Frankie gave the call that let us all know Bumper was returning. I heard the distant reply and the easy trot of hooves just before the shadow came hurtling into the middle of the camp. He side-stepped at the very last second to avoid trampling the two little girls who were sitting on the grassy track playing with an old doll. Their game up to that point had consisted of pulling the doll back and forth between them as they each clung desperately to one of its arms. An identical doll lay on the ground beside them.

Liz was just climbing out of the wagon, trying to lift a big wooden box down off the narrow ledge above the shafts. She dropped the box with a loud clatter and turned to snatch up her children, but the pony had already passed them and skidded to a halt alongside me.

'Come and have a gallop!' he urged me, but I was more interested in feeding myself, and told him 'Maybe, later.' He turned and pranced back out to the road just as Bumper was turning down the track with the two wheeled cart, loaded with the boxes and churns.

Tom called out, 'For godsakes Blue! Will you slap some control on that pony!'

The girl was already making a grab for his halter, saying 'Here, give me that chain.' Tom handed her the tether from the seat beside him and she pulled the pony out of the middle of the track to allow Bumper to get past the wagon and steadily walk his cart into the camp.

'You want this lot here?' Tom asked Liz as he whoa'd the horse to a standstill in front of the big wagon.

'Yeah that's fine, thanks. We'll untack Bumper, you go and help Ben get some wood.'

'Okay. Which way did he go?'

'Down the track.' She pointed beyond the little wagon, over the fence, the way the man had gone with the bow-saw over his shoulder.

As soon as Bumper was out of his harness, he lay down in the middle of the camp and started to roll. Over he went from side to side, kicking his legs in the air; back he rolled, wiggling his rump on the new grass. I'd seen horses rolling before, but none of them ever seemed to put so much sheer enjoyment into such a simple exercise. Bumper rolled over and back four or five times, before climbing back to his feet and shaking himself like a dog coming out of water. A cloud of dust and grass surrounded him as he mumbled, 'hmm, that's better!' and ambled over to where I was tied so that we could have another mutual grooming session.

I was pleased that he chose me instead of Frankie, and as we nibbled and nipped each other's necks we exchanged thoughts in the way of horses. We compared our impressions of the new pony. I probed his mind for feelings about pulling the wagon and the cart, but he dismissed them as 'work'; something that really only occupied a small part of the day. Bumper lived only for the moment. When he was in the shafts he was working. When the harness was off his back he thought no more about it. I decided that was a good attitude, and gave all my attention to itching the part of his shoulder he was twitching.

By the time Ben and Tom clamoured back over the fence with a couple of bundles of dead branches, Liz already had a small fire burning the twigs she and the girl had collected in the clearing. A bent metal bar sticking out of the ground held the kettle suspended above the flames.

'Keep an eye on the twins while we go for more water?'

Two tall metal churns stood on planks spanning the axles of an old pram frame. They rang like dull bells as Liz and the girl pushed the makeshift trolley off down the road. While they were gone the man and boy set-to cutting their firewood, double-handing the bow-saw on the thicker branches. While Tom cut the lighter stuff, his father took the axe off the cart and split the big logs. They were just finished stacking it beside the fresh-stoked fire when Liz and Blue arrived back, struggling to get the heavy churns over the rough ground. Steam issued from the spout of the kettle; boiling water was made into tea.

The family sat around the shafts of the big wagon, drinking from their bright-coloured mugs and talking amongst themselves. The kettle, which had been refilled after the tea was made, was soon boiling again and Liz was pouring the water into a big steel mixing-bowl. She lifted the lid of the metal box beside the fire and took out a bag of flour, which she slowly poured into the hot water, beating it all the time with a wooden spoon. Soon the mixture was too thick to beat and she rubbed the dough off the spoon with her hand and started to knead it into a ball, still in the bowl. When she took the flat iron disc from the wooden box, unfolded its handle and hung it on the bent fire-iron, I knew that bread was going to be baked.

I watched in eager anticipation as Liz pulled a little handful of dough from the bowl and rolled it into a ball between her hands. Then she patted it down on the smooth plank of white wood beside her and rolled it out to a thin round slice with a green marble rolling-pin. The first whiff of baking floated down the air as she sprinkled a handful of flour onto the hot iron. It slowly turned a golden brown. Flames licked the disc as Liz used a metal spatula to scrape the flour over the edge and into the fire.

She expertly lifted the soft slice of dough with one hand and dropped it onto the girdle-iron, which she was slowly turning with her other hand. The delicious smell wafting on the breeze had taken all my attention. Bumper was attracted by it too. He'd strolled casually over to the fire and was nudging Liz in the back to try and persuade her to let him have a taste.

She called to Ben who was still relaxing on the step between the shafts,

'Will you get this horse off my back, please!'

He threw the last of his tea dregs into the hedge and putting his mug on the wagon ledge said 'Come on then Tom, lets see what we can do with this horse!' The boy stood up and got hold of Bumper's forelock.

'Walk on!' He pulled the horse away from the fire and led him down to where I was tied, near the other wagon. I'd rather have stayed and watched the rest of the bread baking, in the hope that I'd get a taste, but it was not to be. Instead, Bumper was fastened to the chain and I was led by the man's firm grip on my halter back up the track, past the fire, where the first slice of bread was being turned on the iron and the second was rolled out, waiting its turn.

Tom, walking beside me said 'Give us that chapati, Liz!'

'It's not ready yet,' she told him.

'Hang on a minute,' he called to Ben, and I stopped in my tracks thinking this was a good idea. But Ben would have none of it.

'Walk on!' he commanded, and I dared not disobey.

'Get that harness together, never mind feeding your face!' he called back to Tom, who was still hovering at the fire. 'You help him, Blue,' he told the girl who was sitting on the end of the wagon-shaft playing with her two little sisters.

She followed us onto the road with the winkers over one shoulder and the collar over the other. Tom hurried on behind her, his arms full of the tangle of straps that comprised most of the rest of the harness. He was blowing the hot chapati he'd just snatched from the fire. When the three of them had finished unceremoniously tacking me up, he gave me the last corner of the warm bread. It wasn't easy chewing over the bit; the dough turned slimy in my mouth and clung to the ridges along the bar, so that I had to slide my tongue over it again and again to get the last of it. The bit was still clanking against my teeth when I felt the reins tighten and the metal sunk firmly into the corners of my mouth.

Tom was still standing at my head, though I could only see his legs now that the winkers restricted my side-vision. Blue was nowhere to be seen. I knew it was Ben holding the reins when I heard his no-messing voice order me to 'Walk on!' There were no poles to drag this time. I started to move forward, leaving Tom standing in the road.

'Good boy,' I heard, over the jingling of the bit which I was trying to chew into a more comfortable position. As I progressed steadily forward the pressure on the bit relaxed slightly, so that I could just feel it. I was striding confidently down the middle of the road when I heard the new command, 'Come in!' accompanied by slight pressure on the bit that inclined my head to the left. I followed the pull until I was walking close to the verge, then the reins slackened and I carried on in a straight line down the road. Each time I started to drift towards the crown of the road the order to 'Come in' was repeated, along with the pull on the bit. I soon learnt.

We walked along the quiet lane as far as the crossroads. Even pressure on both sides of my mouth and 'Whoa!' brought me to a standstill. There was no other traffic. Ben pulled my head to one side and said 'Come a-right' and 'Walk on.' It was easy to understand what he wanted me to do. We walked on past the site of the old camp. A butt-log still smouldered on the bare earth. There were areas of flattened grass, trampled over the past week of dry weather. Other squares were yellowed where boxes had stood. Just beyond the camp, on the left, was another road junction. There was a house on the corner, a little car parked in front of the gate.

I learnt the command 'Come out!' as I was steered into the road to overtake it. Then 'Come-a-left,' as we turned at the junction. I hesitated slightly as a tractor came towards us, but Ben slapped my rump lightly with the end of the reins and I hopped forward and kept going. The tractor slowed right down and crept past us. A short distance further, Ben 'Whoa'd' me to a halt.

'Stand up!' he ordered, folding the reins across my back and walking round to stand in front of me. 'Good lad!' he said, as he patted my nose. I lifted my head so that we could breathe in each other's faces. His was almost entirely covered by a long bushy black beard, tinged at the edges by a few white hairs. His brown moustache was even longer and more luxuriant than Frankie's. It tickled my nose as I brushed against it, tasting his sweet breath, as he blew softly over my nostrils. 'You've the makings of a good horse,' he told me confidentially, 'but don't tell the woman I said so!'

On the way back he had me going through all my newly acquired skills at the trot. When a van came along the straight road and overtook us, I ignored it, and kept up my steady pace. Turning at the crossroads, an old man on a little motorbike sputtered towards us, but I took no notice and trotted on back to the camp with my head held high.

We passed Birch with her front legs up the trunk of a tree she was browsing. Frankie called out to us. I wasn't sure of the appropriate reply, but I muttered something anyway as Ben called 'Easy, now,' in a breathless voice. The reins tightened and I slowed to a walk. 'Come-a-right.'...and we were back at the camp. Liz had just finished baking the days' chapatis. She was wrapping them in a clean cloth on the wooden plank.

'Hmm, they smell good,' said Ben, as we stopped beside the fire, and I agreed. 'Come and help me get this fella untacked, then.'

She was undoing my girth strap and belly band, asking 'How did he go?'

Once I was out of the harness Liz led me back on to the lane where the Shadow was still tethered by my chain. She let him go and tied the chain around my neck, rubbing her hand along my mane and checking to see if the chain had rubbed my skin, but it hadn't bothered me. She was talking to me all the time, asking me how I'd enjoyed wearing the harness, and how did it feel, was it good? I mumbled back at her, nudging the front of her shoulder with my nose till she gave me the bit of bread from her pocket.

'Right then,' she said, as I chewed on my reward, 'tomorrow the cart!'

Pulling a cart.

Naturally I was apprehensive the next day when Liz brought me down to the camp and started lifting my feet and running the hoof-pick around my soles. Then the harness. Each time I fidgeted, I was given a tap on the nose by the girl who was holding onto my halter and told to 'Stand up!' When I tried to put my head down to grab a mouthful of grass the collar rode up my neck and hit me on the back of the ears. The girl put the toe of her boot under my nose and that brought my head up sharp enough.

'Now be a good boy today, Sullivan.' Liz was telling me as she led me out onto the road where Ben and Tom were manœuvering the two wheeler into position. They tipped it back, so that the shafts were pointing upwards, the way I'd seen it parked around the camp.

Liz let me have a good close-up look at the dark green wheels and the varnished wood of the cart body. A bench seat spread the width between the ledges. 'This is called a side-lace car,' Liz told me. 'We call it the side-lace, and your job will be to pull it. And me. And lots of our tat. All over the country! Alright?' She led me round and stood me in the road.

'Now do you think you can back into the shafts?' she asked me, pressing against my chest and saying 'Back? Good boy, back!'

But the memory of the horse-box was still too strong. My fear of stepping backwards would take a lot of overcoming. So I stood in the road as they rolled the vehicle forward and slowly lowered the shafts on either side of me. Liz was talking soothingly to me all the time, just in case any of this new experience should frighten me. They pulled and tugged on the harness as it was fitted to the shafts and body of the cart. The traces were attached to hooks behind me, the braker-straps wrapped around the shafts which were fed through the tugs hanging from the straddle. The belly-band held the shafts firmly by my sides. Ben stood in front of me and looked along the shaft, tilting it with his hand to check the balance. 'Do you think the tugs need lowering?' he asked.

Then he said to Liz, 'Go on then; get up!' and I felt the side-lace rock on its unladen springs as she stepped onto the wheel-boss and climbed aboard. I started to shift around, uncertain what my feet were doing, but Ben had the reins held in one hand under my chin, and pulled sharply on the bit saying 'Stand up!' She gathered up the reins and Ben released his grip.

'You alright?' he asked her.

'Yeah...' came the uncertain reply.

'Walk on!' he said to me, and with the bit trembling slightly against the corners of my mouth I took my first faltering steps. The collar pressed against my shoulders as the traces tightened, but I didn't hesitate. I couldn't see behind me, but I knew the big green wheels were starting to roll when I felt the shafts vibrating. It was nothing like the feeling of the travois poles. Much quieter and smoother. I also felt much more confident in the harness now, less afraid of any traffic we might meet.

'Good boy!' said Ben. 'Now, trot on!'

To Liz he said 'Give him a bit of a slap.' The reins touched my rump and I remembered the command and changed my pace to a slow trot. Ben jogged along just ahead of me, in the middle of the road, as far as the crossroads.

'Hold him!' he told Liz, and she with the gentlest of pressure on the bit said 'Easy now,' and I dropped back to a walk. 'Whoa!' they both said and I stopped and checked the white line across the road to see if it was still safe to pass. The side-lace tilted in the opposite direction as Ben climbed on. Then he said to Liz 'Go straight on,' and without pulling my head to either side she slackened the reins and said 'Walk on, Sullivan!'

I wasn't sure if she wanted me to go left or right, so I tossed my head from side to side as I started forward. I heard Ben say 'Here, give me those reins!' and then a sharp pull on both sides of my mouth brought me to a standstill in the middle of the junction.

'Now! Walk on!' he commanded. I had lost sight of the alternatives, could only see the road ahead. When all four feet had taken a couple of steps to get the wheels rolling he ordered 'Trot on!' and before the reins had even touched my rump I was changing to a brisk trot.

'Be firm with him,' he said to Liz, handing her the straps. 'Don't let him mess you about. He's still got a lot to learn.'

Under Liz's hand the reins slackened and the bit eased off. I kept up my brisk trot for a while till I started to get a sharp pain under my ribs. I slowed back gradually to a much easier jog-trot and the pain began to subside. I was enjoying the feeling of the cart rolling along behind me, trotting steadily along the bog lane, startling the birds and little furry creatures in the hedgerows as we passed.

Ben's voice: 'Trot him on!' and the flick of the reins had me putting a spurt on again. I kept it up for a bit longer this time before the pain had me easing back.

'He's not fit...' I heard Liz saying, and she was right. I could feel sweat under the harness already starting to trickle down my legs and along my flanks.

'Okay. Turn him left just up ahead.'

As we approached a T-junction I was allowed to walk for a short distance. After stopping to see if the road was clear, I was pulled to one side with the direction 'Come left,' Liz's voice making it sound more like a request than a demand. Her touch on the reins was much the same. I knew that if I didn't comply though, the alternative was Ben's harder hand and voice. She guided me round the right-angle bend and invited me to 'trot on' again. The sharp pain in my ribs was still nagging, but I put on the show of a trot anyway. We were heading along a straight road now, no hedges on either side. It was just like a raised causeway across the brown desert bog, flat as far as I could see in all directions. Away in the distance a clump of trees, and a white splash that might be a house. Beyond it the landscape seemed to be tinged green again.

I was making steady progress, and the pain was easing again, when I felt the rumble under my feet. Nothing was coming towards us, no, it must be coming up behind. Liz at once recognised my apprehension. The reins tightened to stop me going to left or right. The panic I felt rising started to subside when I heard her telling me 'Don't mind 'em, Sullivan! Good boy, trot on, don't mind 'em!'

I trusted her not to let me come to any harm. I was no longer afraid of vehicles on the road. I felt sure it would be safe, the road was wide enough for him to overtake without hitting me. The winkers prevented me from seeing its approach, but I could hear the growling of the engine as it pulled alongside the cart. The vibration under my feet told me it was really close, but I just kept up my steady pace. Right alongside me on the narrow road, with the engine revving for a burst of speed, the vehicle let out a high pitched squeal, three or four notes in quick succession, so loud they blasted my eardrums and sent my senses reeling. I'm sure all four feet left the ground as I leapt sideways from the terrifying assault.

'Easy!' yelled Liz, pulling me back onto the road as my left hooves bit into the soft soil of the narrow verge. I swerved about from side to side a few times as I watched the blue and white back doors of the van grow smaller down the long straight road. The exhaust fumes mixed with the tobacco and man-smells in its wake.

'Christ, you nearly had us in the bog!' I heard Ben yelling.

'Me?' retorted Liz, 'What about your friends there? Nothing to do with them, I don't suppose?'

'He'll have to get used to idiots leaning on their horns.'

'I thought he handled it really well.' Liz defended me.

They talked on, and I relaxed once more into the steady trot that brought us eventually to the end of the causeway. The clump of trees was an overgrown hedge protecting the little field at the very edge of the brown bog.

A mixed herd of horses, mares with foals, and ponies were bunched together at the end nearest the house. A big piebald colt was prancing up and down the field as we approached. The side-lace tipped and wobbled as Ben stood up and shouted 'SPRINGBOK!' over my head, then gave his now-familiar 'Whoop-whoop-whoopee!' horse call. The colt responded excitedly, answering with a high-pitched call of his own. He kicked and bucked as he cantered alongside of us. I was glad of the fence that separated him from the road. I overtook the blue and white van parked in front of the house, and stopped outside the gate.

'How's it goin', Larry?' Ben called to the three men standing in the yard.

They had all turned to look at us, and one of them raised a hand and called back 'How's yourself?'

All three men walked down the path and through the creaky gate. They stood around me, patting my sweaty neck and saying 'Fine horse, Ben. Is he a new one?'

'Yes,' confirmed Ben. 'This is his first time out.'

'Nearly his last, back there!' interjected Liz.

'Oh, sorry about that, missus, he was going so well... I didn't realise...' one of the men apologised.

'That's alright,' said Ben, 'it's all good training for him.'

Then he asked 'Any news about the colt, Larry?'

'Aye, the woman is coming down for him tonight. She has some fancy stud farm up in Kildare; wants to train him for a show jumper.'

'Great. He'll be perfect for that. No fear in him at all!'

'Why did you sell him?' asked one of the men.

'Oh, he was just too much of a handful, forever bursting through fences. I was just telling Larry here the other day... I had him tied on the back of the wagon and we're driving past this field full of mares. I'm trying to control the big horse in the shafts and there's Springbok pulling the back wheels up the verge trying to get at 'em! Between 'em they nearly had the whole yoke turned over!'

'Wouldn't you get him cut?'

'Aye, it's not only that. He'd be jumping the ditches out on the bog. He slipped back into one last week and I had to get myself under him to lever him out. I tell you, that's not a thing I ever want to have to do again!'

The men mumbled their agreement, as Ben jumped down onto the road and stood at my head. Fingers tasting of engine oil and tobacco were pushing my lips apart.

Ben said 'This fella's coming a three year old. He'll make a better wagon-horse than yon-lad ever would.' He tipped his head in the direction of the colt who was still calling to him from the field gate on the other side of the house.

'I'd better go over and say goodbye to him!'

'Are you coming in for a cup of tea, missus?' Larry asked Liz. The other two men went ahead of him, back up the path to the house.

'I'll see what Ben wants to do,' was her reply.

She remained seated, the reins slack. Ben met Larry at the side door.

'We'll not stop,' he said, 'we've left the kids back at the camp!'

Their parting handshake was more of a slap.

'How's the little pony going?' called Larry as Ben was climbing back onto the side-lace.

'Ah, he's grand!' lied Ben. Quieter, to Liz, he said 'Bring him round; tell him "come-around".' She pulled my head hard-around to the right and gave me the words of command. I had to side-step, bumping my hips and shoulders between the shafts in order to turn the car in the narrow road. Then I could see the long straight track stretching back over the bog and Liz was saying 'Trot on!' Ben called 'Springbok!' one last time to the prancing colt on the other side of the fence.

I was looking forward to cooling my tongue in the bucket of water as Liz led me back to my tether on the verge opposite the camp. But just as my lips touched the remains of my morning's water she snatched the bucket away and splashed the water deliberately over my feet. Surprised, I asked her 'Why did you do that? I wanted a drink!'

'First things first,' she told me. 'I know you want a drink, but not till you've cooled off.' I could feel the sweat drying off me, rising like mist in the heat of the sun. Liz's hand made a slurping sound as she patted my shoulder.

'First sweat, eh, Sullivan? First of many, I hope! Why don't you have a roll on this nice grass?' she suggested. 'I'm going to get a cup of tea now, and then we've got another surprise for you!'

I pawed the ground to reinforce my demand for water, but she just walked back to the camp calling 'Later, okay?'

'About time too!' I whickered when I saw Tom carrying a full bucket down the lane. Liz walked behind him, a bright plastic brush strapped to each hand. One red, one blue. As I guzzled the water down she started to groom me. I could feel the ghost image of the harness from my earlier sweat. The short plastic bristles separated the hairs again and smoothed my coat. The brushes made no impression on my mane which was thickly matted along my crest. It hung in tufty spikes about halfway down by neck, on both sides. The only grooming it had ever had before was from other horses. My tail likewise had never received any attention. It was a great trailing mass which almost touched the ground. Liz flicked the brushes over it, tugging loose a few stray hairs, but hardly breaking the surface.

'Hmm, this is a comb and scissors job!' she observed.

'Have you brushed his feet yet?' I heard Ben call as he walked down the lane carrying a long wooden box in one hand. He had a sort of leather apron, split in the middle, covering the front of his thighs and belted around his waist.

Liz turned her attention to the long hair above my hooves. The splash of water hadn't done much to loosen the years of accumulated muck. She coughed as the quick brush-strokes released a little cloud of dust around each foot in turn. Tom stood in front of me, holding a rope attached to my halter loosely in one hand. Ben picked up a front hoof, and facing backwards, gripped it between his thighs. He started to cut away the frayed edge of my hoof with a pair of red metal clippers.

As he worked he said 'The bit of road-work has worn 'em down. His feet are long over-grown but they're not twisted. He has a good straight step.'

He held a strip of curved metal against my sole. Liz asked 'Will Bumper's shoes fit him?'

'Yeah, could have been made for him. Here, go put these "fronts" in the fire.'

Ben handed the shoe to Liz who took it, along with another one from the box, back to the camp. She returned as he was running the rasp over my sole and saying 'I probably won't be able to get frog-action on this first shoeing...'

The rasp tickled, taking the hard skin off the frogs in the middle of each hoof. I wriggled and tried to snatch my foot away, but Tom held me by the nose and ordered 'Stand up!'

'Bring him down to the camp.'

Liz picked up the tool box and followed as Tom led me past the wagon to where a bigger-than-usual fire blazed in the middle of the clearing. Ben was already poking at the embers in the heart of the fire. He was using a pair of long-handled grips to pull a glowing shoe from its midst. He lowered the shoe onto a little anvil beside the fire and tapped a short metal spike into one of the nail holes. Holding the hot shoe in one hand, he deftly slipped my hoof between his thighs again and gripping hard on my leg, he pressed the hot shoe firmly against my sole. At first it felt not unpleasantly warm against my hoof, but soon a cloud of smoke was rising from the shoe to envelope the three of us.

'Hold him!' Ben said to Tom, as I hopped my other front foot off the ground, trying to escape this dense white smoke with its strange acrid smell. Tom grabbed the end of my nose in his strong young hand and squeezed so hard that my lip curled back. He dug his sharp fingertips in between my nostrils, which painfully restricted my breathing.

'Easy, boy!' he was saying to me. 'It's alright. You're not on fire. It just smells that way!'

Ben let my foot fall onto the grass and Tom relaxed his grip on my nose. The hot shoe hissed up a cloud of steam as it dropped into the metal bucket of cold water. This performance was then repeated on my other front foot.

Ben put some more wood on the fire, and carefully placed the other two shoes on the top. He covered them with more sticks before coming back to nail the front shoes on. It only seemed to take a few minutes. A few light strokes of the rasp to clear the burnt hoof, then the shoe was fixed to my hoof by short, sharp taps of the hammer. The nails bent as they went through my hoof. As each one came through the front wall, Ben caught it in the claw of the hammer, giving it a twist to break it off short. When all seven holes were fitted with a nail he turned around and held my hoof over his leg so that it rested upon the thick leather apron. He ran a file under each nail, then used another tool to squeeze the nail tip down flat against my hoof. Last thing was the rasp running around the edge of the new shoe to round my hoof for a smooth fit. By the time he'd done the other front one, the back shoes were hot, and ready to be burned on. Tom's vice-like grip on my nose every time I fidgeted soon had me standing quiet again.

When the back shoes came out of the fire, Liz made tea with the boiling kettle, and poured the last of the hot water into the big mixing bowl. The girdle-iron was hung over the fire, and by the time my shoeing job was finished the first of the chapatis was baking over the pile of embers.

'Heat up a bit of Venice Turpentine in an old can.' Ben suggested to his daughter, who was busy gathering up all the shoeing tools and putting them back in the box, while he put the finishing touches to my back hoof. When she brought him the sweet resinous liquid a few minutes later he took an old paint brush from the tool box and smeared it generously over my hooves. He lifted them and painted my frogs too. Then he gave Tom a leg-up onto my back and said 'Let's see him go!' The rope became guiding reins as Tom urged me back onto the road. All the family stood and watched as he trotted me along the metalled surface. The ringing of new shoes under my feet was a little startling at first and made me lift each hoof in an exaggerated trot. The weight on each leg would take a bit of getting used to. At the bend in the lane, Tom pulled my head around to turn me back to the camp. With the new spring in my step, I headed proudly back. The skinny black dog bounded down the lane to meet us. I suppose he was just caught up in the excitement.

Ben called 'Lovely! He's stepping out much better now!'

Liz had gone back to her baking and Ben and the girls went to get their tea, leaving Tom to tie me up again.

'Good lad, Sullivan,' he said as he undid the rope from my halter. 'You're ready to start work now, once we get some muscle on you!'

He patted the flabby flesh on my shoulder and said 'Shouldn't take long ... a few five mile runs before breakfast, eh?'

'Shadow'

He was joking, but there was extra activity in the camp the next morning. When Liz came to move my tether down the lane away from the camp, Blue was with her. The girl caught her pony who'd been standing beside me all night. 'Come on, Star,' she said, slipping a loop of rope over his nose and scrambling up onto his back. Ever the shadow, he jogged along beside me as

I followed Liz. When we got to where Bumper was tied, Blue 'whoa'd' the pony and quickly transferred Bumper's chain onto his neck. The stocky little piebald nudged and bumped the girl as she led him back to the camp. We walked on to the first stretch of good grass and Liz tied the end of my rope to a stout ash-tree. Without saying much she left me there, packing the lush greenery into myself. A short time later she brought me fresh water. Just as I was dipping my nose into the bucket the other horses all started calling. Frankie's high pitched cry came from down the lane beyond the camp. The Shadow, who had only just settled down, renewed his prancing and shouting as Bumper was led onto the road under the shafts of the side-lace. Ben and Tom were sitting up on the driving seat. Blue ran ahead, shouting at the pony to settle down. She grabbed his rope and tried to drag him off the road as Bumper went past, but he reared up and she was thrown to one side. She landed on the grass verge, and soon stood up again, shaking one wrist and brushing down her thigh with the other hand. She was more angry, and shaken than really hurt. The pony she had inappropriately named 'Star' was at the end of the chain, frantically trying to break free so that he could go along with Bumper.

Liz called to her daughter 'You alright, baby?' as the girl came limping towards us. She shook her fist at the prancing pony as she passed him on the road. Ben pulled Bumper to a stop just before he reached us. He turned around and called back to the girl too.

Then he asked Liz 'Anything I need to get from town?'

'Just the usual stuff, you know what we eat!' Then she added an afterthought as the wheels started to roll past us, 'Don't forget the tetanus shots.'

'I won't forget,' he promised as they trotted out of sight.

Blue showed us the gravel-rash on the heel of her hand where she'd hit the road.

'That's one loony pony,' said Liz, and I agreed with her.

Mother and daughter walked back to the camp, hugging each other and hurling insults at the pony who was still calling after Bumper. It was another gloriously hot day. There was nothing to do but fill my belly. As the quiet afternoon wore on I realised that, for the first time in my life, I was not hungry. Feeling satisfyingly bloated, I lay down on the newly nibbled grass and luxuriated in the heat of the sun. I let my head rest against the sweet smelling earth and drifted off into an easy sleep filled with flashing dreams of all my recent experiences.

I was roused from slumber by the distant call of horses and the vibration of hoof-beats echoing down the road. It was the return of Bumper, well sweated from his trip to town. I staggered hastily to my feet, shaking myself to clear my head.

'You alright, Sullivan?' called Tom, as they drove past me. 'Just having a little snooze, eh?'

'Looks to have over-indulged himself somewhat,' observed Ben. 'Hope he doesn't go and get colic, now.'

I lifted my tail and released a quantity of shiny black-green droppings onto the road. The loud squelch caused Tom to look over his shoulder and remark, 'He looks fine to me...'

Later that evening, as the sun brushed the tree tops, Ben brought me more water. He was talking quietly to me as he rubbed a part of my neck with a wad of cotton-wool soaked in astringent smelling liquid. He smelt different too, traffic fumes mingled with his own animal-and-wood-smoke smell. My head was in the bucket when I felt the stab of the needle in my neck. It was over in a flash, and Ben was rubbing the cotton-wool over the spot again and saying 'Good boy. That didn't hurt, now did it?'

'It may not have hurt you!' I muttered back at him, but I gave him a nudge on the shoulder with the end of my nose. There was a dull ache where the needle had penetrated my muscle that lasted into the night, but the next morning it was gone.

The leisurely pace of life continued over the following days. Every morning I was moved to new grass, my water bucket was never empty for long. When the hottest part of the day was passed, Tom came to ride me around the lanes. We were invariably accompanied by the Shadow, with or without his rider. Racing against him should have been easy, but he was considerably older than me, lighter and fitter too. He was also a past-master in the art of Dirty Tricks: swerving in front of me as I tried to pass him was one that had me unbalanced and stumbling in the road quite a few times. He wasn't above lashing a sideways kick as we cantered along neck and neck. He was a thoroughly unruly and ill-mannered lout of a pony. All his boasting of all the different places he'd been began to make sense. I could understand why no-one would tolerate him for very long.

One day, I was tacked up to take Ben and Liz for a jaunt. This was only my second time under the shafts of the side-lace but I felt easy and comfortable as I walked, then trotted steadily down the lane. The Shadow was tied to my chain, which was fixed to an old half-shaft hammered into the ground. Walking past him, he started his usual performance of wanting to come along too. Running to the end of his tether and jerking hard to try to free himself. I could still hear him yelling as we rolled on out of sight down the lane. We'd gone a good distance along the quiet bog-lanes and were approaching the junction of a main road when we heard the intermittent clanking behind us.

His appearance could have been almost silent, unshod feet on grass verge; but this was not the way of this particular Shadow. He was rattling his chain along the middle of the road at a flat-out gallop, the half-shaft on the end whipping from side to side and ringing as it bounced off the tarmac. Ben leapt off the side-lace and grabbed the chain as the idiot pony bounded alongside us. Liz was already pulling me to a stop. The metal spike crashed into the big green wheel before rolling to a standstill in the gutter. Ben and Liz debated what to do now. The main road ahead was going to be my next big test, obviously none of us wanted the extra bother of another horse to mind. But there was nowhere here to tie him; a dense thorn hedge ran along both sides of the narrow lane, the main road had no verges. There was nothing for it but to take off his tether and let him run free. The stake and chain were put in the cart and Ben climbed back aboard.

Doing my best to ignore the triumphant crooning of this foolish creature, I started to roll the side-lace towards the junction. Full of himself now that he'd got his own way, he cantered on ahead, not pausing for so much as a glance to left or right as he ran straight across the main road to the hard shoulder on the far side. He turned around and called to me, but Liz was giving me more than enough pressure on the bit to stop me following him into the path of the traffic. It wasn't a very busy road, but there were one or two cars coming from the left which had to brake hard and swerve onto the hard-shoulder as he came glibly trotting back across the road asking me 'What are you waiting for?'

I could hear Ben mumbling curses at the top of his voice as the lorry came thundering down the road from our right. The pony was standing nose-to-nose with me, blocking the whole of the carriageway. Like the idiot he was, he barely flinched as the lorry roared by, inches from his tail, its air horns blaring.

Liz was saying 'Don't mind 'em, Sullivan!' and slackening the reins to stop me backing the cart into the thorn hedge.

'Go on!' the slap of the reins on my rump propelled me forward and Ben's 'All clear,' at the junction was her signal to keep me going. 'Come left,' she pulled me sharply round and onto the main road. There was a hard-shoulder on my side of the road too. I trotted steadily along it allowing the traffic free passage along the carriageway. The Shadow could easily have trotted along beside me, there was plenty of space before the fence, but that wouldn't do for him. No, he had to be under my feet running just ahead of me, or veering out under the wheels of vehicles that were overtaking us. If part of my training was to get me used to the sound of motor's horns then this was all excellent experience for me.

We hadn't gone far down the road when we caught sight of a couple of chrome-and-white caravans. They were on the other side of the road, parked up at the end of a wide verge. As we drew level with them, Liz pulled me across the road and steered me over the bumps of the rough ground before stopping me alongside the shiny dwellings. Shadow had cantered off along the verge to introduce himself to a little spotted mare who was tied to the fence. An old man was sitting on a white plastic chair outside the door of one of the caravans. He stood up slowly as Ben jumped off the ledge of the cart and the two of them slapped each other on the back in the way of men who haven't seen each other in a long time.

When Liz climbed down too and came to stand at my head, I figured I'd be resting for a while. I gave a shake that rattled the harness and sent a shudder along the shafts, then shifted my weight to relax against the breeching.

The old man gave me an admiring look as he stroked my neck. He glanced over the harness and the side-lace, taking stock of the whole turn-out before settling back into his seat.

'That's a grand sight now,' he admitted.

He took a cigar from a box in his waistcoat pocket and proceeded to puff the blue-white smoke in my direction. A shiny new pick-up truck mounted the verge and stopped in front of the other caravan.

'So you found us then!' the young man called to Ben as he climbed out of the cab. A woman stepped down from the caravan bearing a tray of steaming cups and a plate piled high with sandwiches. I was not to be included in the tea-party; my polite request was met with the response 'Stand up!'

When Liz and Ben climbed back on the side-lace, saying their farewells, the Shadow was still doing his best to ingratiate himself to the little mare.

'Are you leaving this one with me?' waving the cigar stub in his direction.

'I wouldn't wish him on you!' replied Ben, and to Liz he said 'Bring him round...'

'Come around.' She pulled my head to the left and I turned the cart where it stood, so that we were facing back the way we'd come. No sooner had my hoof-beats started to ring the tarmac of the hard-shoulder, than the Shadow gave his 'wait for me!' call and came cantering after us.

Back at the camp, Ben was shouting 'Get this animal away from the cart! Somebody tie him up! Here, Blue! Take Sullivan's chain and tie him to a tree or something!'

The girl finished putting the kettle on the fire, then took the chain and rope from the back of the cart. She slipped the half-shaft off the end and left it behind as she caught the pony and looped her rope-rein over his nose. With the coil of chain over her shoulder, she then scrambled up onto his back. He was still standing beside the side-lace, which Liz and Tom were trying to roll back.

Blue was digging her heels into the pony's ribs and trying to urge him to move, but he was stubbornly refusing to budge. Ben handed her the whippy stick she sometimes needed to get the pony started. She gave a flick on his shoulder and tried to pull him round. He was sweated and still excited from his free-run, and obviously didn't want to obey orders again. He half-reared and bucked with his back legs. The girl was thrown back and forth, but she clung on and gave him another flick of the whip. He spun round then and charged back out to the road. Blue only intended to take him a short distance; she was calling 'Whoa!' and pulling on the rope as he galloped off down the lane, spitefully and wilfully out of control. We heard the chain hit the road.

The girl must have been close behind it. Having thrown his rider, the mindless little animal came cantering straight back to the camp, neatly side-stepping Ben who was running down the road to pick up his daughter.

'Right! That's him FINISHED!' we heard Ben yelling. Tom picked up a branch of dead wood from the log-pile and broke it over the pony's tail. Still brandishing the stump he chased the bad-tempered creature out of the camp. Seeing Ben carrying the girl down the road, the pony took off in the opposite direction. Tom hurled the stick at his fast-retreating rump, and to judge by the squeal of indignation, I'd say he scored a hit.

Liz hastily pulled the last of the harness, the collar, over my head and left me standing in the middle of the camp as she rushed to meet Ben, with their daughter in his arms.

'No broken bones, far as I can tell,' he was saying, 'but she's out-cold.'

He carried her into the wagon, followed by Liz and Tom. The two little girls sheltering from the sun under the wagon played on oblivious as the kettle began to spit water, dampening the bright little fire.

In the gathering dusk, Liz came looking for me. Left to myself I'd spent the afternoon grazing the verge and mutual grooming with Bumper who was tied in the hedge. My chain and rope were still scattered across the road beside him. She straightened it out and clipped the chain around my neck.

I spent the night tied next to Bumper. We couldn't quite reach each other, but we were close enough to talk, to exchange thoughts. Bumper liked Blue; she was forever bringing him treats, and buckets of water. She'd just started learning to drive and was always easy and gentle on his mouth. I don't know if anyone went looking for the pony, but he drifted back, predictably enough, as darkness fell.

Bumper of course had seen him deliberately throw the girl onto the road. Had seen him bolt off leaving her lying in the ditch. He had stood over her limp and seemingly lifeless form, giving her a nudge with his nose and asking if she was alright, the way she often did for him when she found him sleeping. But she hadn't moved, nor made any sound. He'd seen Ben race towards her, then quickly put a hand on her neck and his face close to hers, much the same as Bumper had, to check if she was still breathing. Ben had carefully straightened her crumpled limbs before picking her up and hurrying back to the camp.

And the pony she had called 'Star' was back here sharing our grass as if nothing had happened. Bumper told him in no uncertain terms that he needn't bother staying around here, reinforcing the message with a front-leg kick that stopped just short of the pony's head. He was cute enough to have gauged the extent of Bumper's tether. So he didn't come within range of either of us that night. Frankie had never allowed him anywhere near his range, so from that time he was outcast.

It was only a few days later that the Hi-ace pulled up at the camp. I recognised the little man who had brought me here, although he was towing a decent horse-box. I was tied along the lane, not paying much attention to what was happening. Tom and his sister came walking down the lane. It was the first time I'd seen the girl since her fall. She had a broad white band of cloth around her forehead, and as they walked by I saw her cheek was badly grazed and one eye was bruised a violent purple. But she was talking and laughing unsteadily as her brother slipped a noose over the neck of the pony who had been grazing the hedge with his back to them. Tom had anticipated the reaction and held tight to the big knot on the rope-end when the pony tried to run. The loop of rope tightened around his throat as Tom jerked him round. He made a feeble attempt to rear, but the rope was restricting his breathing, and he quickly submitted. Tom slackened the rope and led him back to the camp.

The little man scarcely glanced at the pony as Tom walked him into the box. As he closed the ramp, we heard the high-pitched whinny for the last time. The man slapped hands with Ben, then with Liz. He took something from his pocket, and after pretending to spit on it, handed it to Blue. She was smiling when the van drove away.

As it disappeared from view, I'm sure I heard all the people in the camp giving a hearty cheer.

Chapter Three

The Derrynaflan Chalice Incident.

Over the next few days, Tom exercised me regularly. Every time we went out, the going seemed to get easier. I no longer suffered the sharp pain under my ribs. I learnt to control my breathing to keep time to my pace and found that I could trot much further without puffing and panting.

He didn't talk to me much, only to give me the verbal commands that matched his movements of the reins. I never had a bit in my mouth on these sessions. The rope tied to the halter was enough for Tom. He never let me canter on the road, but sometimes there'd be a wide grass verge and he'd urge me into a canter or even a bit of a gallop. These were my natural paces at that time, cantering and galloping around a field was the only exercise I'd ever had, and not having anyone to drive me on, I'd never pushed myself too hard.

So you can imagine that learning to trot was a big move for me. It made me ache in muscles I didn't know I had. But the aches soon wore off, and after a good brush-down my coat took on a shine that could only have come through sweating out the dust.

'You're looking better every day!' Liz told me admiringly, after she'd spent a long time combing and trimming my tail. It still reached below my hocks, and without all the matted tangles on the end it made a better than ever fly whisk.

The next time I was tacked up and put under the shafts of the side-lace it was to take Ben and Tom to visit some friends of theirs. Off down the maze of flat lanes with Tom driving. We could hear horses calling, their voices carrying uninterrupted over the bog. We turned off the metalled road, onto a dirt track slightly raised above the stripped brown land on either side. In the distance we could see a line of old trucks and trailers parked on one side of the track. The little herd of horses came cantering down to meet us. They seemed to be all mares and foals, about two dozen of them. There were a few colts amongst them too. They reminded me of the herd I had once belonged to, but of course it wasn't them.

I felt threatened by their attitude to me, which was quite hostile. Ben took the reins and ordered me to 'trot on!', so tossing my head from side to side in response to his firmer grip on my mouth I shouted 'Get out of the way! I have to come through!' and to my surprise they all scattered at our approach, letting me cut a path through their midst. They regrouped at once and came cantering up behind us. Ben and Tom were lashing out with ropes and whippy sticks that they'd gathered before leaving, obviously for this purpose. They managed to stop most of the herd overtaking us, but a couple broke through and hurtled themselves into the shafts as they galloped past. It was a most intimidating game; I'd have liked to get away, run as far as I could over the desolate landscape, but Ben kept my head straight forward and urged me, 'Don't mind 'em, Sullivan! Brave boy! Go ON!' so that I was doing my fastest trot, sweat streaming, heart pounding as we passed the first of the brightly painted caravans beside the track. Yappy, snappy dogs ran out to try and catch my feet. I hardly felt my flying hoof propel some little fluff-ball through the air, we were already past by the time it landed with a bump and a squeal.

The next little knot of vehicles included a wagon, its pale yellow shafts held horizontal by matching props. I snorted as Ben pulled me to a halt and the entourage milled around us. A man jumped down from the wagon and waved his arms at the herd, shouting to drive them back along the track.

'These all yours, Bob?' asked Tom, and the man said most of them were.

'They're not getting enough work!' observed Ben. The man shrugged his shoulders and agreed.

I was glad to stand and let my heart stop racing while the other horses wandered off, and the men went to stand around the smouldering turf-fire in front of the wagon. The track ran straight as far as I could see; only one landmark broke the monotony. It was a bright green mound, standing out like an island on a brown sea. Perched on top, a ruined building, only one gable end still intact. The rest of the walls in varying stages of dereliction, the roof gone.

'Is that where they found the Chalice?' asked Tom, and Ben replied, 'Sure is, that's Derrynaflan.'

It was quiet on the track; I relaxed against the breeching and listened to the story.

'Its a weird place alright…' began Bob, 'd'you remember your sister Becket was camped up here with us last year, before Caramee? Well, one night we were having a bit of a party. It was around solstice and we had a big bonfire an' all. Late on, somebody went to check the horses and there was no sign of them. So a few of us went off in different directions to see if we could find 'em. Becket thought her lot might have made their way over to the 'island' there, so that's where she went. It was a full moon, plenty of light, but real windy, y'know what I mean?

'So she gets out there and climbs to the top of the mound, and its wilder than ever up there, so she gets in behind the gable of the old church there for a bit of shelter; just to get her breath back, like. No sign of the horses, by the way. She looks at her watch in the moonlight and its exactly midnight. O.O.O. This was just after yerman had dug up the treasure and they'd fenced off the bit of ground where he'd found it. Standing there in the shadow of the gable she said the very point of the shadow hit the ground right where the chalice was buried. It was like whoever had buried it used the moon and the church for a marker, so he could find it later.

'Becket legged it back here, toot-sweet, as you can imagine. She told us all about it, but nobody fancied going back for another look!'

'Did you find the horses?' Tom wanted to know.

'What? Oh, yeah. Tim found 'em down on the road...'

Their voices drifted on the hot dusty wind as I half closed my eyes. The last question I heard from Tom before I lapsed into a dream-troubled snooze was: 'Why do they call this place the Loony Line?'

Startled awake by the jolting of the shafts as Tom climbed aboard the side-lace and gathered up the reins, I could hear Ben saying 'We'll see you again, brother. And thanks for the pup, we'll take good care of him.'

A ball of black and tan fur nestled in the crook of his elbow, Ben took my head and turned me around on the track. Without bothering to stop me, he jumped on the ledge of the car and up onto the seat beside Tom saying 'Trot on, now!' to me, and calling back 'Kushty bok!' to his friend.

About half way back to the camp, we stopped beside a dead tree in the hedgerow. The two of them soon had it cut down, pulled clear and sawn up into lengths to fit in the body of the car. Starting off again, the shafts were heavier on my back, the load of wood having upset the balance of the vehicle. Ben soon had me standing again while he and Tom got down and adjusted the seat. Progress resumed with the car once again finely balanced, the shafts floating beside me. It was much heavier to start, but once rolling, the big wheels made light work of it and the extra weight on the springs took all the jolts and shocks of the road so the car rolled, if anything, more comfortably. Tom pushed me on at a brisk trot. By the time we got back to the camp, my coat was streaked with white lines of sweat, but I held my head up proudly when Liz came to untack me.

'Good boy, Sullivan! Good load of wood, men.'

Ben handed the fluffy pup to Blue, who said 'Aw, he's lovely. Thank you.' And gave Ben a quick kiss on the cheek before burying her face in the black and tan fur. She went to show the little creature to the twins who were bouncing up and down and shrieking for a look.

First trip to Town.

'We'll see how he is in the traffic.' Ben said the next morning. I was led into the camp and tacked up again.

'Its a miserable day to be taking him to town,' said Liz, as they settled the shafts into the tugs.

'Miserable day to be going,' agreed Ben, 'but it has to be done, and he may as well get used to it. We're moving out of here tomorrow, remember.'

Liz helped him move the seat forward on the ledges, and Ben and Tom got up on the car. They were wearing shiny green waterproof jackets, with hoods. I was wet from the heavy drizzle that had been falling for most of the night. The blanket under my straddle warmed my back as we set off, and soon the raindrops I shook from my mane and forelock were mixing with the sweat running from under my collar. Ben had the reins, and he pushed me on at my fastest trot for the first few miles. Then he would let me ease off the pace for a while before pushing me on again. He used a thin whippy stick which he flicked against the side of my rump when he wanted me to go faster. It didn't hurt for long, but the sting was enough to make me jump-to-it. The stick made a whirring sound when he waved it over my back, and after he'd stung me with it once, it was enough just to hear the sound for instant acceleration.

We crossed a hump-back bridge as a train was chugging slowly underneath. It let out a high pitched whistle which hurt my ears and made me toss my head and call out. But I had no time to panic; Ben had firm control of my mouth and the flick of the whip kept me going so that the imagined danger was soon passed.

We were in the town, traffic everywhere. Stop in the street surrounded by motors, overtaking on my left as I face the oncoming traffic before turning right. People milling along the pavements and crossing the street in front of me. A van full of men driving alongside us, slowly overtaking, calling out, 'New horse, Ben?' and 'He's going well!' as he urges me on with a wave of the stick. With Tom at my head, I stand amongst the parked vehicles outside the big grey building. Ben returned with half a dozen other men who stand around me and mutter their comments. One gratuitously shakes a shaft, then pulls at the top of a wheel as he eyes the side-lace over. Another peels back my lip to look at my teeth.

'Yes, get me out of here!' I whicker. The two men climb aboard and Ben turns my head back to the road saying 'See ye, lads!' and 'Walk on, Sullivan. Good boy, now trot on!'

We turn back down the street and head for the middle of town. Some of the streets and lanes are narrow and all are mad-busy with traffic, but Ben steers me with a firm hand and a clear voice. Next stop is a wide-open space with a few cars parked at one end, close to a big square windowless building. At the other end, a patch of rough grass. Ben jumps down at the back entrance to the building and leaves Tom to take me to the bit of grazing. He removes my winkers and throws a blanket over my back. I send a shake the length of my body, nose to tail.

Tom adjusts the blanket and says, 'There y'go, boy. That better? See if this grass is fit to eat...' He squats down on the edge of the weedy grass and I pull a mouthful.

'Its pretty rank,' I tell him. He can see for himself the drinks-cans and crisp-bags, the plastic wrappers and old newspapers. The rain has freshened it up a bit, and in from the edge of the tarmac some of the tufts of grass are succulent enough. I munch slowly, wishing we were back under the trees on the quiet lane, instead of in this rain-soaked town, all noise and exhaust fumes. Tom eats his apple to pass the time, and feeds me the core.

Ben returns pushing a wire trolley on little wheels, piled high with cardboard boxes exuding white plastic bags. He calls to Tom from half-way across the car-park, but the boy has seen him coming and is already putting the bit back in my mouth. He shakes the blanket and folds it again before putting it back on the seat. They load the boxes and abandoning the trolley, we head back down the wide main street and out of town. Over the railway bridge the road is empty and I need no encouragement to get back to the camp as quickly as possible.

The moving next day went off uneventfully enough. Frankie led the way, pulling the big wagon; all I had to do was follow on behind. The side-lace was heavier than ever before, but the load was well-balanced so it didn't rock or tip and it rolled along smoothly. Bumper with the little wagon and Tom driving brought up the rear. The worst nuisance was the nanny-goat who had to have her legs tied together before she'd submit to travelling on the cart. Ben and Liz had to lift her aboard and she protested loudly, wriggling and kicking to try to escape. Once we started moving however, she soon settled down and apart from the occasional bleat, she seemed to accept the situation.

Frankie set an easy-enough pace, having the heaviest load to pull. The wooden wheels looked light under the wagon, wobbling uncertainly on their axles as though they might buckle or crumple at the next jolt. But they somehow managed to withstand all the jarring potholes and road-drains, despite a decidedly soft spring on the back of the wagon.

The day was still overcast, but the drizzle had finally abated. It was better than travelling in hot sun; we were a good few miles down the road before I started to break sweat. When we reached the main road, there were a few hills to contend with, but they were gentle enough, nothing I couldn't manage. Going up was easier than coming down, at first. The breeching pushing against the backs of my legs felt strange.

Liz was saying 'Hold it back, Sullivan. Easy boy. Good boy. Brave horse! Hold it back!' and holding the bit firmly in my mouth to let me know I mustn't let the harness push me forward. With the back of the wagon blocking the road in front there was nothing for it but to shorten my step and hold back on the breeching.

The sun rose above the low-lying cloud as we pulled off the road onto a large area of rough ground on the outskirts of a village. A few bungalows lined the road, but beyond the new camp scrubby trees marked the horizon. Only in one place did the distant ridge of low hills show over the hedgerows. The grass-centred track leading off the road ran alongside a grey stone wall. Behind this a high dark green hedge bordered a cottage garden. As soon as we were all untacked and tied out on the rough pasture, Liz and Tom scrambled over a tumble down gap in the wall, carrying an empty water churn. When they had filled the four buckets that Blue brought to the gap, they went back to fill the churn again. The water was carried back to the camp and the fire lit with wood that Tom had carried along in his little wagon.

Then, while Liz and the girls set about clearing out the wagons and arranging the kitchen boxes around the fire, Ben and Tom disappeared beyond the hedgerow wielding bow-saw and axe. My favourite smell, baking bread, wafted across the wasteland as they returned, each burdened with a bundle of dead wood as big as himself.

Over the next few days there were many visitors to the camp. Most of them drove their vehicles along the track till they were opposite the fire, then off-loaded whatever they were delivering. First thing I saw arriving was a pair of metal spoked wheels on narrow tyres. Then the new timber came off the back of a pick-up. Everyone who came to the camp was given a drink from the ever-boiling kettle, many stayed to enjoy a meal with the family.

Ben set to work on the wood and soon had the shape of a flat-cart put together. The springs were the last thing to arrive, but once they were wire-brushed and painted the little cart was assembled and ready for the road. While Ben was working on it, Liz took me out a couple of times. Bringing Blue and the twins along for the ride we'd go and visit other camps in the vicinity. One place had horses, and a mule, along with the motor vehicles. Raggety children ran about the camp, scruffy mongrel dogs were tied under old caravans. The little black lurcher called 'Jet' had run along with us that day. He was a good dog to have alongside the cart, taking seriously the job of stopping other dogs that charge out of gateways and snap at our heels.

The slim, dark woman who gave Liz and the girls a cup of tea made a huge fuss of him. Jet was delighted by the attention.

Liz said 'He looks just like you, Caroline!' and they all laughed and compared the woman's thick black plume of hair to the dog's bushy tail. When it was time to leave, the woman called the dog into her caravan and closed the door. She spoke to Liz through the window: 'I'm sure he'll be alright, but I'll just keep him in 'til you're gone.'

'Sure. You know where we are, just bring him back if he doesn't settle down.'

But Jet obviously took well to his new home. A few days later the woman and some of her friends visited the camp in an old car. Jet stayed close by her side as she sat at the fire, and when they left he had no hesitation jumping back in the car with her.

Another day, we visited a roadside camp of curiously painted vehicles. On the narrow verge next to a big brown car stood a wagon more lavishly decorated than any I'd ever seen. Its narrow little doors opened outwards and were lined with mirrors which reflected the overhead trees. The caravan parked next to it was also a riot of elaborate scroll-work. On its roof sat an assortment of objects all painted the same bright sky-blue and ornamented with red and yellow flowers and white borders that looked like rope. An old watering-can, a dented bucket, what might have been handle-less pans, all given a new lease of life as flower-pots.

Strangest of all was the high-sided truck alongside of which Liz had me stand. The window had red stained-glass panels that looked like curtains. This was only one of many illusions. The whole side of the truck that I could see was divided into different sized panels and each of them contained a scene so startling realistic that I couldn't help shying away. Mountains and sky-scapes, a stormy sea set in an octagonal frame of plaited ropes; in each corner a spray of roses. Other panels had geometric designs, squares within circles, all bordered with intricate interlacing. The carved wooden panels around the window were salmon-pink, the upper part of the truck and the areas between the paintings was an insipid pale lilac.

A white strip defined the top of the wheels. Below that, the black paintwork was decorated only by a fine red outline. A ledge hung on chains from the back of the truck. A woman leaning over the half-door shouted at her dogs which were going crazy on the end of their chains. She came out to greet us, jumping lightly onto the road beside me.

'Another new horse, Liz?' she asked, letting me sniff her hand. She wore a soft black dress which covered her legs but left her arms and back bare.

'Hmm, this is Sullivan. We've had him a few weeks now.'

'Where d'you get him?'

'Off some fella from New Ross. Swapped him for a couple of ponies.'

'Was he worked before?'

'No, he's just learning. But he's lovely; its like driving a new car!'

The girls had climbed off the side-lace and were rummaging through a pile of old clothes outside the caravan.

'You having a clear-out?' asked Liz.

The woman said everything got musty packed away and she was just airing some stuff. A pink metal trunk stood with its lid open and garish cloth draped around.

'Is Dave about?' Liz stepped down to the road.

'He's just getting up. DAVE!'

'Who wants me?' came the gruff voice from inside the truck. Almost immediately the grizzled blond head appeared at the door, one hand scratching at the spiky thin hair.

'Liz! When did you get here?' still fastening his belt, he jumped off the ledge to land beside her. Arms around each other, hugs and kisses.

'Just a few minutes ago!' she laughed.

'You know what I mean!' he said, his hand still resting on her shoulder.

'Last Friday. We pulled onto the back of the quarry.'

'Holy Cross?'

'Yeah. We thought you were up there.'

'We were. But we got a lot of hassle, so we pulled down here last week.'

'Nobody bothered us yet, touch wood...' said Liz, lightly brushing the end of the shaft with her fingertips and reaching up to pull my forelock free of the brow-band.

'So, admire my new horse!' she told him.

'Seen one, you've seen 'em all.'

'Ah! no! This one's different! Let me introduce you. Dave, this is Sullivan. Sullivan, meet Dave.'

He patted the end of my nose with a hand that was laden with the smell of paint and tobacco.

'Hello, Sullivan,' he dutifully intoned.

I said to Liz 'Who is this guy?'

He turned to the woman shaking a scarlet coat from the trunk and said 'Any chance of a cuppa, Vicky?'

'I thought you might be finally going horse-drawn when I saw the wagon.' Liz was saying.

'No chance. Not me. Its just a paint job I'm doing for one of the local travellers. Come and have a look!'

Saying, 'Mind the horse, Blue,' Liz strolled back to take a closer look at the fancy wagon.

The twins were having great fun dressing up in all the theatrical silks and velvets. A smooth haired white terrier with a brown eye-patch was joining in the game, allowing itself to be draped in the mildewed fur of a long-dead fox.

The Party at 'Mary-Ellen's Bog'.

After a week of sunshine and showers, of dramatic sunsets over the distant hills and hazy mornings, the flat cart was finished. So was the rough grass. Time to move on.

One morning Frankie, Bumper and I were brought to the camp and tacked up amidst the shouting and bustle of last-minute packing. Everyone helping, even the little ones rushing around collecting up chains and stakes, and walking around the embers of the fire with their heads bent to make sure no bits of kitchen equipment got left behind.

Ben got Frankie under the shafts of the wagon before calling 'Here, Blue, hold this horse. Liz! Let Tom hold Sullivan, I need you to help me tie-on the flattie.'

Tom told me 'Stand up!' and stood in front of me with the reins in one hand as we watched them attach the newly built cart to the back of the wagon. Bumper stood unattended some way off. He was in the shafts of the little wagon, patiently helping himself to a few last mouthfuls of grass.

The cart bumped and swayed as it was towed behind the wagon, but once on the road it rolled along smoothly enough. We'd made an early start, and put a good few miles behind us before the sun was overhead. In the midday heat we pulled in to a lay-by and after untacking us and tying us along the wooded hedge, Ben and Tom pulled armfuls of dead branches and twigs. Liz soon had a bright little fire with a kettle hanging over it.

The family were eating their lunch when the dark blue van drove in to the lay-by and stopped alongside the wagons. The driver leaned out of the window to talk to Ben, who stood with his back to the fire, a mug of tea in one hand. He gestured an invitation to share the meal, but the driver shook his head. Their conversation only lasted a few minutes. The orange cone on the roof of the van flashed a couple of times as it pulled out of the lay-by and headed back the way it had come. Ben saluted the driver, middle finger standing out of his clenched fist.

As we rested, Tom and Blue were busy pulling more of the dead wood out of the hedgerow. They piled it into Tom's little wagon. Liz washed-up the cups and plates, then tipped the last of the water from the big churn into a bucket and offered it to me, to Bumper, to Frankie, to Birch. The goat took as much as she wanted before Liz poured the dregs over her own hands.

There wasn't much packing to do, the hardest part was tying Birch back on the cart. She never submitted gracefully to this indignity, and having to endure it for the second time in one day, she put up more than her usual resistance.

Back in our warm, sun-dried harness, we were moving again in the afternoon heat. I was glad we'd rested a while because soon we were facing a long uphill pull. It was steady enough, but it had me flagging, not being used to hill-work. Liz jumped off the cart when I slowed to a walk and slapped the reins off my flank to trot me on again. I could hear Tom's voice behind yelling something too, so I put my shoulder to the collar and pushed on as best I could. Without Liz' weight, the cart should have been easier to pull, but the goat was having one of her panic-attacks, bleating and thrashing around so that the shafts kept tipping, alternately casting the weight between my back and the belly-band. Apart from that it was, surprisingly, easier to keep going at a jog-trot than a walk. When the hill levelled out, Ben brought Frankie to a standstill and we stopped behind him, glad of the chance to get our breath back.

Liz was patting my neck with one hand and saying 'Good boy, Sullivan!' while she pressed her other hand against her midriff and drew deep breaths.

'Phew! I'm not as fit as I should be,' she told me.

'How do you think I feel?' I snorted back.

Almost as soon as my heart had stopped pounding I heard Ben calling 'Y'alright?' to Liz, and 'Ready Tom?'

With Liz back on the seat, the side-lace found its balance again. There was a gentle breeze across the open road as we rolled along the top of the hill. Liz was probably enjoying the miles of scenic views, but I could only catch glimpses to left and right by moving my head sideways: the winkers severely restricted my vision.

The downhill run started gently enough. I was trotting-free in the harness, collar and breeching both sitting loosely about me. The wagon with its little cart in tow was bowling down the hill away from me, and my instinct was to stay close, but Liz held me back so that I was obliged to hold the same pace. I felt the breeching pressing against my legs, a few stray tail hairs trapped under the leather tugged as I tried to swish them free.

We were closing in on the wagon, which had slowed down in order to make a right turn. An oncoming car cut through at the last second, as Frankie was already over the white line and obviously committed to his move, but the lorry behind it stopped. Oblivious to our intentions, cars were still overtaking Bumper and weaving in and out between us as we crossed the road.

We were back to a single-track road, overgrown hedges on both sides, and the downhill drop was suddenly steeper than any I'd yet encountered. The wagon looked to be hurtling out of control as it raced away with its extra two-wheels bobbing crazily along in its wake.

Liz was still letting me trot, but the breeching was pushing so hard against my legs that when my front feet started to slip, my back legs buckled under me and I kept losing control too. At one point a sharp tug on the already-tight reins saved my nose colliding with the loose chippings as I slid all-four-feet into the ditch.

Approaching a cluster of farm buildings, the yapping black-and-white dogs came belting out of the wide gate snapping and snarling at Frankie's legs. I wished Jet was with us. He'd have sorted them out. He wasn't afraid to bale-in and see them off. Dogs that are used to bullying sheep and cattle soon back off when faced with the likelihood of having to defend themselves. But the only dog we had at that time was 'Pip', the armful of fluff who still rode in the wagon. So the sheep-dogs launched their attack on Frankie. The two of them disappeared under his legs and must have grabbed onto the masses of hair over his hooves. He shied off to one side, rearing to kick free the front dog, lashing out behind to try to shake off the other. The wagon and flat-cart were snaking about the road in front of me. Liz was pulling hard on the bit and shouting 'WHOA! WHOA!' I could hear Tom shouting the same to Bumper.

I wanted desperately to stop, but the weight of the fast-rolling cart on the breeching just kept propelling me forward. Feet locked into a skid, I could only see the back of the wagon looming nearer, hear Ben's curses as he struggled for control. I jerked my head to one side as my chest rammed into the back of the flat-cart. A holding rope snapped and its shafts flew upwards. One of them crashed in through the window in the back wall of the wagon. The tinkling of breaking glass and the thud of the other shaft as it bounced off the wagon must have really terrified the two little girls who were inside. Their wailing became another element in the confusion.

The farm was out of sight behind us when we finally managed to stop. The pair of collies slinked back past us, one of them holding a front paw in the air. Tom gave it a resounding kick in the ribs as he ran by on his way to help Ben. He took hold of Frankie's head, but the big horse was already standing quietly enough. All Ben's anger seemed directed at Liz, and at me. He rounded the wagon waving his arms, raging fists punctuating his fury as he cursed and shouted. Liz yelled in our defence, but he wasn't listening as he pulled the shaft free of the broken window and let the cart drop back onto both wheels.

'Are the twins alright?' Liz called to Tom. Saying 'Stand up, Sullivan!' she left me trembling in the shafts, with Ben continuing his tirade. She went around the front of the wagon and hugged the crying children who clung one each side of her, burying their faces into her neck.

'If you put those brats down you could do something useful... like help me tie what's-left-of my flattie onto what's-left-of my wagon!'

Liz took over Tom's job at Frankie's head and tried to calm the frightened children while Tom helped his father fix the two vehicles together again. The road soon levelled out and we were on bog lanes again. A few more miles we trudged wearily along in the late afternoon sunshine.

A voice I'd not heard before called out, 'Welcome to Hairy Melon's Bog!'

And I heard Tom's 'Yo! Becket!' as Liz turned to see the girl overtaking Bumper. A squeal of brakes as she slowed her old black bicycle and let it cruise alongside my head. I turned to get a better look, but only caught a glimpse of long dark hair and long pale arms before Liz straightened my head.

'Hey, baby!' she was saying to the girl, 'How much further's this camp?'

'Not far. Have you come all the way from Holy Cross?'

'Yeah. We stopped for a break before the hill and the Shades were on us before we'd had a cup of tea!'

'You'll not get bothered down here, but there's not a lot of grass left!'

'I suppose we'll only be stopping a night or two. The mood yerman's in we might not stop at all!'

'Right. What happened to the window? Don't tell me ... I saw the glass in the road. Those dogs want shooting!'

Frankie must have been about as tired as I was by this time; we were plodding along at a trot no faster than a walk. The banter between the women helped keep my mind occupied, and before too long Liz was Whoa-ing me. She didn't even bother to tighten the reins. The wagon in front of me stopped. I stopped. I gave a weak bit of a shake that barely tinkled the harness-buckles. It seemed to take the last of my energy. My knees were still wobbling involuntarily, my chest felt sore where I'd hit the flattie.

As soon as the goat was untied, she struggled to her feet, rocking the side-lace as she leaped clear onto the grass verge. She immediately squatted her back legs and relieved herself of a long-held bladder full of frothy golden liquid. Lifted her tail to release a cascade of shiny black pellets. Bleating her relief, she shook her silver-grey coat free of dust and headed into the hedgerow to start feeding. Becket wheeled her bike off the road and came back to help Liz untack me. They soon had me out of the shafts, and tied to a stout fence-post. The verge was only a bit wider than the wagons but the grass was knee-high. After following the goat's example, I let my knees buckle under me and collapsing on the soft grass tried to roll the way Bumper was doing on the other side of the lane. Over he went and back again, kicking his legs in the air. I got about half-way over, then rolled back onto my side. Legs twitching, I tried again but didn't even get half-way. Too tired to care about my unsuccessful attempt, I just lay on my side, soaking in the late afternoon sun and fell fast asleep.

A pair of massive stallions had launched an unprovoked attack on me. Their screams and threats had me cowering in terror as their great hairy feet lashed out at me. Backing away and half rearing to defend my head from their kicks, I caught a blow to the chest that tumbled me over on my back. I tried to right myself but they were towering over me, one each side, their manes streaming, their nostrils flaring blasts of hot breath in my face.

I woke with a start, blinking away the horrific vision, shaking my ears to get rid of the stallion screams. But they were real. Fortunately, Frankie and the other horse didn't seem to notice me as I struggled to my feet between them. The big white horse was tied further along the verge, behind the wagon. The object of his fury was coming down the road under the shafts of a flimsy metal-framed two-wheeler, a 'sulkie' of sorts. He was another stallion, and quite prepared to face Frankie for the show-down. He was an unmarked black, taller than Frankie, though not so heavy. As he approached, he seemed to accelerate. He was moving faster than I'd ever seen a horse move. The man up on the high seat was doing his best to exert some control.

Ben was half-way between me and Frankie, bringing me a bucket of water. The big black horse had passed me by unnoticed when the man finally managed to stop him.

'Whoa, Lightning!' he shouted. 'Stand up, there!'

Ben had put the bucket down and tried to catch the horse's head, but Lightning was too quick for that. The man on the sulkie had the horse standing.

'Hey! How's it goin'?' he called to Ben.

'Middlin' to bad!' The unenthusiastic reply.

'What's up? You over for the party?'

'Looks like it. Her ladyship wanted to come. You know me, I wouldn't be bothered. Only to see our Becket again, the rest of 'em, well, you know what I'm like about parties, crowds. I'm dying of the 'flu as well!'

'So have you been over to Charlie's?'

'Yeah. Went over to say 'hello' when we got here and ended up skinning and butchering a couple of badly-killed goats. Honest-to-god, I don't know how I get involved in other people's trips!'

'They've been brewing for weeks, there'll be gallons of booze... oh, you don't drink these days, do you?'

'Not so's you'd notice. I wouldn't be drinking anything that crew would make; there's no telling what goes in the mix!'

Frankie was still calling for a fight and straining at the end of his chain. Lightning started to prance in the road. The man said 'Better see if I can get this lad back to the camp.'

'I'll get Frankie off the road.'

With both horses determined not to lose face, the men had to exert powerful influence to stop them trying to kill each other. Away down the road, the black horse kept screaming his threats. Even when he was tied back at his own camp, out of sight, the two of them kept up the barrage of abuse.

There wasn't much rest to be had that evening, with old motors driving by us on the lane, noisy, smelly, rusted under layers of paint. Most were packed with people; kids and dogs hung out of windows.

Darkness was a long time coming. The stars finally showed themselves against the night-sky when Liz came to say 'Goodnight' to me. I was standing half-asleep tucked under the hedgerow. I called softly to her as she walked down the lane. She came to stand beside me in the pitch-black shadow of the thorn trees, running her hands along both sides of my neck, smoothing the hair down my chest and finding the painful swollen area where the phantom stallion had kicked me over.

'That's a nasty bump.' She soothed me as I flinched at her touch. 'Didn't do the flattie much good either. Or the wagon...' she added.

Her voice sounded different somehow, and her breath smelt bitter, acrid. I told her so, with a snort of disgust, but let her put her arms around my neck so that my head rested over her shoulder. She buried her face in my mane. We stood there in the total darkness for a few minutes before she started to make little sobbing sounds and her shoulder under my chin trembled and shook.

'What's wrong?' I asked her, and she just said, 'Oh, Sullivan, my lovely, lovely boy, you give such a lovely hug...' and she squeezed my neck in her arms. Letting out long moaning wails, she rubbed her face against my neck to smear the tears on her cheeks. I just stood there, with her crying on my shoulder 'til she'd cried enough. Then she wiped her eyes on her scarf and patted my neck, saying, 'Thanks. I needed that! Early start tomorrow. Get us out of this place. Oh, Sull., I'm so sorry about this...' she gently stroked the swelling on my chest, '... about all of it. Ben was right, we shouldn't have come here at all.'

A damp mist descended in the night, and with the dawn it turned to an incessant drizzle. Tom was the first out of his wagon, gamely trying to coax fire from a pile of wet twigs. The white smoke hung like a flat cloud over the camp. Eventually the flames sputtered to life and the kettle was boiled. Liz and Blue brought us water. There was a lot of shouting in the camp that morning. Bumper, Frankie and I had eaten all the good grass on the narrow verge, Birch picking between us. It was time to leave.

Liz folded a wool blanket under my straddle, and struggled with the tangle of wet straps as I stood patiently accepting the inevitable. The drizzle got heavier, so that I could feel the beat of raindrops against the harness as we set off, leaving only the hissing embers of the breakfast fire to mark our stay.

Turning left at the first junction, we could see another camp along the lane. Mares and foals that were scattered in the adjoining field lifted their heads and called as we passed. A few of them trotted a short distance towards us. The big black horse, 'Lightning' was tied on a running line in the hedge. He pranced along to the end of his tether at Frankie's approach, and the two of them renewed their challenging. Ben had to put the wagon on the opposite verge to get past Lightning, who trotted beside the shafts, tossing his head and kicking sideways. I stayed close behind the wagon hoping the big horse wouldn't notice me.

When he had run the length of his rope, he stood in the road calling after Frankie, mercifully ignoring me and Bumper. Three wagons stood on the roadside, a smoky fire burning between the first two.

Liz whoa'd me in, but she stayed on the side-lace as she talked to the people around the fire. Becket was making tea and asked did she want a cup? Liz said they'd just had some.

'You're off early,' observed a man I hadn't seen before. His long red hair hung in tight curls that sprayed rain when he shook his head.

'Yeah. Not a moment too soon!' replied Ben.

'So you're still heading for Puck?' asked the man who was driving Lightning the day before.

'Looks like it...'

'We've got a present for you, then,' he said, and ducked out of sight behind one of the wagons. An alarmed bleat and he emerged with a pure white goat kid in his arms.

Offering it to Ben he said 'A puck!'

'Just what we needed!' Liz said sarcastically. Birch started to thrash around in the back of the cart, calling in response to the kid's pathetic bleats.

'You can always eat it,' said the red man.

'Sure, what else would they do with it?' put in Becket.

Ben called back to Tom, 'Will you carry this yoke?' indicating the animal still in the man's arms. Tom glanced back into his wagon and agreed to take the puck. Birch almost managed to free herself and tipped the cart as the man walked by, delivering the kid to Tom. Liz leaned over the back of the seat and shouted at the goat.

Ben said, 'Come on, let's get this mad-house on the road before we pick up any more passengers!'

Becket said, 'You're not going to change your mind and come to Caramee with us?'

'Next year,' said Liz, as she slackened the reins and said 'Walk on,' to me.

The wagon was already rolling, Ben calling 'Kushty Bok!'

Liz reached down and touched hands with her daughter saying 'Take care, honey. Be lucky.' 'You too!' said Becket, adding 'Give our regards to Kerry!' as we broke into an easy trot.

The Roadside Fight.

We plodded along the quiet lanes in the morning rain until we joined the main road again just before a small town. Over a hump-back bridge with a tumbledown tower guarding its flank we were competing for road-space with heavy traffic. Cars and lorries revved impatiently as we negotiated the narrow little streets of the town, turning left and right, stopping for traffic lights, hurrying around roundabouts. A long pull uphill past petrol stations and cottages before the road widened again and we had the hard shoulder to ourselves, main road traffic spraying past us.

I suppose everyone shared my relief when we pulled onto the raised verge. It was a big half-circle, on a bend in the road, separated from the fields by a grey concrete 'post and rail' fence. Liz tied my rope to one of the posts and went back to sort out her camp; the two wagons side by side, back to the wind, the side-lace with her kitchen boxes standing, shafts-down, in front of them.

For the first time that day, the rain eased off and away down the valley we'd just climbed out of, a rainbow poured from the blanket of white cloud and drenched the horizon in its colours.

Tom and Blue trundled the water churns to a farm a short distance way on the opposite side of the road. They were soon returning. The girl was pushing the old pram-frame along at a half-run, her brother glancing back over his shoulder. The noise of the churns as they clattered together rang hollow. They were still empty. Their excited voices in the camp telling their parents how the man had not only refused them water but told them they couldn't camp here, they'd have to move. Ben picking up the axe and making a dash towards the farm. Liz grabbing him by the arm, spinning him back into the camp. The two of them shouting, Ben gesticulating, Liz trying to hold his arms and stop him leaving. Blue crying and yelling at them to stop. The twins wailing in confusion.

Tom, in exasperation saying, 'Look, I'm going down to those houses on the hill to get some water. Are any of you coming with me?'

Ben: 'Alright son, wait for me,' dropping the axe and following the boy. Liz picks it up and leans it against the wheel of the big wagon, then puts an arm around Blue and strokes the girl's hair saying 'Its alright, don't worry about him, he's just some buffer.'

'But he said the last time travellers stopped here all his horses broke out of the field and one got hit on the road.'

'So, maybe he should fix his fences. Hey, its not our problem, don't worry, okay?' and to the twins, whose wails had subsided to snivels she shouted 'Will you two ever shut up!'

They were soon back with the water and Liz was struggling to tip some into the empty buckets when the big silver-grey car stopped on the road. Ben was intending to go find some firewood: he had the bill-hook in his hand. Three hardy-looking young men were crossing the field from the farm. They climbed the fence on the other side of the road and stood there glaring at the camp as the driver got out of the car wielding a short-handled lump-hammer. Ben was at the roadside, facing them. A passenger got out of the car.

'We're not looking for trouble, just pack up and get out of here!' said the driver.

'So what's the hammer for?' asked Ben, who was still carrying the blade.

Liz bundled the little girls into the wagon and told Blue to stay with them before rushing to the road where the men were already shouting and threatening. She tried to pull Ben away and he had to shake her off as the unarmed man took the opportunity to swing a punch at his face. Caught off-balance Ben only partially avoided the blow which connected with his cheek-bone. Liz was screaming as she was thrown backwards onto the grass, not knowing what to do as the two men set about Ben. The hammer was aimed at his head, but he managed to deflect it with the back of the bill-hook, knocking it out of the man's hand. It landed with a thud on the broad bonnet of his shiny car.

'Tom! The axe!' as Ben was punched in the stomach, doubled up. Tom hefted the big axe and ran from the camp, but one of the men crossed the road and stopped him before he reached his father, easily snatching the axe and pushing the boy away from the fight.

One of the men had Ben's arm bent up his back and was holding the blade of the bill-hook against Ben's neck while the other man punched him about the body. Ben was raging and kicking, but every blow he landed only increased the men's anger. Liz was still screaming at them to stop. She wasted minutes trying to wrest the axe from the grip of the farm labourer, wasted more imploring the motorists who were driving slowly by, watching, to help, to call the gards.

Blood was pumping from a wound under Ben's ear. He was pinned helpless under the blade of his own tool while the big fat farmer continued to use him as a punch-bag.

He only stopped at the sound of cracking glass as Liz beat the hammer with all her strength against the big curved windscreen of his car. She took three swings at it before the glass finally shattered. He spun around and I thought he would turn his attack on Liz, who was standing in the road, still holding his hammer. He rushed around the car shouting 'Give me that!' and making a grab for her wrist. She dodged him, threw the hammer so that it punched a hole in the crazed glass of the windscreen, right above the steering wheel. He reached in through the open side-window, and picked it up off the seat. Cars were driving by and overtaking, some slowing right down, others sounding their horns. Calling to the other man who was still holding Ben in an arm-lock and digging him in the back with the metal-bossed handle of the bill-hook, the driver got back into the car. The other man threw Ben's limp body aside and dropping the blade onto the back seat, he climbed in next to the driver. Glass fragments crunched under the wheels as they spun a U-turn. The man with the axe crossed the road and climbed the fence with the other two, back across the fields. Liz helped Ben to his feet and she and Tom half-carried him between them back to the wagon.

Sitting him on the step between the shafts she filled a steel bowl with water and called to Blue to bring the cotton-wool and witch-hazel from the wagon. She tore the blood-stained tattered shirt away from the wound on his neck and pressed a wad of soaking cotton-wool against it. He flinched and complained loudly before snatching the blood-soaked wad away and looking to see how bad it was.

'More cotton-wool, girl!' he shouted. He ripped away the rest of the shirt, popping buttons as he yanked the cuffs over his hands. Liz was fussing around asking what she should do, where was he hurt. Ben was still angry as well as hurt all over.

'You can shut those brats up!' he told her and she climbed past him into the wagon to try to quieten the twins, who had redoubled their moaning at the sight of their father's blood.

Tom was dabbing white ointment onto the worst of the red marks on Ben's back when the dark blue van stopped, front wheels scattering the glass on the road. The two men put on peaked caps as they walked into the camp. They stood in front of the wagon, talking quietly to Ben. I didn't hear everything they said but they seemed to be insisting that we'd have to move. Ben was arguing that the horses were tired, the children were hungry, it was raining again. All these things were true, but the men from the farm were standing by the road outside their gate and didn't look as though they would leave.

The men in the dark suits were pointing down the road saying, 'Just a couple of miles...' so reluctant and weary, we were tacked up again. Tom caught the little white puck who was running around trailing a length of light chain, and lifted him into the wagon. Birch jumped lightly in after him, and they put the half-full water churns up on the side-lace in her place. Nothing had been unloaded from the cart or the wagons, so we were very soon on the road again. The men sat in their van and watched across the road. By the time we passed the farm we were trotting miserably. The men stood in their waterproof coats watching to see that we were really leaving. Ben hadn't bothered to put another shirt on; the rain ran down his arms and mingled with the blood on his chest that still trickled from the wound under his ear.

'This isn't finished!' he shouted as he passed the little group. 'It's only just begun!'

The men jeered back at him, keeping up their abuse as Liz drove me by, even shouting at young Tom and brandishing the axe they'd taken.

'I want those tools back!' Ben yelled to the men in the van as they overtook us and went on ahead. They were waiting, parked at the roadside at the bottom of a steady hill a few miles on. A bend had been taken out of the old road, a wide verge built at the intersection. A high mound of gravelly soil formed a barrier that stopped us taking the wagons onto the old road, but once untacked we were easily led over it. It must have been a few years since the new road went through. The old tarmac under our feet was cracked and pot holed and overgrown with creeping plants. Grass encroached from the narrow verges. Because there was no traffic we were tied on long lines to reach both sides of the road, and the goats were left free.

The blue van drove back up the hill and returned shortly afterwards with Ben's axe and bill-hook. The rain eased off in the evening, and with plenty of dead wood that Tom and Blue pulled from the long-neglected trees along the old road there was a good big fire that night.

Liz carried two buckets full of water and set them down on the edge of the road across from where I was tethered. I strolled over to investigate, but the steam rising from the buckets surprised my sensitive nose.

'Back off, Sullivan!' said Liz, pushing my head away and giving me a slap on the rump. 'Don't you know that's a whipping offence, drinking the officer's bath water!'

Ben brought another hot bucket. He had a couple of towels over his shoulder and a big jug in his hand. They were standing next to the densest part of the old hedge, an effective screen between them and the traffic out on the new road. Ben took off his shoes and trousers; that's all he was wearing. He started to pour jugs full of water over his head as Liz was undressing. She handed him a plastic bottle and he squeezed thick liquid into the palm of his hand, then rubbed it into his hair and beard.

As he rinsed away the grime, I could see that his cheek was grazed raw, and his eye bruised a deep purple. All over his body and legs red marks were developing dark shadows. The deep cut on his neck had formed a crusty scab.

Liz quickly shampooed her own hair, then they took turns with the jug, pouring the last bucket over each other, letting the suds run down and wash their bodies. Wrapped in the towels they bundled their dirty clothes into the empty buckets and hurried back to the camp. The heat-haze that rose like a shimmering column from the stove-pipe of the wagon said it was a warm dry space inside.

Liz brought me water before she went to bed. She smelt more like her old self, but sounded really tired. The sun was still hours away from setting, but it had been a long day.

An uneventful night, stars bright. Sun high before we saw signs of life at the camp. A slow start to the day. Another visit from the dark blue van. Just checking? The men didn't bother to get out, or put on their hats.

After them, an old yellow Hi-ace van rattled up to the camp. A little man wearing a tattered tweed jacket a few sizes too big for him climbed out and joined the family around the fire. He took the mug of tea, pushing his greasy trilby to the back of his head as he spooned in the sugar. He lit a cigarette and sat himself on the metal box next to Tom.

We'd picked the best of the grazing from the old roadside by the time the camp was packed. It must have been mid-afternoon, the hottest part of the day, but a cool breeze meant it wouldn't be too unpleasant to be working. The bump on my chest was no more than a dull ache by this time, but after a few miles it was starting to throb and my front legs tingled, a sort of numbness spreading down from my shoulders. I stumbled a couple of times, and Liz knew something was wrong. She told me we didn't have far to go, called me her Brave Boy. I did my best to ignore my discomfort and keep up with the wagon. It wasn't far to the next town, and we didn't have to make our way through the traffic.

Just before the town a wide expanse of rough grass fronted onto the road. Behind and to one side stood grey concrete factories, bright signs proclaiming their business. On the side nearest the town, two-storey houses spread in rows, uninterrupted by gardens or trees. A sagging wire fence strung between concrete pillars backed onto the gable-ends. A small white caravan was parked on the edge of the grass, just a few feet from the pavement. Beside it stood the tatty yellow Hi-ace. The little man came out to greet us again as we pulled onto the rough ground, jolting the wagons up the curb. The big wheels of the side-lace mounted it easily, and heavily laden it rode the uneven ground smoothly and quietly.

We pulled as far from the road as we could, Frankie and Bumper leaving the wagons with their shafts facing the blank wall of the factory on the other side of the fence. There was grass enough for a few days, so we all rested up and fed well. The pain in my chest disappeared, and the day before we left Ben replaced the broken glass in the window and repaired the split in the end of the cart-shaft.

Through the twisting little town, over the bridge, past an imposing castle on a cliff overlooking the river. A steady uphill gradient pulled us onto a level road that ran straight for mile after mile. Patches of plantation forest on the high ground to our right with breaks in between for a large house or a cluster of little cottages that looked over the road to the low-lying plain. We stopped for a midday rest at a gravelled lay-by. It had a lower terrace reached by rough stone steps. There were wooden tables and benches where the children sat to eat their lunch and enjoy the scenery. Not a lot of pickings for us horses; spiky grass on the sloping bank above the low stone wall was littered with the leftovers of many a picnic.

We made camp that night in the entrance to a forest track, a half-moon of hard-standing defined by dark wood post-and-rail fencing. We were led through a gap at the end of the fence and up the track to where the growing trees were. There was a big area between there and the road where only stumps remained. New grass showed through the rough ground cover of saw-dust and twigs. Frankie was tethered to his stake at the edge of the track but Bumper and I were left off that night, along with the goats.

'Don't wander off now,' Liz told me as she unclipped the leading rope. I was too tired to make much of my new-found freedom, and just settled down to the job of searching out the best of the grass. The gap was blocked to stop us getting onto the road during the night. I rambled a short distance into the forest, but soon returned to the sunlight.

The next day's travelling was along the same straight road. A lunch stop down one of the many side roads that led to the farms and villages in the valley. It was a narrow lane with even narrower verges, so that two of the wheels of the wagons were on the tarmac. A farmer squeezing by on his massive tractor asked if they were intending to stay, but Liz assured him they'd be gone just as soon as they'd rested the horses. Ben and Tom brought in water from a nearby cottage, and pulled sticks out of the hedgerow. Soon a bright little fire boiled the kettle, and Liz baked a few chapatis for their lunch.

The sweet roadside grass grew up the earthen walls of the ditch. Never cut, self-seeding year after year, it was a wild meadow assortment of every grass that had ever been planted in the adjoining fields. Midsummer ripe heads of seeds were succulent and filling. Heady-scented flowers added to the rich flavour.

An overnight stop just before the hill that led down to the next town. The old man who supplied our water crossed the road from his cottage and sat awhile by the fire talking with Liz while she prepared their evening meal. Ben dropped off his bundle of firewood and leaving Tom to cut it he brought the old man round to meet me and the other horses.

'You're off to Puck Fair, your wife was telling me...'

'That's right. Were you ever there yourself?'

'I was. Good few years back now, mind. When I was a young-fella. Meself and me two brothers, we took a string of horses there.'

'From here? How long did it take you?'

'Why, we were there the same day. Starting first light.'

'Were you riding?'

'Aye. Riding different horses as we went along, you understand, to let the others rest.'

'And you went from Mitchelstown to Kilorglin in one day?'

'We did.'

'Begod, you were hardy men in them days!'

'Ah, but there wasn't the traffic like today....' reminisced the old man as a giant tanker almost bowled him over with its slipstream.

Kildorrery.

Down the hill, turning right at the first set of traffic lights we were soon through the town and heading along a country road that rose and dipped between neat hedges which left no room for stopping. We'd put a good few miles behind us and I was wishing we could stop for a rest when we were faced by a long uphill pull. The road had been widened as far as the stone walls on either side, but it was still not wide enough for more than two vehicles so we were soon trailing a convoy of motors anxious to overtake.

I was forced to pull back from the wagon to allow cars to cut in front of me, as they saved a few minutes on their journey time. The hill peaked and dropped again almost immediately. Going down the other side we had the extra hazard of oncoming traffic overtaking slow moving vehicles. Frankie was having a hard time holding back the wagon, its sideways motion accentuated by the little flat-cart that bobbed along behind. I was slipping and sliding too, pushed down the winding hill by the breeching pressing hard into my rump. We'd no sooner reached the bottom of the hill, when it started to climb again. Steeper than the first hill, this one soon had Frankie walking and I was glad to do likewise. The cars continued to push their way past, some giving a blast on their horns, whether aimed at us or the oncoming traffic I couldn't tell.

One hopped by with a revving of its engine that put more than the usual amount of choking exhaust gas into our lungs. Grinding the gears, the woman driver leaned across the passenger seat as she overtook us to shout something at Liz, who was long-reining me from the middle of the road.

'Get out of the road!' yelled Liz, the car coming towards us on the other side echoing the sentiment with a flash of lights and a passing howl.

The car struggled on until it was past the wagon and level with Frankie. Ben was also walking in the road and the woman was again leaning across, this time to shout at Ben. I could see him shaking a fist at her and waving her away. The car sputtered on but the next thing I knew, Liz was saying 'Whoa!' and pulling back on my mouth. The moment I stopped the collar seemed to catch me around the chest and pull me back down the hill.

'Hold it, Boy!' shouted Liz, an edge of panic in her voice as the big wheels started to slip. I rocked forward to stop the side-lace dragging me backwards, but there was no grip on the road and my feet were sliding away from under me. The bit pulled my head to the left so that I caught a glimpse of the rough stone wall just before I felt the back of the cart collide with it. At least it was no longer pulling me back, though I was still struggling to find purchase on the slippery road.

'What's going on?' shouted Liz.

I could hear Ben's voice raised to a furious level as he screamed abuse at the woman who had been driving the car. She was standing beside him in the road, gesticulating towards Frankie. In her hand she held a small black box, a short cylinder protruding from its front.

'Get that bloody camera out of my face, you stupid old bat!' shouted Ben, and 'Giddup, there, Frankie!' he lashed the reins across the big horse's back to get him started again. The wagon lumbered forward, crossing the road to get by the car which the woman had left on the corner of what was probably the steepest part of the hill.

In her haste to get out of the car, she had left the door open. It protruded across the road, and as the wagon pulled out to overtake it lurched to one side and the front corner just tipped the leading edge of the door. With a dull thud it folded back against the body of the car, leaving a deep dent in the panel. The woman, who had been pointing her camera at me, spun around at the sound of crumpling metal. Liz was saying 'Walk

ON, Sullivan! Don't mind 'em!' the way she did whenever there was anything that might frighten me. Woman and camera stepped back to let me follow the little flat-cart that trailed behind the wagon on its slow progress up the hill.

The knees were almost buckling under me by the time we reached the broad street of the little town perched on top of the hill. We pulled over to stop alongside the footpath, between parked cars. The sweat dripped from our bellies to collect in frothy puddles in the gutter. I was panting and blowing, my heartbeat racing the blood around my overheated body. The pulse behind my eyes pounding my head so that I was sure I could go no further. My nose was almost level with the kerb as I waited beyond caring for what would happen next. Liz stood at my head, still getting her breath back. Tom was holding Frankie's reins, Blue stood beside Bumper, though none of us were going anywhere.

Liz was waggling the top of my mane and talking quietly to me. I don't suppose she even noticed the black boots walking the pavement behind her. Startled by the voice her hand gripped my mane: 'You can't stop here!'

'What?' she spun round without letting go of me. I nodded my head for a fleeting glimpse of the big round man in his dark suit. He wore the same hat as the men who drove the blue vans.

'Does it look like we're about to make camp, or what?' she asked him.

'You can't stop here,' he repeated. 'You're obstructing the traffic. There's cars wanting to park here.'

Liz laughed. A mirthless sound.

'I'm not joking!' said the fat man. 'I'm telling you to get these horses out of this town!'

'And I'm telling you that your little no-horse town is by no means our final destination, and we'll be out of here soon enough!'

'You'll be out of here NOW!'

'Oh, come on, get real...' Liz was starting to lose her temper. 'These horses have just trotted from the other side of Mitchelstown. Look at them! They'll be dead in the road if we try to push them on before they've had a rest! Now will you just go arrest criminals or whatever it is they pay you for...'

'It's you I'll be arresting if you don't keep a civil tongue...' he was saying, but he hadn't seen

Ben coming out of the hotel with two buckets of water.

'Is your lad ready for one of these?' he called to Liz, ignoring the uniform standing between them.

The fat man turned and started to repeat his orders to Ben, who responded in much the same vein as Liz, only throwing in bits about harassment and 'Offences Against the Animals Act' and the European Court of Civil Rights. A few locals drifted out of the pub and stood on the pavement, ostensibly looking at Frankie, but their attention drawn to the altercation between Ben and the fat man.

'Move along there,' he told them after a few minutes. 'Don't be blocking the way!' They all shifted their positions, some moving forward to lay hands on the big white horse, others retreating back to the bar. A couple of them turned their backs, as though just having a conversation with their friends. The water in the black buckets stood on the pavement. A big man wearing a grubby white apron came out of the hotel carrying a shiny little kettle. 'Are you still wanting this hot water?' he asked Ben.

'Oh, yes. Thanks a lot, pal, I'll just put it in here.' He took the kettle and poured the boiling water into the buckets. 'You can't give the horses cold water when they're sweated like this. Give them colic,' he explained.

'I thought you wanted it to make tea!' laughed the man.

'Nice idea...' agreed Ben, 'but I don't think our friend here' a tip of the head, 'would want the likes of US drinking tea in HIS town!'

The man took his kettle and went back into the hotel, stopping at the door to call back, 'Plenty more if you want it!'

Liz only let me drink half the warm water, giving the rest to Bumper. Frankie must have had the other bucket.

Slightly refreshed, we walked the length of the town's main street. At the bottom of the hill a curiously shaped building was set back off the road with a big car-park alongside. We pulled in there and were glad to get out of the harness.

'There's a little field with loads of grass behind the church,' reported Blue as she scrambled over the low wall.

'It's probably the old graveyard!' said Liz.

'So? The horses won't mind, will they?'

We had a few hours rest and some good feeding, then it was back into harness. Another hill lay before us, not so long as the other two, but steeper at first. Setting out, Bumper's traces were tied to the front of the shafts of the big wagon, ahead of Frankie, and the two of them together trotted the big wagon up to the top of the hill. I didn't like having to wait in the car-park when I could hear their hoof-beats fading into the distance, but it wasn't long before we heard the brisk tapping of Bumper's return. He was only wearing half his harness: winkers, collar, hames and traces. Tom jumped off his back and soon had him fully tacked and under the shafts of the little wagon. Blue held my reins and told me to 'Stand up' while Liz loaded the goats into the wagon. Then she jogged beside my head to the top of the hill where Frankie stood waiting for us.

We put in a few more miles that afternoon, after the road levelled out, making the travelling easier. Pulling in to an old farm-lane that looked long-abandoned we were turned loose, for the night. The wagons parked at the road-end to stop us escaping that way, the short lane was blocked by a gate at the other end. It would have been good enough for an overnight stop, but a woman came from the house along the road and invited us to spend the night in her lush little acre.

Maybe our luck was changing.

Chapter Four

Kilorglin.

High summer, travelling into the west. Early morning starts, the sun at our backs. Lazy afternoons and long evenings packing in the luscious grass. Sometimes a late hay meadow would send delicious messages on the breeze; mostly the fields beyond the fences were suffering their second cut of the season. The best of the grazing was to be had on the long acre, the side of the road.

Every day we'd pass through another little town, stopping in the street so that Ben could visit the shops. A box of provisions and on to the next camp. The weather seemed to change abruptly as we were crossing the bridge over the wide river before the town. A dark cloud obscured the sun and cast a heavy shadow over the streets and houses that clung to the hillside before us.

The road began to climb steeply beyond the bridge, and heavy drops of rain quickly became a downpour. We took a road off to the right, parallel to the river, but still climbing. Another right turn dipped down before levelling out again. Houses with steeply-sloping gardens on the left. Below the wall on the other side the gravelly banks of the river. A short distance down the lane an old bridge of iron lattice-work spanned road and river, two stone columns towering from the bed of the estuary. A narrow verge with overhanging trees, just enough space to get the wheels of the wagon off the road.

This was the first time we'd camped in a town.

The trail of boys, most of them about Tom's age that had followed us from the first bridge, tipping the side-lace trying to jump aboard, running ahead and grabbing at the reins, were joined by others as soon as we stopped.

'Can I jock the horse down to the river?' they were shouting, and 'Hey, missus! Not him! He's no good. Me! Me! I'm good! Let me jock the horse for you!'

Several of them were making jumps at my back before Liz even had the winkers off me. In the end she selected one blondie-haired boy who'd been pushing all the others aside and said,

'Okay. You! What's your name?'

'Johnny.'

'Right, Johnny, you ride him down with Tom, and don't be racing him up and down, alright? He's tired and hungry, so just take him down to the river and tie him where he can get some grass, but not so he can reach the water. Will you do that?'

'Will you pay me?' asked Johnny.

Liz made a grab to pull the boy off my back, but he dodged sideways and pulled my head around, digging me in the ribs to urge me down the lane after Tom who was already trotting away on Bumper.

'Only kiddin',' he called back to her, then 'Hey, Tom! Wait for me!'

The boy was a good rider, he relaxed back with his legs straight so that his feet were almost kicking my chin. He had my tether clipped under my halter and coiled over his shoulder. To rein me in, he jerked hard on the rope so that the nose-band cut into my face.

'Give you a race, Tom!' he called when we were out of sight of the wagons.

But Tom said 'No way! Come on, we just have to let them get some grass.'

He walked Bumper down the short bank that led to the dried-out river bed. A deep channel flowed fast under the high arches of the old bridge. Tom tied Bumper's rope to an old thorn bush that grew under the wall and then had to argue with the boy on my back to get him to give up on the idea of riding. Eventually the boy handed Tom the rope and chain, but he stayed on me as Tom led me further along and tied me to a disused fence post.

The shower had passed and the sun glistened the river. The boy rocked back and forth, swinging his legs as he talked to Tom asking where we'd come from, how long had it taken us to get here? He said his Daddy kept horses, but he'd never lived in a wagon. They'd moved around in their caravans in the summer, stayed in a house in the winter. They talked on, getting to know one another, while Bumper and I searched the river-side weeds for something to eat.

The rest of the boys had followed us down and they spent most of the afternoon pestering Tom to let him take me or Bumper for a ride. He refused, but it didn't stop a few of them trying to scramble on our backs. Tom shouted at them, pulled them away. Scuffles broke out, they were tough lads. At one point three of them held Tom down on the grass shouting

'Now, Mikey! Now!' to a ginger-headed youth who was determined to get a ride on my back. Mikey threw his leg over me and leaned forward to try to unclip my tether.

'Get the chain!' he shouted to one of the others, as Tom squirmed helplessly.

A lad in a bright yellow jacket made a grab for my rope and was fumbling at my halter. It was all too much for me. I reared as high as I could, surprising even myself at the new-found strength in my back legs. I took several steps backwards, lashing out to kick the yellow jacket smartly in the ribs as he fell away.

Mikey slid down my back, but clung desperately to my mane with both hands and locked his skinny legs around my gut. I shook from side to side as I brought my front feet down, and kicked out with both back legs to clear the space behind. Mikey lost his grip and slid over my neck, his fingers still grasping hands full of mane. When I reared again I lifted him off the ground. He fell under my feet on the hard pebbles, long black hairs still clutched in his fists.

The whole gang were shrieking and cheering at this performance. The three who'd been holding Tom had leapt to their feet and scrambled away up the bank and over the low wall. Mikey shook his ginger hair as he backed away, wiping his hands on his trousers.

'I'll get you for that!' he threatened. I don't know if he was talking to me or Tom. 'Ah, don't mind him,' whispered Johnny, standing next to Tom, 'he's just a big fool. He's always trying to do things he's not able!'

'Why didn't you help me when they were holding me down? Why didn't you stop him?' asked Tom.

'He's my cousin,' replied Johnny, as though that explained it all.

The gang drifted back to the town, leaving Tom to throw stones at the water. Some time later, Ben came down to the river.

'You alright, son?'

The boy didn't complain.

'Come on, we'll move these lads up onto the old railway track with Frankie. There's plenty of grass up there.'

Next morning, the promise of another scorching day. Ben and Tom and Blue collected us from the hollow between the embankments and led us back to the camp. Liz was baking at the fire; men and women were standing around talking. Some of the lads I'd met yesterday were hanging about in the road. As soon as they saw us coming, they were at Ben, begging for a ride.

'No,' he said, 'we're just taking the horses down to the river to wash them.'

Whatever he said the gaggle of whining voices kept up their insistent pleading. Ben helped Blue up on my back after leaving my chain in the wagon. She had a rope tied to my halter, the way she always rode me. A lad tried to snatch the rope from her as we stood in the lane waiting for Tom and Ben to mount up.

I shied away, spinning right round and giving a kick with my back legs to let him know I didn't want him near me. Blue was taken by surprise. She lurched forward and landed with an unsteady bump. She wobbled a bit, but stayed on and righted herself. I was facing Bumper and Frankie, who had been standing behind me.

'You alright, Blue?' asked Ben. 'Do you think you'll be able to handle him in the traffic?'

'I will if these little pigs just leave him alone!' she spat venom at the boys jeering her from behind.

'Maybe he'd be safer in the winkers?' suggested Liz and she went in the wagon and returned a few minutes later unbuckling the long driving reins.

With the rope tied to the bit-rings, Blue had full control of my mouth, and with the winkers over my eyes I had very little idea of what was going on around me. Frankie and Bumper went on ahead and I just followed at an easy trot. Back down the road to the bridge, now packed solid with slow-moving traffic. We moved steadily amongst the cars and vans, many of them towing horse- or cattle-boxes whose occupants called out to us. They sounded unhappy to be confined amongst the exhaust fumes. I would have been, too.

It felt good to have water lapping around my ankles as we waded through the shallows under the bridge. Frankie and Bumper splashed ahead of me, wetting their rider's feet as they cantered across the river to the other side. They snorted in exhilaration.

Ben called back, 'Come on, Blue! Its not too deep!'

I could sense the girl's apprehension, even share it: I wasn't at all happy about wading an unknown depth of water either. Bumper came charging back through the water, spray flying shoulder-high, with Tom on his back calling, 'Giddup there, Sullivan!' and 'Kick him on, Blue!'

They were beside us, somehow managing to splash even though the river was less than knee-deep.

'Go on!' urged Tom, and Bumper was away again, spraying us with his wake.

'Oh, what-the-hell...' I heard Blue mumble, 'we can't get much wetter!' and she gave me a dig in the ribs and 'Trot on, Sullivan!' had me high-stepping over to the other side before I had time to reconsider.

Ben was pouring buckets of river water over Frankie's back, and sluicing them away with the plastic brush strapped to his palm. When he'd finished, he got Blue down off my back and did the same for me. The first bucketful was a cold shock that made me jump, but after that I enjoyed the cool water being brushed through my coat and by the time he'd washed me all over, I was feeling really good. Tom took the bucket and brush and started to give Bumper the treatment. Ben gave Blue a leg-up onto my back, leapt astride Frankie and waded leisurely back across the river calling to Tom, 'We'll see you back at the camp, okay?'

The sun had the water steaming off our backs as we made our way through the ever-increasing number of vehicles crawling into the town.

The main street rose steeply from the bridge, with a crossroads about a quarter of the way up where we had to turn right. Traffic everywhere, parked along both sides, we picked a way between the double-parkers and those just waiting for a break big enough to squeeze through, until we reached the crossroads. Frankie was right in front of me, Ben on his back with right arm outstretched to indicate clearly his intention. He started to turn, to cross the road. I was right on his tail. I'd seen the red car coming down the hill at the last minute as Blue was pulling my head round to the right. Then it was lost from my restricted field of vision. I'll never know if he was trying to stop, or just not bothering.

The front of the car hit my left side and knocked my legs away from under me. As I tumbled, my ribs bounced off the front of his bonnet and Blue rolled off my back and landed against the windscreen.

Blinded by the winkers, in my confusion and panic I staggered to my feet and bumped into Frankie. Ben was leaping to the road, shouting 'STOP!' at the top of his voice as the car that had hit me carried on down the hill. We were boxed in on all sides by stationary traffic. I stood next to Frankie, turning this way and that to try to see what was happening. Blue was picking herself up out of the gutter.

Cars were starting to honk their horns. Ben ran down to the little red car, stuck behind a cattle lorry on the hill. The driver was frantically winding up his side-window. He got it closed just as Ben grabbed the door handle, furiously trying to wrench it open. Ben banged his fists on the roof of the car, but the man at the wheel stared straight ahead as though none of this concerned him. The sound of shattering glass as Ben punched his fist clean through the side window and grabbing the driver by his shirt front, dragged him half out of the hole. He shook the driver, whose arms were pinned helpless inside the car. The honking of horns had become a blaring crescendo. Ben dropped the man back into the driver's seat and ran back up the hill, ignoring the other traffic. He gave Blue a quick hug, ran a hand over my side and down my legs before lifting her up on my back. He was up on Frankie and away up the road leaving me to follow unsteadily, frightened that every car might not avoid me as I'd expected it to.

Liz was fussing over us; Blue had finally burst into tears as she recounted the story in her mother's arms. Ben pulled off my winkers and threw them into the wagon. Bright sun full in my eyes dazzled me.

I heard him say 'Gards'll be here any minute!'

As if on cue, the dark blue car rolled to a halt beside the fire. Without preliminaries, a shouting match began. The two gards got out of the car, leaving the driver of the car that had hit us sitting in the back seat. A small crowd gathered, forming a half-circle around the camp. Some of them added their voices to the general confusion. One little man, well-the-worse for drink, was determined to take Ben's side in the altercation, even though he didn't have any idea what it was about. He kept bobbing up in front of Ben, wagging a finger at the Gards, repeating 'Thish man's my friend!'

At one point Ben's voice rang through 'Damages? I'll give him damages!' he pushed past the gard and caught the handle of the back door. It was locked. 'Let me in there with him and I'll give him damage alright!'

Tom arrived back on Bumper, the bucket slung over his arm.

'What's happening?' he asked Liz, as he wormed his way through the assembly.

'This one of yours?' the gard asked Ben, and the shouting started again.

Untimely ends.

Eventually the gard-car left and the crowd dispersed. We were taken back to the railway track and tied on long lines so we could graze the embankments on both sides. Tom and Blue stayed with us, leaning on the old fence that blocked access to the iron bridge, looking out over the lane and the river. The two cousins from the day before joined them there, talking for a few minutes before jumping over the fence.

'Don't go!' said Blue, putting a hand on her brother's arm.

'It's alright.' Tom assured her.

The boys called, 'You comin' Tommy?'

They were already crossing the lane and heading towards the first of the bridge supports when Tom climbed the fence and hurried after them. The bridge hadn't carried trains in many a year. It was a rusted hulk, a skeleton with less than half its original sleepers. In places the boys were making their way along the metal girders, finding hand-holds where they could along the rotted railings. Blue sat on the fence, watching her brother and the other boys as they hopped and jumped their way across to the other side of the river. I looked along the once-elegant curved arch at the death-trap path they were dancing, and wondered what motivated boys to play these games.

On the way back Tom was in the lead, closely followed by the blond-haired Johnny. They stopped for a while over the fast flowing river, looking over the rail, then looking behind them, through a gap where several sleepers were missing. Johnny dropped something and they all waited for the splash.

Mikey was on the opposite side of the bridge, daring the others to cross the last sleeper as he had done. Tom and Johnny were laughing and shaking their heads. They started to move way, edging along the iron girder.

'Hey, lads, watch me!' yelled Mikey and they looked back just in time to see him leap into the air. He must have been trying to jump across the gap, but he seriously misjudged the distance, or his own ability.

The boys both shouted 'NO!' but it was too late. They saw the ginger head disappear under the metal framework and hit the water. Stood transfixed by the horror of it as the river carried him quickly out of sight. Then they got off that old bridge as fast as they could. Blue still had her face buried in her hands when they reached her.

'You didn't see that!' Tom told her 'Okay?'

The goats were scaling the near-vertical sides of the old railway cutting when Liz came walking along the track. She stopped to say 'Good Morning!' to me and I checked the white plastic bucket she was carrying, but it was empty. Her voice echoed back from the shady hollow as she called 'Birch, Birch, Birch!' and rattled the handle against the side of the bucket. The nanny-goat answered, the way she always did, scrambling down the bank and jogging along the track. After their usual greeting ritual of rubbing and scratching, the goat stood quietly under Liz's legs and allowed the milk to be squeezed into the bucket. This happened every morning and evening, but always fascinated me to see the way the woman and goat seemed to blend into one strange six-legged creature with a head at either end. Two young lads drifted along the track and stood a short distance from the milking scene.

One of them piped up, 'Is this the one he's goin' to kill, missus?'

Liz looked up, briefly. 'He'd better not!'

The bigger boy nudged his companion and pointed to the white puck still innocently munching near the top of the cutting.

'Is that the one?' asked the first boy, but Liz didn't bother to look up.

'Will we catch him?' asked the boy.

'Time enough,' Liz told them, but taking no notice they were already on their way up the track.

'We'll catch him for you!' called back the bigger boy as they started the ascent. The puck saw them coming and made a run for it, but the lads were nimble and soon had the chain he was trailing. They were dragging the loudly-protesting creature down the track when Ben arrived with a small entourage of mostly older boys. Tom was amongst them, carrying a steel basin. A white cloth was draped around his neck.

Liz teased the last drops of milk from under the goat and stood up straight. She tapped Birch's rump and the goat obligingly walked off saying 'Thank you, that feels better.' 'And thank you, too!' said Liz.

She watched the goat pulling bramble bushes for the soft leaves.

'You've plenty of helpers for the job.' she said to Ben.

'Bunch of spectators, this lot!' he replied. 'Come on, lads, its not a tug-o'-war!' he called to the two boys straining at the end of the chain as the little goat dug-in with all four feet and shook his head about wildly.

Ben entered the shadowed cutting and took the chain from the young lads while Liz was making her way carefully down the embankment with her bucket full of milk. The bunch of lads formed a half-circle around the little goat as Tom struggled to hold his knee against the animal's neck, pinning it to the ground. 'Here, you!' said Ben, looking at the tallest of his audience, 'Don't be standing there like a spare part. Help him keep the goat still!'

The lad made to take a step backwards, but the others caught him and pushed him forward. 'Wha'?'

'Hold his back-end down,' suggested Tom, and soon the two of them had the puck lying quietly on its side.

Ben produced a short blade from a sheath at his belt, and flashing it briefly at the sky said 'Hold him now, lads!'

The puck's last bleat was never finished. I lost sight of Ben for maybe a minute as he crouched over the prostrate animal. When he stood up, he was clutching its head in his right hand, the blood-stained knife still in his left.

Just then, the first rays of the morning sun cleared the top of the cutting and illuminated the scene on the tracks. Seizing the moment's dramatic effect, Ben hoisted the little white head by its horn and pointed it at arm's length to the sun.

'Ra!' he chanted, and the boys responded with a nervous sort of cheer '....'Raay'

Tom and the other lad stood back and I watched along with all of them as the brainless body pumped its dark blood into a pool where its head had been. The younger boys were stifling giggles and wriggling their limbs as if in imitation. They started to drift away, leaving Ben to skin the carcass. When he'd finished, Tom helped him wrap it in the white cloth. Only the two boys who'd caught the goat stayed till he'd finished.

'Who's going to bring the head back for my pup?' Ben asked them.

One of them picked it up by the horn, but quickly passed it to his friend. The other boy dropped it as though it was hot. Tom put the head on top of the folded skin in the basin and followed Ben who was carrying the shrouded meat over his shoulder. A last look at the pile of entrails on the track and the two boys ran from the cutting as if they were being chased. Scavenging birds put out the cry and soon a black and white flock descended to make a meal of the offal.

Later that day, Bumper, Frankie and I were taken into the town. Tom was riding me this time, Blue was up on Bumper. Birch was hoping to come with us, but Liz caught her as we passed the camp and tied her behind the wagon. She called plaintively after us until we could no longer hear her for the noise of the traffic.

The steep main street of the town was crowded with people. Temporary stalls had been set up on both sides selling every kind of thing, toys and tools, curtains and clothes. Vans backed onto noisy generators sold greasy smelling food. Still there were cars making their way through the crowds.

At the top of the hill was a sort of square with roads going off to left and right, where other horses stood, aimlessly resting in the afternoon heat. Men held reins or ropes, one or more horses. Groups of animals, noses together, tails to the traffic, patiently standing as men walked slowly along the pavement, looking them over. Suffering the indignity of having their mouths examined, being prodded with sticks.

The occasional Hunter or child's pony under saddle shared the road with us. Their riders disdainfully whipped their mounts past us as quickly as possible in the throng. Frankie was calling all the time, challenging the other horses, flirting with the mares. Bumper put in the odd word, mostly defending himself. I was just overwhelmed by it all, letting Tom take control of all my actions.

'There's nothing here I'd swap Frankie for!' I heard Ben telling his children.

'I know what you mean,' said Tom. 'Maybe we had to come here just to appreciate how good these lads are.'

He patted my neck, saying, 'I'm heading back to the camp. You coming, Blue?'

Birch greeted us like long-lost family, though we'd only been gone about an hour. A scrawny young man who had been sitting at the fire talking to Liz called 'Hey, Ben! How's it goin', boy?' and rushed into the road to clasp hands with Ben as he dismounted. They all had cups of tea while we stood on the narrow verge. Liz brought my chain and tethered me behind the wagon, where Birch started to make a huge fuss of me; rubbing the ridges of her horns along my flanks and scratching my chest with the points. I nibbled her neck where her mane should have been. She gave little grunts of approval, and squealed if I bit too hard.

The camp fire attracted a crowd, even in the heat of the day. Liz seemed to spend the whole time dispensing tea, and washing cups.

Ben led Frankie down the lane, the young man at his side barely as tall as the horse's shoulder.

'I'd say he's the biggest horse at the fair,' he was saying.

'He's certainly the best!' replied Ben.

'I'll bet I can leap him,' said the little man.

'D'you reckon?'

'Will he stand still?'

'I'll hold him for you,' said Ben. 'What way do you want him standing?'

'Just across the road, any way at all...' and the young man stood and sized up the horse as Ben positioned him, blocking the narrow lane. Then a short run, a mighty leap, and the man had cleared the big white horse and landed nimbly on the other side.

'Well, fair-play to ya!' said Ben, genuinely impressed,

'Where d'you learn to do that?'

'It's just something I do,' shrugged the young man, modestly.

'Shall we go back up the town and give the buffers a bit of a show?' suggested Ben 'I'll call for you...'The Amazing Flying Finn!'... and we'll get the kids to pass the hat, d'you fancy?'

'Alright!' agreed Finn.

Puck Fair.

I was beginning to think that I'd seen it all, the world could hold no more surprises for me. Which just goes to show how wrong we can be.

When Liz tacked me up next morning there was no sign of the other horses. She'd also spent a long time grooming me, not at all like the usual once-over with the brush of our travelling days. As I left the camp under the shafts of the side-lace, Bumper came cantering alongside, Tom in his easy bare-back pose. A family outing, Liz at the reins, with Ben beside her on the high seat. Blue and the twins with their legs dangling over the back of the cart. We were just heading up the main street of the town, the stalls open for business but quiet in this early part of the day. A party of girls in identical chequered skirts were blocking the road as they walked steadily down the hill towards us. They seemed to be moving as a square; straight lines, in ranks they approached, carrying curious tartan bags with dark wooden pipes poking out at odd angles. The girls on the end of each row had drums slung to their hips, and they twirled long pale sticks as they walked.

I pulled right in to the kerb to allow them to pass us by. Just as we drew level, the most appalling noise burst from their ranks. It was as if each of the girls had turned Banshee, an unearthly cacophony of mournful wailing.

Liz must have been anticipating something of this sort, for she had a tight hold on the reins even before I jumped. But even she must have been taken by surprise at the suddenness of it, jerking my head down to stop me rearing. In the same moment, the drummer girls all started to beat their tattoo as the squeal of pipes settled into the rhythm and the painful drone became music.

I snorted and shook my head, and Liz slackened the bit and gave me a slap of the reins to drive me on; any verbal command she may have given drowned out by the passing band.

'Well, if he can handle that, the parade shouldn't be too much for him.' I heard Liz commenting as we neared the top of the hill where a high tower of decorated scaffolding had been erected. Near its top, a canopied platform stood empty.

We took the road to the left a short distance out of town and turned into a yard in front of a plain grey building. People were milling about, some of them in fancy dress. Others were putting the finishing touches to bizarre displays on the backs of lorries and low-loaders. Liz, Ben and the children climbed off the cart. It must have been about midday, the sun hot and high. I was offered water, but made to stand much longer than I'd ever had to stand in the shafts before. Tom rode around on Bumper for awhile, then left him to graze the edges of the car park. I'd have liked to do the same, but still I had to stand, to be looked at, admired, ignored, by the bustling crowds.

After what seemed like an eternity, a subdued cheer rippled through the crowd to announce the arrival of a tractor towing an ornately decorated float. Tied on the raised platform, an unhappy-looking puck goat. He had a long shaggy, multi-coloured coat and a magnificent set of horns that swept over his back. A fancy collar and chain held him securely in place.

'At last!' said Ben. 'Now maybe we'll get started! Climb aboard, kids!'

It wasn't long afterwards the procession of vehicles started to make their way onto the road. I watched them slowly turn and drive past on their way back to the town.

The pipe and drum girls all assembled and took their place in the cavalcade. Others wearing short skirts and tall hats waved sticks as they marched in formation. We fell in line behind the last of the lorries leaving the yard. Slowly making our way back around the narrow streets of the little town, now lined with crowds gathered to watch us pass. Blue jumped off the cart and ran alongside me shaking a bucket at the crowds. Ben was doing the same on the other side of the street. People were throwing coins into the buckets, the clink of metal echoing our hoof beats as we half-walked, half-trotted to try to keep pace with the procession.

The puck goat must have been at the head of the convoy, because by the time we rounded the corner into the crowded square at the top of the hill, he had been elevated to the platform at the top of the tower. The other floats were inching their way through the cheering throng; we were forced to a halt outside the bleak stone building on the corner. Four men, three of them in dark blue uniforms hurried from the building and grabbed Ben and Blue, who were trying to climb back onto the side-lace. They were bundled off the street, still clutching their buckets of money. Liz shouted after them, but had to stay with me and the twins, standing outside the dark doorway as the town carried on its festivities, oblivious.

As the last of the parade disappeared beyond the crowd, Ben and Blue emerged from the building. She was rubbing her fists into her eyes, smearing tears down her cheeks. Ben had a protective arm around her shoulder as he helped her aboard. He threw the empty buckets under the seat and said to Liz, 'Get us out of this godforsaken hole!'

She whipped me on with Ben yelling at the milling people to get out of the way!

An early start next morning, impatient to be out of the town.

'The Scattering' one man called it as he said his goodbyes to the family. The roads out of town were already a solid mass of crawling traffic when we pulled out of the lane and joined the road into town. At the cross roads on the hill we had to wait a good while for a break. Eventually, Frankie edged into the flow, the wagon still trailing the unsold flat-cart. I was following close behind when a big cattle lorry came bearing down the hill, air-horns screaming.

Liz pulled me back as the massive bulk with its stinking load ground to a halt right across our path. We pulled out behind the lorry and followed it down to the bridge at a slow walk. People were still crowding the pavements and crossing the road between the almost stationary traffic.

We were about half-way over the bridge when the lorry stopped abruptly. Bumper and his little wagon were behind me, Frankie had his load free of the traffic on the wider road to the left of the bridge. The lorry had itself jammed across the road as it was attempting a right turn. Its bonnet straddled the white line, its ramp still blocked our exit from the bridge. Every car, van, horse box, seemed to start the horn blowing as pedestrians giggled and pointed cameras at us.

Ben left Blue holding Frankie and came striding back along the road. He shouted and waved his fists at the passenger in the cattle box, who flung open the door and jumped down from the cab wielding a heavy iron bar with a vicious beak at its head. Ben saw him coming and was already running back to the wagon as the man pursued him down the road, weapon slung over his shoulder.

Ben reached the wagon well-ahead of his assailant and grabbed the big axe from the inside ledge. The man with the iron bar stopped short when he saw Ben re-emerge, armed. The driver of the cattle lorry was shouting to his passenger and blasting his air-horns as he started to inch forward in the road. The passenger legged-it back to the lorry and jumped aboard, slamming the door just before the axe crashed into the metal panel. It stuck there and Ben was jerked forward as the lorry started. The axe shook free and the passenger hung out of the window flailing the iron bar inches from Ben's head. Liz held me back while the lorry made its halting progress across the junction. Even so, the axe-head passed dangerously close to my face as Ben whirled it through the air and brought it crashing down on the rear lights of the lorry. The cattle on board started bellowing, adding their frightened voices to the shouting of men, the protests of passers-by and the blaring of car-horns.

Somewhere behind us, stuck fast in the traffic on the bridge, a mournful siren cried a loud, slow, 'Nee, naw, nee, naw...'

A cloud of black exhaust fumes belched in my face when the lorry revved away. Ben ran back to the wagon and 'upped' Frankie. The big horse must have sensed the anger that was transmitted through reins and voice as his driver urged him on. We headed out of that town at a brisk trot; I was glad to be out of the traffic and the crowds, but it must have been a hard pace for Frankie to set, pulling his load.

We made camp that night on a patch of grass tucked in behind echoing vacant sheds. High roofed, their concrete floors divided by many stout metal barriers that the children used for climbing frames. The buildings carried the faint lingering smell of disinfectant, partly disguising the stale odour of cattle.

The fire was lit and the meat roasting over the flames soon permeated the whole area. Two old ladies pushing a dilapidated pram hobbled onto the green and set up a tarpaulin make-shift tent. They put their little tin kettle on a miniature gas-burner and as they waited for it to boil, Ben strolled over and invited them to share the fire. They brewed their own tea, but accepted the invitation to the meal.

The following morning they were up early and one of the women brought her little teapot to the wagon and poured the hot dark liquid into the two china mugs that stood on the ledge. She talked for a few minutes with Ben and Liz, while the other woman folded the tarp and humped it on top of their other possessions. The two of them were on their way with not a trace of their passing by the time Tom had the fire lit.

'Service'.

After an overnight stop in a lay-by, we arrived in the next town the following morning. The main street was wide and flat, two rows of cars parked nose-to-nose along the middle between statues that looked down from their pedestals.

Half a dozen immaculate caravans were already parked on the wide verge of the new road that skirted the town. We bounced the wheels up the kerb and onto the fresh cut grass. Ben was soon surrounded by a group of men who all seemed to be talking at once. Liz led me back across the black tarmac to tie me to the chalky concrete fence that backed the verge on the other side. The grass was almost knee-deep, freshly seeded, abundant clover. I started packing it in to myself, ignoring the fast moving traffic. Ben was still holding Frankie in the midst of his audience when Liz arrived back with churns of water and Tom struggled into the camp under a load of old building-wood he'd retrieved from a skip outside one of the factories on the other side of the fence.

'That's no use!' Ben shouted at him, as he dropped it in the middle of the camp.

'It'll do for the washing!' called Liz, dragging the trolley of water alongside.

'Go find some decent wood for the cooking!' ordered Ben, and after a few more words with Liz the boy set off out of the camp again, the bright orange bow-saw over his shoulder.

Blue helped Liz smash up the lathe and painted boards and light a toxic fire around a blackened tin bath. White powder turned to foam as they poured half a churn of water into the old bath and soon their dirty clothes were simmering.

Ben had finally crossed the road to tie Frankie out when the high-pitched whine of a grass-cutting machine started up on the verge beyond where I was grazing. Liz left the camp and went to talk to the young man operating the machine. He cut the motor for a few minutes as she remonstrated and pleaded with him, but he soon had it running again, sweeping away the sweet grass in relentless swathes. As he moved ever-closer she had no choice but to untie me and move me back across the road to the camp. I was put on a short tether under some bushes that grew out of the bank at the back of the verge. The grass had been cut, probably the day before, and chopped up weeds were mixed with the litter of shredded paper and plastic under my feet. The young man across the road emptied his box of clippings into the dumper truck, and carried on with his job as Ben brought Bumper to stand beside me. Frankie had maybe half an hour of the good grazing while the man drove off to empty the dumper truck, then he was back and the big horse too had to be tethered amongst the caravans on the verge.

Tom arrived back as Liz was squeezing the dingy water from the clothes. She took the basket across the road and draped the wet washing over the new concrete fence. The boy dropped the bundle of dead wood beside the glowing embers of the fire and collapsed onto the step of his wagon.

'Well done, son,' said Ben, who was sitting on the shafts of his own wagon, drinking tea with a dark-haired man. Liz broke the smaller sticks and kindled a bright clean fire for her kettle before filling two buckets with water from the second churn.

'This is for Bumper, Tom.' She indicated one of the buckets and carried the other one over to me. Tom obediently brought the water to his horse. He groaned as he lowered it under Bumper's nose.

'Are you alright?' asked Liz.

'No, I'm not; I nearly got killed getting that wood!'

'Where? How? What happened?'

'I hope you're not intending to stay here,' he began. 'There's no wood to be had in this town, only the stinking old off-cuts from the factory. I had to go miles to get that bit of thorn. Up through the housing estate, where I was set-on by a load of kids, throwing stones, the lot! So I had to leg-it over a great big high wire fence to get away from them and on the other side there's the railway line! So I crossed the tracks and then there's fields and a few hedges, but no dead wood. That thorn bush was growing out in the middle of a field... its probably some kind of holy-tree or something...'

'I wouldn't worry about that too much,' Liz assured him 'it's burning grand.'

'That's not half of it,' he continued. 'After I'd hacked away at the tree, cut my hands to ribbons...' he showed her the lacerations, 'I'd just got it bundled up and on my back and I turn around to see a herd of bullocks heading across the fields. So I just ignore them and head back for the gap in the hedge, but the stupid things caught up with me, and surrounded me, y'know, and they were pushing and shoving and I couldn't get through them. They just stood around me and when I tried to push them out of the way they just barged me back. Honest to god, I thought they were going to trample me to death! So, eventually I got back across the field, threw the wood over the fence and it rolled down on to the railway tracks. I wasn't intending to walk along the lines, but once I was down there I couldn't get back up the bank with the load on my back, so I had no choice. Then the worst of it!

'I was going along this single track, between the high embankments and the bloody train come up behind me! There was no way it was going to stop, so I just had to press myself against the embankment with the thorns digging me in the back, and pray! The train went hurtling past, I thought it was going to drag me under the wheels. Then I still had to pick myself up and carry on to the end of the cutting and climb another high wire fence... this one had barbed wire along the top! ... and carry that load back through the town, with everyone jeering at me and shouting abuse. I hope he thinks it's worth it!'

He finished his story with a nod towards the bright little fire that had already attracted a group of men, who were standing around it, listening to Ben.

'Well, I think it is, Love,' Liz assured him, putting an arm around his shoulder and patting his back.

'Ouch!' he protested.

We were hungry the next morning. Early, before the factories opened their gates, a mare arrived in a horse-box. She was paraded up and down on the new-mown verge across the road while Ben tried to control Frankie who was rearing and screaming amongst the caravans. Bumper was joining in the excitement, and though I didn't really know what all the fuss was about, I gave a bit of a call as well.

Two men led the mare up the verge and along the slip-road that led to the factories. Ben had Frankie on a short lead-rope as they followed close behind, the big horse still shouting and prancing. As far as they could go off the road, the men stopped and turned the mare to face the stallion. She gave a high pitched quavering cry in response to his deep-throated rumbling voice. They stood noses-together for a few seconds, before she spun round and lashed him a kick to the chest with both her back legs. He reared and gave her a dab on the rump with his great hairy hoof. She squealed and gave a little buck in protest, but then she settled down. Two men were holding her head to steady her as Frankie reared on his massive hind legs and brought his front legs down over her shoulders. He sunk his teeth into the base of her mane. Ben was under the mare's tail, pushing it aside to ensure the horses' connection. Bumper was still prancing back and forth on the end of his short tether. After a few minutes, the big horse slid off the mare. The man at her head trotted her away, just as the first car drove up to the factory gate. A thin little woman got out and went to open the padlock, waving her arms at the men and horses, berating them in her squeaky voice. They laughed and called after her as she drove her car through the gates.

The mare was back in the box and gone by the time Ben had tied Frankie on the verge and come back to the camp where the kettle was just starting to boil. He had the cup of tea in his hand when the white car stopped. Driver and passenger put on their caps as they walked the few paces to the fire. 'There's been a complaint...' one of them began.

'So, tell me about it!' Ben smiled up at them.

As soon as the morning rush-hour traffic had filled the factory car parks we were on the road again. We pulled a few miles out of town to a place where a road-widening scheme had provided a long straight stretch of wide verge. The wagons were parked at the end of the hard-shoulder, in behind a line of reflector bollards. The same kind of concrete fence that marked all the new roads separated us from the harvested fields. The grass was a rich clover mix; ripe seeds and sweet flowers, delicious and satisfying.

Children from the nearby farms visited us bringing apples and carrots and sticky sugar mints. Day after day we lazed in the sun and had no work to do.

One hot afternoon Tom and Blue and the twins were playing in the little river that ran along the other side of the fence. They'd just finished crawling all over Bumper who was quite content to lie on his side and let them. The game over, he was stretching his legs and having a sort of half-roll to scratch his ribs on the ground. A car pulled on to the hard shoulder and a woman got out.

She called to the children 'Is this your horse?'

'He's not for sale,' answered Tom.

'I don't want to buy him!' she snapped back,

'He's obviously in distress! Has he had water today?'

'Of course he has.' Blue told her, indignant.

'There's nothing wrong with him, he just does that!'

Bumper scrambled to his feet and shook the grass from his back.

'Nothing like a good scratch!' he chuckled as the mist of black and white hairs slowly descended.

The woman got back in her car saying 'Horses need lots of water in this weather.'

'Yeah, yeah...' said Tom, but he threw the warm dregs from Bumper's bucket and replenished it from the stream. He climbed the fence and offered the water to the horse, who only dipped his nose for a taste before shaking the cold drops off his bristly moustache.

'Alright?' Tom asked the woman. She revved away leaving us with the lingering aftertaste of her perfume and exhaust fumes.

'Rose of Tralee'

The next day, Tom rode me into the town. The carnival atmosphere spilled over onto the side-streets, with stalls erected along every stretch of pavement. We picked our way amongst the cars that inched forward, pushing their way towards the middle of town. The wide main street was like an open-air market, packed with people, but unlike the other fair, no animals.

Tom was content to let me stroll through the crowd. A small boy smeared his candy floss against my chest, then began to wail to his mother. A toddler in a push-chair pointed up at me as we passed, saying 'Donkey, mammy, donkey!'

Tom smiled down at her, 'I don't think so!'

In a little square off the main street a big black truck blared loud music for the benefit of a few disinterested teenagers who leaned against the statues or shop windows in little groups.

A park with tall iron gates locked together with a stout chain. Beyond, on the grass, donkeys were running around a track much to the amusement of the spectators.

'What do you think of that, eh, Sullivan?' Tom asked me, a laugh in his voice as one of the riders slipped, saddle and all, under his donkey's belly. I gave a chuckle in reply, hoping he didn't intend to involve me in any such spectacle.

We made our way past a big empty stage, loudspeakers filling the street with the strains of some sentimental ballad. Past vans where queues waited patiently for their bags of greasy chips. Past caravans of gleaming chrome where gold-bedecked matrons solicited passers-by to have their fortunes told.

Through an open gate we could see an area of grass-land that had been turned into an amusement park. A giant wheel with seats slung around its rim revolved slowly, taking its passengers high into the air. Another circular dish of a ride had its people standing around its outer edge while it dipped and wheeled at high speed. Tom urged me closer, though I found the flashing lights and the confusion of loud noises most unsettling. He had to give me a dig in the ribs with his heels to get me past the massive engines that sat on the backs of lorries, a throbbing perimeter for the hostile territory within. The colours of the stands, the sudden irrational movements, the mad screams of the people as they spun out of control in gaudy little half-circle seats rocking on an undulating deck or deliberately drove their odd-shaped cars into one another, it was all way-beyond my understanding.

The air was charged with electricity that set my ears tingling. I shook my head and pleaded with Tom to get me out of this place. 'Alright, Sull.,' he assured me with a pat on the neck, 'Easy, boy! Let's go get something to eat.'

We fell in behind a laughing crowd who were making their way back to the streets. A man had a wood-fire burning in half of an oil-drum, and he was cooking little circles of meat over the flames. Tom climbed off my back and joined the queue of people waiting to buy. He had the rope rein looped over his arm as he searched through his pockets, counting loose change. A dapper little man with a shock of white hair stood beside him, inquiring politely, 'Have you enough?'

'I hope so...' replied Tom, pulling another silver coin from his back pocket.

'Is he your horse?' asked the man.

'Yeah. Well, he's my mother's horse really, but I'm riding him.'

'And does your mother ride him sometimes?'

'Not very often, she drives him mostly...'

'Do you live in Tralee?' the man wanted to know.

'Only this week.' Tom told him, adding, 'We're Travellers.'

'Oh, Travellers?' repeated the man, 'and where are you staying now?'

'Well, we were in the town, but we got put out, so we're camped on the road, about three miles out.'

'Who put you out?' They shuffled forward as the woman at the front of the queue moved away, clutching a pile of meat-filled buns.

'Oh, you know, the Gards, the council...'

'But where would you camp in the town?'

'Out on the new ring-road. There was loads of grass, but they came and cut it the day we got here.'

The man tutted his commiserations and then asked Tom what his horse was called.

'Bumper.' replied Tom.

'Hello, Bumper!' smiled the man as he gingerly tapped my nose.

'Oh, no, this is Sullivan.' Tom apologised. 'Sorry. My horse is called Bumper.'

'And where's Bumper now?'

'He's back at the camp.'

'Of course. And what's your name?'

'I'm Tom. Who are you?'

'Don't you know who I am?'

'Should I?'

'Do you ever watch the 'Late Late Show'?'

'What's that?'

'It's on television. Do you have a television?'

'No,' said Tom, simply. They had reached the front of the queue.

'Burger, please,' he said to the man, and handed over the collection of coins. He took the burger and led me onto the pavement.

The white haired man called after him,

'Nice talking to you, Tom!'

'Yeah, see ya!' Tom replied through a mouthful of food as we edged our way amongst the crowd.

The bright morning sky clouded over about midday, and thunder rumbled the distant mountains. Liz finished her baking and hurried along the fence gathering her washing. Ben piled wood on the fire as the first heavy drops of rain sizzled on the hot girdle-iron. The children ran for the shelter of the wagons, their shirts pulled over their heads. I turned my tail to the road.

The downpour soon had a shallow river flowing along the hard shoulder and I was catching wheel-spray from every vehicle that raced by. It wasn't cold, the change in pressure as lightning sparked overhead was refreshing. The thunder rolled by, seeming to take the rain with it. Light drizzle followed. The wet grass was more succulent than ever.

I looked up at the little black car that came hurtling along the hard shoulder, arcing water to both sides. All four people in the car were looking at me, but the car didn't slow down. Seconds later the driver was swerving to avoid the white plastic bollards that marked the end of the hard-shoulder. The water under his wheels prevented them responding to his urgent tugging at the steering wheel. The front corner of the car flattened the first two bollards and bounced off the third. The car rolled over onto its roof, skidded sideways across the road and tumbled back onto its wheels as it landed in the field on the other side, flattening the low hedge. The mangled wreck faced back the way it had been travelling.

Almost in slow-motion the two doors opened and the driver and his three passengers spilled out. They stood in the field, patting each other on the back, stretching legs and flexing fingers. One of them had blood trickling from a gash on his forehead. They were scrambling through the gap they had made in the hedge when Ben rushed across the road to see if they needed any help. The fire had survived the downpour and was boiling the kettle. Liz gave the men cups of tea and Ben tied a bandage around the bleeding wound.

One of the men went walking down the road. The first car that came along stopped to give him a lift. Shortly afterwards, another car arrived at the camp to pick up the other three. The next day, a lorry with a winch hauled the heap of scrap out of the field.

We moved to a camp beside a river, wide but shallow enough to wade across. High banks on both sides were overgrown with dense vegetation. The wagons were parked up at a junction where three roads joined the bridge. I was tied on a long line so that I could graze the bank and reach the river. The water was cold and clear and tasted wonderfully alive. Frankie and Bumper were on the other side. Birch, who was untethered as usual, chose to stay with me rather than wade across the river. She didn't like the water at all, would always seek shelter from the rain, hardly even took a drink!

We were still packing the grass into ourselves when Ben and Liz reappeared and pulled up our stakes, gathering in our ropes.

'What's happening?' I asked, as I was dragged reluctantly away.

'Sorry, boyo,' she said, 'but yerman up there has a mortgage on all this grass, and even though his cattle can't get at it, he'd rather see it wither and die than let you get the benefit!'

The man she was referring to stood on top of the bank watching as Ben led Frankie and Bumper back across the river. Liz had been looking at him as she spoke and he'd obviously heard her. He scurried back into his motor and drove off. We trotted down the bank and back along the lane to the wagon-camp. The junction had been gravelled so there was hardly a pick of grass around the edges. Ben tied Frankie on the verge across the river. It wasn't a good place, the sparse vegetation polluted by the exhaust fumes of every vehicle that slowed for the narrow bridge.

As if to put yet another damper on the day, it started to rain. Birch pushed in amongst the harness under the wagon and the children clambered inside. During the shower, the same thin little man drove up to the camp in his battered motor. He sat behind the wheel tooting his horn, sort-of politely at first, then more insistently. No-one came out of the wagons to see what he wanted, so that eventually he ventured into the camp and presented himself at the wagon-door.

He waved his arm in the direction of the river-bank, talking urgently to the people inside. Before he left, Ben offered a handshake and the little man clasped Ben's hand in both of his, as though his life depended on it.

When the rain stopped we were led back up the lane and tied in more-or-less the same places we had been originally. Liz held the metal stake while Ben hammered it into the ground with the back of the axe.

'The poor man...' She had a smile on her face, 'the bit about his wife committing adultery must have really got to him!'

'More likely the bit about the bank foreclosing his mortgage!' Ben laughed.

Chapter Five

Road Works.

Birch continued to travel in Tom's wagon. She was much happier with this arrangement as it meant she didn't have to be tied. She would jump willingly on board just before we left each camp, and stand looking out the door as we rolled along. Tom and his sister would usually occupy the ledges on either side and the goat in the middle would be listening to their chatter. If it started to rain she could retreat inside the wagon and lie in some convenient hollow amongst the things stacked under the old tarpaulin, or stand on one of the ledges, leaning against the curved canvas wall. It also meant that my load had been considerably lightened.

The morning we were getting ready to leave the river camp, the little flat-cart was tied on behind the side-lace. Liz tacked me up and got me under the shafts then left me standing while she went to catch Birch and put her in the wagon. Ben was in a hurry to be moving once he had Frankie ready.

'Get a move on, woman!' he shouted from the step between the shafts where he liked to stand when driving.

'Alright, just give us a minute!' she called back. Birch was squatting to relieve herself as she always did before jumping into the wagon. Tom was feeding Bumper's reins through the terrets on his straddle.

Blue was inside the little wagon, spreading the tarp out to cover boxes and tools. Liz handed her Birch's leading rope and the goat scrambled aboard.

'Right!' shouted Ben. 'Giddup, Frankie!' and the big horse threw his weight against the collar and started the wagon rolling. Both the wagons were facing the road and the horses only had to move forward, but I was in the shafts of a cart that still had to be turned. Looking sideways I could see the wagons slowly moving away and I called out, 'Hey, wait for me!' I wasn't used to travelling behind.

Liz shouted 'Stand up, Sullivan!' as she hurried towards me, but I'd already started to turn, intent on following the others. She caught the reins under my chin and jerked me to a standstill. I over-reacted, taking a couple of steps backwards. The breeching dug into my rump as the the braker-straps tightened and with a creaking and a cracking of wood the two carts jack-knifed and the damaged shaft of the flattie was crushed under the ledge of the side-lace.

Tom glanced back when he heard Liz frantically 'WHOA'ing me. He saw our difficulty and shouted to Ben who already had Frankie going down the road at a trot. Both horses had to stop. Blue ran forward to take Frankie's head. Ben came storming back, ranting and throwing his arms in the air. His anger was mostly directed at Liz, with just the occasional reference to my own short-comings.

'I should have sold this yoke when I had the chance!' he shouted as he struggled to lift the back of the flattie out from under the ledge.

'Help me!' he ordered Liz, who was standing at my head trying to keep me calm while the shafts tipped and jerked at my belly-band. 'Stand up!' she growled at me, and she went to help free the jammed-together carts. Furious, Ben broke the splintered end off the shaft and threw it into the river.

'Maybe you could have fixed it...' Liz began, but he shouted her down.

'Fix YOU would be more like it! I don't know why I bother! It'll be a pile of firewood before the end of the day at this rate!'

'Look, I'm sorry...' she offered, but added, '...if you weren't in such a hurry...'

'Oh, yeah, always somebody else's fault!' He stormed back to the wagon and whipped Frankie on down the road leaving Liz to bring me around and follow on. The flat-cart was tied-on by its one good shaft. I could feel it wobbling drunkenly as I picked up speed. With Ben's anger pushing Frankie on at his fastest trot we were soon bowling along the main road, drenched in our own sweat.

New sections of road petered back to country lane barely two vehicles wide. We picked up long convoys of impatient motorists, overtaking me and cutting in behind Bumper's wagon as though they might reach their destination quicker. By the time the road widened again there would be maybe a dozen assorted vehicles between me and Frankie. They would all pull out at once when a straight stretch of road presented itself, vying amongst themselves for the foremost position.

Then there were road works. Temporary lights made us wait while a stream of traffic poured down our side of the road. At the green signal we were driven on between flickering ribbons of crackling red and white plastic. On the other side of the road, men pounded the tarmac with deafening drills that shook the whole surface. Great yellow lorries stood by, rumbling engines idling. Just beyond, another new section, bright black tarmac marked out with fluorescent cones that seemed to jump out at me from the roadside. A big square orange board proclaimed its warning from the verge but nothing could have prepared me for what was to come. Around a bend in the road the dancing cones appeared in the middle of the carriageway as well as along the edge so that I had to negotiate the narrow track between them. Liz tried to pull my head up to take my attention away from these distractions, but I was convinced they would attack my legs at any moment.

Worse, the line in the middle became a double row, quickly fanning out to surround the strangest vehicle I'd ever encountered. It was a dazzling yellow box on little black wheels, flashing orange lights flickered along a panel on its roof.

'Easy, Sullivan! Don't mind 'em! Brave Boy!' Liz was doing her best to reassure me as we approached. It crawled along the middle of the road between its flanks of striped cones, belching foul-smelling fumes, not only from its upthrust exhaust pipes but also from a steaming vat attached to its rear-end. The driver had his back to us, enclosed in the glass cab at the front, but on a platform behind him two men in glowing orange jackets were operating levers. As we drew level with the back of the vehicle it suddenly let out a high-pitched sigh and a cloud of steam.

Hot white paint streamed out of the vat and left a sparkling line on the new road. I'd been watching the flashing lights and was totally convinced that the expected attack had been launched when the vibration hit my ears. Liz pulled on my mouth, as if she expected me to bolt. I half-reared in the shafts, tipping the side-lace so that it pressed down on the flattie, pushing it backwards. There was the crump of wood on metal, and the tinkle of shattering glass. Again the wagons had to stop and Ben came running back down the road while the line-marker pursued its relentless course. He grabbed the reins under my chin and pulled me out of the ditch shouting 'I don't believe this! How do you manage it?' at Liz, and 'That'll teach you not to drive so close, won't it?' to someone else who was also shouting at Liz from somewhere behind.

He led me past the yellow machine as it was pouring the next line. I was still convinced that it meant me harm, but was also terrified and at-the-same-time reassured by Ben's grip on the reins. His 'walk on' was not a polite request, it was an order, and I had no choice but to obey.

Wheels and Deals.

Big new houses peered down on the road from balconies supported by fluted white columns. Their driveways defined by sparse rows of thin trees. Ivy-clad farmhouses nestled snugly amongst outbuildings and stands of mature oak and feathery pines. Skeletal elms pointed bleached fingers from the hedgerows between fields. Satellite bungalows brooded on their little acres. Some were decorated with hanging baskets and iron cooking pots dripping flowers, others with scrap cars. Petrol stations, the edge of town. Terraced houses lined the road, brightly painted signs swinging over the spiked railings. The road narrows, the front doors of the houses are only a step back from the pavement.

A down-hill run to the busy town centre, the surface smooth as glass under our feet. Frankie has slowed to a walk, Bumper too. Liz pulls me in just in time to stop me colliding with the back of the little wagon. I lose traction and three metal shoes slide away from under me, the fourth stabs at the road seeking grip.

We stop to allow traffic up the hill, then have to pull out to overtake the cars parked half-on the pavement, their wheels straddling the double yellow lines. At the bottom of the hill a set of traffic lights on red. Cars streaming up the hill. The breeching pushing my legs along the slippery road, so that I have to back-step constantly just to stay in the same place. The green light, the wagons sway as they start to roll, turning left. Two cars have pushed in between me and Bumper, so I lose sight of the other horses as the drivers dither at the lights, the front one intending to turn right. Black smoke clouds the junction as the car hops and revs away. The other car slips left as the lights go back to red.

I hear Frankie calling 'What? Again?' and the clop of their hooves slows to a halt. In front of me, in the middle of the road as it attempts a right turn up the hill a massive cab sits over a protruding engine, chrome fenders flashing. Its trailer an open frame work of latticed metal, two tiers of sparkling new cars, creeping across the narrow junction. Panic tells me 'Go back!!' but Liz is urging me on. She must think the transporter will stop and allow us through. She's wrong.

The teetering load jerks forward, air-brakes hiss. Liz is trying to stop me turning too sharp, but I side-step to save myself going under the wheels of the trailer which is inches away from my face. The big wooden wheel of the side-lace mounts the kerb, tipping the shafts at a precarious angle, setting the little cart behind into a sway that bounces it off the metal lamppost. The car in front of me blares his horn as he overtakes the two wagons. In the noise and confusion, with the two carts behind me still jostling themselves into line, I give in to blind panic and let Liz steer me down the line of motors ticking-over as they wait for the lights to change.

The pavement is busy with women carrying shopping bags, little kids in push-chairs, their brothers and sisters swinging alongside. I catch a glimpse of gaudy cloth, an image of someone stepping into the road, back to me, a black box held up to the face, pointing at the wagons.

Liz shouts 'Look out!' and pulls my head right so that all I can see is the great rolling bulk of a cement mixer on the other side of the road. I feel the shaft connect with the soft body, the rubber-tyred wheel of the flat cart bounces again and Liz is pulling back hard on my mouth, her 'Whoa!' carries an edge of hysteria, an echo of my own panic. I stop behind the little wagon hearing Liz call back

'Are you alright?' Ben, standing in the middle of the road, reins in one hand says 'Never mind the tourist, are you alright?'

'Yeah, but...'

'But nothing. Let's get out of here!' He jumps back onto the shafts and 'Ups' Frankie into a brisk trot. Bumper and I stay close behind as we make our way through the narrow winding streets. The road splits, a triangular 'island' of grass and flowers to our right as we stop at another junction waiting to turn left. Lined up along the kerb opposite are horses under the shafts of wooden wheeled vehicles, more than I'd ever seen. Mostly two-wheelers, some had seats that faced inwards, some had their passengers sitting sideways, looking out. There was a four-wheeled carriage with a high seat in front for the driver. The horses stood patiently, their noses in canvas bags. Men on the pavement leaned against the wall talking amongst themselves, accosting passers-by.

Frankie is calling to the mares as Ben steers him around the kerb. A couple of them look up and answer him. A man clutches the reins of his little bay mare when she makes a move to leave her post. On the road out of town we pass several more of these horses, heading in the opposite direction, carts full of passengers, black boxes dangling against their chests. Frankie must have been as surprised as I was at the sight of all these other working horses, but he kept up his challenging and flirting as though he was still leader of the herd.

A motor that was overtaking slowed right down to match our pace.

Leaning out of the passenger window a man called to Liz 'Are you selling?'

'I wouldn't swap!' she replied. The engine sounded rough; it sputtered and coughed as the driver accelerated forward to drive alongside the wagon in front. It was the familiar Hi-Ace, this one a barely-recognizable wreck. The back window was shattered, replaced by a sheet of board. The back door waggled from side to side, unable to close, the whole body of the van leaning uncomfortably towards the gutter. A black mist belched from the exhaust pipe that rattled off the road as the van screamed forward again and stopped in front of Frankie. We all had to stop and wait while Ben climbed down from the wagon and stood in the road talking to the three men. After a few minutes he waved his arm in my direction and the four of them trooped past the wagon and came to stand beside me.

'He's a fine horse, Ben!' one of them said.

'Nothing to do with me. He's the woman's horse.'

'A fine little horse, ma'am!' he said to Liz.

'Yeah, I know.' she replied.

'Would ye sell him, ye would!'

'I might swap him for a better one!' I didn't like the sound of that, but she added, 'You know where I'll find a better one?'

The man said his brother had the finest piebald mare in the country. Liz laughed, saying, 'Sure, he wouldn't be wanting to swap for a bit of an auld gelding then, would he?'

'He might take money to swap,' the man persisted.

'I'll bet he would!' she agreed.

The shafts of the side-lace vibrated as one of the men shook the top of the wheel. 'Good side-lace.'

'Indeed, I built it myself.' Ben told them. 'The flattie too. Newly built, never been used, but it's getting a battering towing it about the place.'

'How much?' asked a voice.

'I'd have to get a hundred.'

'Would you take forty?'

'Forget it!' Ben was already walking past me on his way back to the wagon.

'Hang on a minute!' called one of the men. 'We've got some auld harness in the van, we might have a deal?'

'Show me!'

They all walked back to the van.

'Good boy Sullivan, stand up!' as I shifted my weight to take advantage of the rest. The group of men were soon back, untying the flat-cart from behind the side-lace and wheeling it away down the road. As one of the men counted out notes into Ben's hand I could hear their conversation.

'Did you lose your back number plate there?' Ben indicated the door of the van, wobbling droopily on its hinges while two of the men struggled to load the flat cart.

'Er, no, we never got round to registering it,' the man admitted.

'What?' Ben was incredulous, 'You mean that's a brand new van?'

'Well, it's about three or four months we've had it.'

'Jeez, how'd you get it into that state? Did you crash it?'

'No, it wasn't ever crashed... just some of the young fellas, they do be a bit rough, learning to drive, an' that!'

Ben shook his head and slapped hands with the man.

'I'm glad it's not a horse I'm selling you!'

'Would you buy a good horse?' the man asked.

'What? Off you fellas? If that's the way you drive your motors!' He laughed, already walking away and taking the reins from Blue who had been holding Frankie. The driver climbed into the Hi-Ace and it hopped and jerked away down the road. They hadn't managed to fit the flattie inside. One of the men sat facing backwards, holding onto the shafts as they towed it behind.

The little wheels bounced along the pot-holed road almost in time with the mangled door that bobbed along at roof-level.

Glad to be rid of the encumbrance of the flat-cart, we continued with our travels. We'd be travelling all day with the autumn sun at our backs. Through villages with dog-leg roads leading over narrow bridges. Fields ploughed and mown hay meadows trampled by cattle seeking the last of the grass.

The steady trot that covers the miles through rich farm land and roads lined by trees turning from green to every shade of yellow, gold and red. On days when the sun cast shadows and burnished the branches the land seemed to come alive with a spirit of abundance.

The talk we overheard was all of 'The Great Fair' but to me each day was just another adventure on our journey away from the sun. The weather held good, and the grass was plentiful on the wide verges of the quiet country roads we mostly travelled. The routine of finding wood and water, of unpacking the cooking pots and preparing food every evening continued, even though it would often be full-dark before the meal was completed. Then fine evenings would be spent sitting round a bright fire, a kettle steaming constantly over the flames. Sometimes visitors would gather. Sometimes music and song would echo round the camp. Other times the children would be put to bed early and Liz and Ben would disappear into their wagon and light the stove. Only on the stormiest of nights would the canvas curtain ever be dropped over the doorway.

Ballinasloe

Something seemed familiar about the skyline as we approached the town. The powerful aroma of horses overwhelmed all the other scents of the place. After days and nights of the riverside air, cooking smells and peat fires, the town was an assault on the senses.

I followed as close as I could to the back of Bumper's little wagon, not wanting to be separated from the others as the roads got more crowded.

By the time we reached the middle of town we were at a standstill. Moving forward a few steps as we negotiated a narrow street lined with stalls selling everything from fried food to sparkling ornaments. Step by careful step we made our way through the throng. Men of all ages calling out a greeting to Ben at the head of our procession. Hands reaching out to touch my face, my flank, tug on my tail. Liz's voice 'Back off, lads!' not aimed at me.

Through a gateway and a rutted muddy entrance leads into a field already occupied by a semi-circle of wagons similar to Frankie's. I watch the canvas top swaying precariously as the big wheels navigate the uneven ground. Ben is driving him on, partly for show, partly to avoid getting stuck. Bumper puts on a burst of speed too; his little vehicle bouncing along on its car-tyres.

Taking my cue from the other horses, and Liz's gentle encouragement, I lean into the collar and find the weary strength to keep the wheels rolling.

That evening seemed to come earlier than any in the year. Each day seemed noticeably shorter than the one before, but this day ended abruptly with a dark menacing cloud spilling its load of sleet and icy rain. Liz had just finished staking me out on the green behind their wagon. The last resounding clang of the heavy hammer on the half-shaft rang out like a signal for the start of the storm. A rumbling clap of thunder was followed by a flash of lightening which had Liz running for the shelter of their wagon. She wiped the moisture from the back window and looked at me. I called to her, reassuring her that I was not afraid, only glad to be off the road and out of harness. I shook the first of the rain out of my mane and tail, then shook the rest of my coat to revive the areas flattened by the harness. Turning my back to the wind, I looked again at the little window and saw the faces of all the children staring back at me, and at all the other horses standing sentinel across the field.

Our water buckets that night consisted of rain-water, dusty tasting from the smoke laden atmosphere of the town. We were not too thirsty, having eaten the wet grass during and after the storm. It ended almost as abruptly as it began. The strong wind seemed to be driving the rain, the whole storm, ahead of itself. The clear sky could be seen approaching, golden red with the setting sun. Woodsmoke mingled with peat for a distinctive mood as people emerged from their shelters and re-kindled their cooking fires. A big communal fire in the middle of the circle became the haunt of the men of all ages. Smoking and spitting like the fire spirit they are drawn to. Men who talk of times when they lived this way. Their fathers and grandfathers, lost in the mists of time and memory. Young men who've heard it all before, without ever having experienced it first-hand. Some respectfully basking in the flames' heat, steam rising from their wet clothes. Some playing with the fire, throwing in logs and anything they can find; plucking burning branches and waving them at the nearest person. A loud voice calls to them to stop messing with the fire, and a few quiet words from the older men has them stopping their game, kicking a few stray logs into the burning centre, drifting off to somewhere else.

It was as if the storm had brought all the week's bad weather and given it to us in an hour. The following days were bright and sunny once the morning mist was gone. I was tied each day on a slightly different patch of grass, always alongside Bumper and Frankie. Quiet days for me, not expected to face the rabble on the street, or take part in any of the events of the town.

Bumper came back one evening after spending the day 'on the fair' with Tom. Through his eyes we were introduced to horses of every type from the finest thoroughbreds to the tiniest Sheltie. And donkeys everywhere, being given away to anyone who would take them.

A few men, mostly young lads, came and tugged on my chain and tried to look into my mouth. I learnt very young that it is less painful to relax and let them look at my teeth than to have a fist gripping a top lip. Usually there would then be a discussion on my age and condition, wildly at odds with one another.

The dogs have barked, someone is coming from the camp to say 'He's not for sale.' After a few repeats, and some 'would ye takes...?' they will drift away.

The grass is gone, it's time to move on. Some of the wagons have already left.

'We move on tomorrow,' I hear Ben saying to Liz as she brings me my night-feed and checks my water bucket.

I relish the warm mash of cereal and beet-pulp, to fill my belly on these cold nights. My winter coat is shedding old hair to make way for the new. The last few days, I've been groomed to a greater or lesser extent, every afternoon. Great tufts of hair thrown to the wind, catching in the weeds to be collected during the night for some other creature's comfort.

Another clear day to resume our travelling. The dry windy weather left the field rutted but hard. We soon had the show on the road. Back along the main street where a few big vans were being packed down with the contents of the makeshift stalls. Litter still blew around the pavements, almost all the horses were gone.

Almost. At the very end of the town, a man was tying a little mare to the upright post of a road sign. There was no indication of anyone living nearby.

Pulling Frankie to a halt, Ben calls out 'Is that your horse?'

'It is. Unless you want her, then she's yours.'

Liz keeps a firm grip on my bit as the traffic overtakes us. When oncoming traffic stops them, I'm the first to hear the blaring of horns and even shouts from motorists.

I see the man untying the short rope attached to the rope-halter and handing it to Ben. They slap hands. The man lights a cigarette as he walks by me on the verge. Mutters something to Liz. Tom is right behind him, leading the nondescript little animal. He ties the end of the rope to the curved bracket under the bed of his wagon. She turns her head sideways to look at me, standing over her, feet stamping, impatient. Her look of resignation coupled with complete acceptance transmits experiences I hope never to endure.

'Hup!' and we're off again down the road. At the first tug of the rope, she turned forwards and quickly matched her pace to that of Bumper.

That was the first time I ever saw Misty. The quiet little old mare that nobody wanted.

Back at the bog camp she was tied out for the night alongside me. Her story emerged in different scenes throughout the night. Our mutual grooming session let me know that she was familiar with other horses. She was also recovering from mastitis, left untreated when the foal she had been suckling was taken from her. Never to be seen again. Just as her own birth-foal had been left behind when she was taken to the riding stables, two days after his birth.

I realized how blessed my young life had been.

The next morning, Ben put a set of shoes on the mare, and she joined the family as an instant matriarch. Frankie and Bumper were as deferential as I towards this wise and brave little mother.

We had to be out on the road as soon as the sun was risen. Even so, yellow buses and streams of cars and lorries impeded our progress away from the town. We would try to find a place to rest for an hour or so until the worst of the traffic subsided. Then pull a few more miles into the sun.

Having had her worm-dose, Misty started to show an improvement in her condition. The seed-heavy grass in areas that had escaped the mower was high-energy food. We all packed as much as we could eat at the end of each day's travelling. Some evenings would find poor enough pickings. Other horses may have camped ahead of us. Or other horses already there with the best grass taken. But most nights we hardly need our 'mash'.

One whole day was spent trotting along a road which followed closely the shore of a vast body of water. Some of the time, we couldn't see across to the far shore, even though the day was clear and bright. That night, we pulled onto a long narrow field nestling between the road and a fast flowing river. High steep rocky banks flanked the road and the far side of the river. The grass had not been cut in recent times, and was deep and lush. We all enjoyed a good roll on the clean ground. Little Misty kicked her legs in the air and wobbled unsteadily as she shook herself upright. She was fast-regaining her strength and vitality. Even the young twins were running wild and free through the long grass; throwing themselves down to hide in their imaginary games.

As darkness descended, Liz was boiling water over a blazing fire and washing clothes in big buckets. She hung the dripping garments over the roadside wooden fence. The sunset that night was blotted out by dark clouds gathering as the day ended.

With complete darkness came the first of the rain. Soft to begin with, then squally as gusts of wind whipped it cruelly in our faces. No moon shone through the clouds that black night and the rain never ceased. Before dawn we were standing in water up to our knees as the river burst its banks and continued to rise steadily. The cloud cover had still not broken, nor the rain abated by the time the sun brought full-light to the day.

The family must have been unaware of our predicament, even though we called to them several times during the night. Each time, a light would shine over us, check that we were still there. But they didn't notice the gradually rising level until a sudden onslaught of water sent a wave racing over the land, engulfing the wheels of the wagons and cart, lifting our feet as it washed under our bellies. The little mare Misty was swept to the end of her chain, struggling to swim against the relentless current.

A confusion of shouts and screams as Ben and Liz and the two older children waded out to where we were each tied. Blue ran along the edge of the new-fledged river until she reached the stake that Misty was tied to. Resting both feet against the half-shaft buried in the bank, she leaned back, tugging at the end of the rope until it slipped free. The mare was swept away downstream. Blue watching in dismay, unable to do anything else to help in any way. Tom waded out waist-deep to where Bumper was tied, and tugged valiantly at the stake holding him. It slid from the wet ground. The boy threw it over his shoulder, and coaxed the horse to follow him out of the midst of the raging river. Ben did the same for Frankie.

Liz was struggling with the chain pulled taut from my necktie to the metal stake. The others were clear of the water and I was anxious to join them. I gave a mighty tug and the water-logged ground gave up the tether. Dragging it behind me, I heard Liz scream as it hurtled past her in the water. It may have knocked her off her feet, or she may have just stumbled on uneven ground, slipped, or been upended by the fast-flowing water. With a backwards glance I saw her fall sideways into the river. I didn't look again until I reached the safety of the road. Ben had handed Frankie's rope to Tom, and was swimming back out to reach her as she struggled to re-gain her footing against the current. Clasping hands together, falling into each others arms, they emerged from the ice-cold water.

'Get into the wagon and light the stove. Get out of these clothes!' Ben ordered her. Then he and Tom untied the stakes from our chains and left us standing on the road. There was no traffic. The short stretch of tarmac disappeared from view under water in both directions. The wheels of the vehicles were almost covered by the flash flood. Before he joined her in the wagon, Ben tied a stout rope to each of the vehicle's axles and secured them to the sturdy fence along the road. Then he rescued the last garment still clinging to the rail, a pair of his denim jeans.

From somewhere downstream we heard Misty calling; knew that she had somehow scrambled out of the water. Heard her newly shod hoofbeats on the road, saw her splashing back through the flooded section. Joyful calls from all of us as she trotted back to the inundated camp.

White smoke rising in a tall plume above the green canvas of the wagon signalled a rare daytime fire in the stove. We shuffled about on the road, trapped between the torrent and the steep bank of scrub woodland. The rain had finally stopped, high winds pushing clouds away. By midday the sky was blue as a summer's day, but the chill in the breeze reminded us that we would need to eat again soon.

Taking turns to mutual groom with each other, I enjoyed the attentions of Misty, who could reach up just high enough to tug on the base of my mane. I nibbled along her back, making the flesh twitch. She was in very poor condition when she joined us, but was already starting to fatten up and get fit again.

Ben and Liz emerged from the camp at the sound of an approaching engine. An old pick-up truck was making its way slowly through the deluge, spraying a high wake from its big wheels. Once on the dry road, two men climbed out and greeted Ben. Indicating the load of hay-bales on the back of the truck, one asked 'Have you any use for these?'

The first of the bales was cut open and shaken out onto the road. We all whickered our excitement and jostled together to take mouthfuls of the sweet meadow hay.

Ben was insisting he must pay the men for their generosity, but they wouldn't hear of it. Liz was offering them a cup of tea, but they just turned the vehicle in the road and headed back the way they had come. So for the next few days we lived on hay, with smaller rations of mash at dusk. Our water came from the steadily falling overflow.

Liz poured the last of their drinking water from the big black container and announced that 'someone' would have to go find more.

That was the morning we were back in harness and continuing our journey. Water was still high in all the rivers we passed by but the days were dry and the roadside acres refreshed by the deluge.

We reached the outskirts of a big city one evening and stopped for the night on a large expanse of rough ground beside a swollen river. A few other horses were already running free on the land, but we were tied out as usual. The bright fire in the camp attracted a small crowd as Liz fed the family from the big iron pot. The men talking quietly to Ben. The young lads calling 'Can I jock him, missus?' as they dragged me around by my chain.

'No! Get away from them!' Liz calls back. With a few more slaps to my flanks they return to the fire. A big woman brings a gaggle of children to stand around me, grabbing my legs until she snatches them from under my feet. Over to Misty, where she sits the two smallest kids on the mare's back. Misty carries on eating, moving one step at a time seeking out fresh morsels.

Next day finds us on a ring-road round the city. The traffic is constant. Lights slow us at many of the junctions. Roundabouts are even more of an hindrance. Impatient motorists not waiting for our entourage to make its way round, cutting in between us to save a few seconds on their trip. Wide pavements with high kerbs. No place to pull off the road for a break. Sweat dripping from our legs despite the cold air. The exertion of stopping and starting, the terrifying close encounters with speeding vehicles. The exhaust fumes and smoke from the chimneys of the houses lining the road in places making it hard to breathe.

We leave the road briefly to pull into the car-park of a shopping precinct. There is nothing for us to eat, or drink. We relax between the shafts, glad of a rest, while Ben goes into the supermarket and returns with a box of groceries. As soon as this is in the wagon we are moving again.

The light is fading when we eventually find a place to camp for the night. A new motorway will soon be linking in to the ring-road, but for now only construction traffic is allowed onto the access lane. Ben and Tom easily move the temporary barrier stopping public use of the road and we pull a short distance and park up in a turning-place left vacant for the night. On one side of the roadworks the land is churned to mud, but across the way the grass has not yet been disturbed, and there is plenty for us to eat that night. The water containers are all filled from a convenient standpipe. A fire is kindled from sticks gleaned out of the old hedgerow, now partly uprooted and demolished to make way for the new highway.

Each morning sees us on the road shortly after sunrise. When it reaches the highest point in the sky there is always a lay-by or a picnic spot to rest for a while as the family light a fire and boil kettles and cook up some food. Liz's bread is always a favourite. Then, if there are still enough daylight hours left, we will travel on a few more miles and hope to find an overnight camp.

A Bad Hill.

Storm force winds drove dark clouds across the sun as it set behind the mountains on the opposite shore of the lake. We had stopped for the night in a little wooded area that bordered the gravel shoreline. There wasn't much grass amongst the trees, only along the edges of the paths, but it was a bit of shelter. The wind increased during the night, so that the trees swayed and howled in reply to the pounding of waves whipped up on the lake. Intermittent bursts of rain had us turning our backs to the water and hanging our heads. The wagons creaked on their springs, occasionally brushed by dipping branches.

Next morning saw no let-up in the storm but the sun broke through the flying clouds, and we were tacked up and driven back along the rough track to the road. After a couple of miles we turned left and started a steady uphill pull. The road was narrow, a few passing places. A long sweeping bend and suddenly we were faced by a straight steep stretch. The wind in our faces must have made the wagon harder than ever for poor Frankie who struggled and slipped as Ben jumped from the shaft and jogged along beside him, shouting encouragement and shaking the reins against the horses' rump.

We were less than a quarter of the way up the hill when he stopped. Liz pulled me up as the wagon in front of me teetered and swayed and started to roll back. Blue had been following behind with a wedge of hard-wood in her hand, and this she now slipped under the back wheel of the wagon. She hesitated for a split-second before standing up, glancing at the towering bulk of the wagon bearing down on her. A scream startled my ears and caused Liz and Ben to shout 'What is it?'

'What's happened?'

The girl was staring in horror at her own hand as blood poured down one of her fingers and dripped from her wrist. Liz dropped the reins and leapt to the road, reaching Blue just ahead of Ben. She wrapped her arm around her daughters' shoulder, hugging her close. Ben grabbed the red hand and shouted to Tom,

'Water! Get us a bowl of water!'

The blood sent a ribbon of scarlet into the water, soon turned it all a deep red. Cotton wool was called for and fresh water to rinse away the blood. A car, creeping slowly down the hill past us, stopped. Rolling down his window, the driver asked, 'Is she alright? Do you need to get her to a doctor, a hospital?'

An exchange between the three of them, Blue shaking her head, determined.

'No, thanks. She'll be alright. Thank you all the same.'

'You're sure?'

'Yes, she's had her tetanus shots.'

'What about stitches?'

'Doesn't look like there's anything to stitch.' Liz was considering the fingertip. 'It's gone. She's lost the end of her finger.' With a nervous little laugh she asked the girl 'Think you can grow a new one?'

Blue buried her face against her mother's chest and let Ben tie a pad of cotton wool over the stump of her finger, then bind up the whole hand. The car drove away. We were still stuck on the hill. Liz stood beside me, hugging Blue while Tom unhitched Bumper from the little wagon behind and led him past us. They must have tied his traces to the front of the big wagons' shafts because after a few minutes it rolled away from the block and away up the hill, Tom long-reining Bumper from the middle of the road. Ben strode alongside Frankie, whipping him on with a springy branch torn from a young ash tree in the hedgerow.

Liz asked Blue if she wanted to ride up but the girl said 'I'm okay, I'll walk. It's not much further, is it?'

'Well, it's a few more miles. Are you sure? How do you feel?'

'A bit wobbly...' the girl admitted. 'Shock, I suppose. I'll walk up the hill anyway, and see how I feel.'

'You're one brave girl, Blue. If that was me I'd have been in yerman's car and off to the hospital!'

'Ugh! I hate hospitals! I hate the smell, and all the sick people! What could they do anyway? Pour disinfectant over it, or something!'

'You're probably right.'

Starting the cart on the hill wasn't easy. Liz gave me slack reins and a slap on the rump to encourage me. I leaned into the collar but my feet slipped away from under me and I grazed the skin off a knee as it connected with the loose chippings. I recovered and followed the wagon to the top of the hill, walking. The girl striding ahead of me holding her bandaged hand to her chest said 'This is a bad hill, Sullivan; it's had blood off both of us!'

We turned right and the road levelled out. Liz brought me to a standstill behind the big wagon. Tom led Bumper back down the hill to bring up his wagon, leaving us to get our breath back.

We had climbed onto a high moorland plateau; to our left the land was strewn with pale grey rocks. Some small enough to fit in a child's hand, others so big that two men couldn't join hands around them. To our right, the land fell away sharply leaving an unrestricted view over the lake. In front, the road seemed to lead into a small mountain range, curiously wrought peaks changing colour as the clouds blew across the sun.

Bumper rejoined us and we walked on, buffeted by the wind until we came to a track leading across the moor. Here we turned and I held back as the big wagon rocked and swayed ahead of me over the ruts and boulders, humps and dips of the grass-aisled track. A bend swept along the very edge of a deep, sheer-sided hole, its bed littered with every kind of rubbish from black plastic bin-liners spilling household refuse to abandoned cars. The rotten decaying smell swirled with the wind.

'Argh! What a stench!' I gagged, snorting, turning my head to try to rid my nostrils of the cloying, gut-wrenching stink.

'Easy, Sullivan. Good boy, don't mind it!' Liz pulled on the reins to point me in the right direction, and I broke into a trot to catch up with Frankie. Ahead of us a stand of dark green trees swayed and rustled. When the track ran between low walls built of the grey stones, the trees on either side seemed to be talking, the rush of their voices overhead a calming, soothing sound that captured the wind. The same low walls enclosed tiny fields as the track bent this way and that. We stopped at a fast flowing river of peaty-brown water, and turned left into a gently sloping field.

Ben urged Frankie diagonally up the slope into the corner farthest from the gateway and then had him turn the wagon so that the shafts faced over the river. I pulled the side-lace alongside and Liz started to untack me. Blue carried a bucket of water from the river and poured about half of it into a steel bowl. The astringent smell as the brown liquid from the flat bottle turned the water milky. Liz dunked a handful of cotton wool into the icy water and pressed it against my knee. I'd almost forgotten about the graze until the sting bit into my flesh.

'Don't be such a baby, Sullivan!' Liz chided me when I flinched and complained. 'Blue has to soak her hand in this stuff.'

The girl shuddered as she peeled away the bandage. The pad was a bright red blob clinging to the tip of her finger. She screwed up her face and gave a squeal, lowering her hand into the bowl.

'Wow, that's cold!' she breathed through clenched teeth.

'Try and keep it in there for a while.' Liz told her.

Tom rigged a makeshift gate of branches and baler-twine across the entrance to the field and we were turned loose. I made straight for the river, longing to quench my thirst in its delicious mountain freshness. There was a part of the wall that was half tumbled-down, the rounded rocks having slid into the river where the bank had eroded. I had my front feet in the gap sending boulders splashing when Tom grabbed my halter and pulled me around.

'You trying to kill yourself, you stupid horse!' he berated me, slapping my rump to head me back into the field.

'I only wanted a drink!' I complained.

'You'll get a drink later,' he said, 'when you've cooled down! Now, go eat grass with the others, why don't ya?'

I left him piling the loose stones back into the gap and went to see what Bumper and Frankie were doing. It felt good to be free in the little field, free to roll, to groom one another, to wander into corners and find the choicest feed. The three of us, and Birch, had grazed the best of it by the end of the following day, but there were other little odd-shaped fields adjoining and we were let roam during the day.

'Tetanus'

About a week later, Liz drove me back down the hill into the town. I was left to pick over the mown grass borders of the car park for a couple of hours, before being tacked up again and driven round the narrow streets. We stopped outside shops to load up boxes and sacks of food. Some of it was for the family, but the sacks were feed for me and the other animals. The mountain grass, which we had to share with a seemingly infinite number of sheep, was not the best of grazing, and now our diet was to be supplemented with hard feed. Oats and beet-pulp, barley for Birch. Now that we were camped so far from the shops there was also a sack of dog-food for Pip, who was getting bigger by the day.

At one of the shops, a sweet-smelling place with a display of fresh fruit and vegetables on the pavement outside, we picked up sacks of carrots and apples, and others stuffed with the outside leaves of cabbage and cauliflower. These were to be mixed with our buckets of feed to make them more enjoyable. The delicious flavour of all this food on the back of the cart was making my stomach ache as we left town. I hadn't realized how hungry I was! A shower of rain poured in from the lake as we were hurrying along the shore, making the steep hill slippier than ever, but I tried to step on the points of my hooves and somehow managed to keep from going down on my knees again. The track leading over the moor was dry, as though the rain hadn't fallen here at all. I could feel the sun making steam rise off my back as we trudged the last mile or so along the rutted way. Feeling strangely weak, I stumbled a couple of times over boulders, into hollows. When we got back, I stood with my head between my legs so that the collar slipped up around my ears, but I was too exhausted to care. Liz was off the cart and starting to unhitch the traces, calling to the children, 'You didn't get the washing in!'

'Why? Was it raining in the town? You're all wet! It never rained here!'

Ben left the log he was sawing to help get me untacked.

'He looks jaded. Did you push him hard?' he asked Liz.

'Would I ever? You're right though. He was tripping over his feet coming along the track.'

'Hmm, they're getting a bit long alright.' Ben pushed aside the hair that hung over my front hoof and glanced at the shoe. 'How long has he had these on now? Must be a couple of months; his feet are well over-grown. I'll get them off him in the next day or so.'

Liz said 'Walk on, Sullivan. Good boy.'

Ben gently lowered the shaft to the ground as I stepped forward. Tom and Blue helped take the harness from my back and spread it on the low wall to dry. I felt a slap on the rump and Liz said, 'Go on, find the others, have a roll on the grass. You'll get a good feed in a while.'

I took a step forward and my head began to spin. I felt myself swaying and thought I would stumble.

'You alright, Boy?' Concern in her voice.

Ben called 'Go get the tools, Tom. I'll have those shoes off him now!'

Knees buckling under me, I tumbled onto the grassy verge alongside the track. A spasm ran through my legs, causing them to stretch and twitch uncontrollably. My head lolled back, the muscles in my neck suddenly too weak to allow me full control. I lay down on my side, legs rigid. The soft grass under my face buzzed with disturbed insects. Eyelids drooping, I felt my whole body relax into an exhausted heap. Never before had I felt so totally weary.

Ben was standing over me, buckling on his leather apron.

'Right then,' he was saying, 'get him up on his feet!'

Liz was patting my neck, then taking hold of my halter.

'Come on, Sull., up you get!' she gave a gentle tug that caused the top strap to dig me behind the ears. The pain shot down my neck, around my throat. A lump I couldn't swallow seemed set to choke me as I lumbered unsteadily to my feet. The trees overhead swirled with the rocky ground, the whole scene swimming as I tried to hold my head up. Closing my eyes made no difference, the dizzy feeling still persisted.

Ben's voice again: 'Pick it up!'

He lifted my front hoof and rested it between his thighs. He started to hit the front of the hoof where the nails attached the shoe. I swayed and wobbled, shifting my back feet on the uneven track.

'Stand up!' he ordered, and I searched amongst the stones for a level space. He gripped the metal shoe with a pair of pincers and working his way around the nails, gradually eased it away from my foot. With a final wrench, it came away, and he lowered my hoof gently to the ground.

By the time he'd repeated this on all four feet, I was so exhausted I could barely stand. Dragging the bare hooves over the rough track, I followed Liz as she led me down to a sloping field beside the river. No sooner had she let go of my halter than I fell onto a bed of spiky rushes. They crumpled under me with a soft rustling sound, and the water that oozed up felt cool against my side. Another spasm in my legs had me rolling over towards the river. 'Easy, Boy.' Liz was saying 'You'll be over the edge if you're not careful!'

I stopped with my feet dangling over the river bank, and relaxed again.

'Come on, you're not going to lie here, are you?' she asked. Then 'Are you alright, Sullivan?'

I tried to tell her that I felt weary, that the world was spinning inside and outside my head, that my throat had a lump too painful to swallow. The only sound that came out was a strangled moan. With a gentle pat on my neck, Liz stood up and hurried back along the track, leaving me lying beside the river. The rushing water noise soothed my aching head, and with my eyes closed the swirling gradually subsided into a sort of pattern of rolling waves. When Liz returned some time later, Ben was with her, saying 'You're right, he's obviously not well. Where did you have him tied in the town?'

'In the car park. Why?'

'Oh, I don't know, some eedjit could have fed him something...'

'I picked up all the plastic and rubbish before I left him there.'

'Sure. It looks a bit like bracken staggers. Typical! Saturday evening, no chemists open till Monday. We'd better call the vet.'

Sleep overtook me, blissful oblivion from the pains that were racking my whole body. It was dark when I awoke to the sound of voices.

Liz: 'He hasn't moved.'

Ben: 'She had him in town this afternoon, and when he got back... well, you can see for yourself he's not right.'

The stranger who stood between them:

'Yes. Can we get him up, and away from the river?'

Ben took hold of my halter saying,

'Up you come! Good boy, Sullivan!'

Tucking my legs under me, I staggered to my feet. Liz stood between me and the river bank as I swayed from side to side.

'What do you reckon?' Ben asked the dark haired man, who was shining a bright little torch over my body. The light hit my eye with a dazzling intensity. I could feel the membrane from the corner pull over the eyeball when the man tapped underneath my chin with the back of his hand.

'Hmm, when did you say he had his tetanus shot?'

'Must be a couple of months back, now. He should have had his follow-up weeks ago, but the chemist in the town there wouldn't sell me it. Said I'd have to get a vet to give it him, and we've been pretty strapped for cash since we got here.'

'You'd have saved yourself money in the long run,' the man told them. 'I'm sorry to say this horse has tetanus. Has he injured himself at all in the past week or so?'

'He took a bit of a tumble the first time we came up the hill. Here on his knee.' Ben ran his hand over the bare patch of skin where the graze had healed but the hair had not yet grown back. The man shone the torch to examine the wound.

Liz had her arms around my neck and was sobbing 'Oh, no. No, Sullivan. Oh, no.'

She wiped the tears from her cheeks with the back of her hand, asking the man, 'Can you do anything for him?'

The man said, 'I have to tell you now that I've never managed to save an animal with tetanus...'

'Oh, no...' a fresh onslaught of tears.

'...but having said that, I've never been called out this early to treat a case. They're usually on their last legs before anyone recognises that anything is wrong. So I'd say we have a good fifty-fifty chance of saving him at this stage.'

'Whatever it costs...' Ben was saying.

'Indeed,' said the man. 'He's a fine horse. Now did you say you have a shelter for him? He needs to be kept quiet and calm. Feed him whatever he can eat. I'll start the course of treatment straight away.'

Ben led me unsteadily out of the field and along the rough track to an old shed with a metal roof. I'd noticed the building before, but with its door closed had never paid it any attention. Now a white van was parked alongside the gable and the door of the shed leaned open at an angle to the wall. The man lifted the tailgate of his van, as Ben walked me into the cool musty interior of the shed. The floor had a deep covering of freshly cut rushes which felt springy and creaked when we walked on them. A clean bucket of water stood in the corner nearest the door. Another bucket held my supper of oats and barley and beet-pulp. Slices of carrots and apple were mixed in with the grain, and a handful of cabbage leaves sat on top. The man came in from his van, slipping tiny bottles into his pocket. In one hand he held a white plastic syringe, its upturned needle glistened in the light of the torch that Ben was now holding.

'Easy, now, lovely boy,' Liz soothed me, stroking my neck and fondling my ears. I tried to shake my head, and almost lost my balance again. My skin flinched but I was too weak to react to the stab of the needle as it sunk deep into the muscle of my neck. A numbness started to flow through my whole body, almost immediately.

'That's just a painkiller,' the man was explaining. 'Now I have to give him these other shots to fight the infection.'

When he had finished sticking his needles into me, Liz brought the bucket of water over and held it up to my nose. I wet my lips, tried to take a drink, but the cold water seemed to burn the back of my mouth in a strange way, making it more painful than ever to swallow.

'You might put a bit of hot water in that for him,' suggested the man. 'He'll find it easier to drink.'

And Tom was dispatched from the shed to bring a boiling kettle from the camp. Liz brought the bucket of food to me, and setting it down under my nose, offered it to me a handful at a time. Eating was a slow and painful business, the numbness having reached my lips, making it hard for me to even get the food into my mouth. Chewing sent sharp pains across my throat and down my neck. Hunger made me persist, but by the time half the bucket was gone, I was too tired to take any more. Liz gave me a last hug, before taking the little paraffin lamp from the nail in the rafter, and shutting me in the dark little shed. As soon as she'd gone I lay down on the soft rushes and let the drugs in my bloodstream take me back to dreamless oblivion.

The next few days and nights I was kept in the shed. Liz brought me more rushes every morning, and shovelled out my droppings. As each day progressed, the cramps and spasms that racked my body would get gradually worse, so that by the time the white van arrived just after dark, I would be rocking and swaying on my feet, trying in vain to relax. The man would put the needle into my neck, and the numbness would gradually overwhelm me, so that I could at least take some feed, and sleep for most of the night.

Outside there seemed to be a storm blowing. The trees howled and thrashed, the tin roof of the shed rattled and clattered. Draughts whistled around the old door, and moaned under the edges of the roof. I was glad of the shelter, at least I was warm and dry, though at first I found the noise of the lashing rain on the tin quite frightening. Like a crowd of drummers surrounding me, closing in on me as I lay trapped and defenceless, too weak to even run away. By about the fourth day in the shed these morbid imaginings passed over, and I began to feel much better. When the man arrived in the evening, I scrambled to my feet, greeting him.

'I'd say we've made it,' he told Liz and Ben.

She rushed in and threw her arms around my neck, laughing and crying at the same time. 'Oh, Sullivan, Sullivan, my lovely boy...' she was fussing over me.

Ben was asking the man 'How long will we have to rest him up?'

'Well, he'll not be ready to pull a wagon for about six months.'

'Hmm, looks like we're stuck here for the winter then.'

'He'll not be going anywhere under his own steam, that's for sure.'

Liz asked 'Can we let him out? I'm sure he'd rather be out with the others than cooped up in here the whole time.'

'Well, you're supposed to keep them 'quiet', but I suppose if the weather gets better he'll be alright to go back out, if that's what he's used to.'

That night, I was able to eat without the tightening of my jaws that had made chewing so painful all week. I crunched up the cabbage leaves, looking forward to the prospect of getting out and tasting fresh grass again.

After the man had left, Blue came to visit me, bringing an armful of sweet meadow hay.

'You able for this, now, boy?' she asked me, shaking it into a loose heap in the corner of the shed. I walked the few steps, slowly stretching the muscles in my legs that were still very stiff and painful to move. The girl held out a handful of the hay, examining it in the dim light of the paraffin lamp.

'Look!' she tried to interest me, 'there's all sorts of flowers and stuff in here!'

I took the food she was offering me, steadily chewed all the flavours of summer that it held. By the time I'd finished the first mouthful she was holding out another. When I wrapped my lips around it, I noticed a strip of rag tied around the finger that she had damaged under the wheel the first time we had come up the hill. Green stains seeped through the grubby white cotton, a faint smell of decay mixed with the astringent.

'How's your wound?' I asked her, nudging it as gently as I could.

'Ouch! Careful, Sullivan, its still pretty tender. Yours is all healed up now, isn't it?' She ran a hand softly over my knee. 'Oh, well, at least I didn't get tetanus. And this Herb Robert is doing a great job of healing. Liz thinks I might really be growing a new fingertip. Won't that be great?'

Blue checked my water bucket before she left, taking the little lamp. The wind was still beating the tops of the trees, and shaking the tin roof overhead. The moon flashed bright when the clouds blew away, then darkness again when they obscured it. But the rain held off that night, and the storm passed over.

Next morning I was allowed out of the shed. At first the sun dazzled me, making me hesitate in the doorway.

Liz said, 'Good boy, Sullivan. Don't you want to come out yet?' and stood half-in, half-out of the shed with me for a few minutes until my eyes got used to the light. Then I stepped forward, stumbling slightly on the uneven ground where the mud had dried leaving deep ruts and holes where our hooves and footsteps had been. Away from the shed, the air smelled good. Rich Autumn scents of ripe fruit and leaves already withered to brown along the paths. I tried my voice, a tentative call that sounded unsteady to my own ears, but which was instantly recognised by Frankie and Bumper who were in a field nearby, but hidden from view by the walls and hedgerows. Their answering calls carried a note of concern, as well as the usual 'oh, it's him again!' sort of banter. As soon as I was in the field with them, Bumper came bouncing over to see me.

'How's it goin', pally-boy? Where've you been the past week?' He grabbed me by the mane, his playful tug sending stabs of pain along my body, down my legs. I winced, groaned, and he knew at once that I was not well, and eased back, apologetically. For the rest of the day, he stayed close by me, grooming the dust from my back, gently nuzzling my neck, expecting nothing in return

Chapter Six

Recovery.

So began my winter of convalescence. The days grew shorter, the nights colder. The summer grass had gone to seed and died back, the bitter bracken drying, brown-tipped. We saw the sun set behind the mountain peaks, falling a notch closer with each passing week.

Bumper took over my job of going to the shops, the side-lace was too small a vehicle for Frankie. Every few days, Ben or Tom would drive him down the track, returning later with the springs groaning under the weight of supplies. Sometimes a stack of hay-bales, sometimes sacks and boxes from the shops. All our food had to be carried in, there was little nourishment to be found in the sparse mountain pasture we were sharing with the multitude of sheep.

Although I never left the vicinity of the camp over the following months there was no shortage of things going on. Ben and Liz had visitors most days. Friends they'd met all over the country would come and camp up for a day or two, sometimes a week or two.

The first person I remember seeing again was the big girl, Becket, who arrived in an old van with a couple of her friends. Liz brought her out onto the moor where I was roaming free. They stopped to say hello to Frankie who was tethered nearby. Then they wandered over to me, bringing a bucket of water from the river that the big horse had declined after dipping his moustache. I wasn't particularly thirsty that day either. The dew from the overnight mist saturated the pick of grazing, so we never felt much like drinking until the evening, after our buckets of dry feed.

Becket walked right up to me, raising a hand to grab my mane. I edged away, anticipating the twinge in my neck. Lifting my head still sent a shaft of pain across my throat, but it was a reflex action. I looked sideways at her, standing beside me with her hand still half-raised.

'He's gone quare head-shy!' she was saying to Liz.

'You should have seen him a week back,' Liz replied. 'He was too weak to even lift his head.

Bad order, the poor beast. We didn't know if he'd survive at all. Only for the vet coming when he did, we might have lost him altogether.'

'So, will he ever recover?'

'Who can tell? Yerman reckons he'll be alright again by the Spring. We can only wait and see. Hope and pray. Y'know,' Liz went on, 'I'd most likely jack it all in if he'd died on me. None of the other horses meant as much to me. Oh, I know we could get another horse to pull the cart, but it wouldn't be the same, y'know what I mean?'

'Sure, but life goes on, Liz. How do you think I felt when Belle keeled over last winter? Stuck on the bog with a new wagon and no horse to pull it!'

'How did you manage?'

'Tim lent me Gwen till I sold her foal, and bought 'Patches'.'

'She good?'

'She's lovely. A bit young to be doing the sort of miles I'd like to cover, but she's well-strong. I put her in foal to the Young Sham. If I get a decent filly foal I'll probably keep her on.'

While they were talking, Liz had sidled up to me and started to gently stroke my neck. It was still very tender from all the needles that had been stuck in it the previous week, and I could feel it flinching under her hand, but I made no attempt to stop her. Fingers lightly detecting the lumps under my skin, and firmly massaging the crest of my mane, she spoke softly in my ear.

'Poor Sullivan, you've lost all the fine condition we put on you last summer, haven't you?' She was right, I had no energy at all.

'So what do you think about me taking Blue away for a while?' Becket was asking. 'Can you manage here without her?'

'Ah, sure. It's not that. What about you?' Liz leaned forward and touched the girl in the middle of her body. 'How's the parasite treating you?'

'No bother. It's not due for months yet. Past the morning sickness stage. I'm feeling okay these days. Besides, Blue's a great help in the camp. She loves Jed, and he's really good for her. It's just good to have someone to babysit, someone he doesn't mind being left with for a few hours.'

'Well, see what Ben says, then...'

They turned to leave, Becket holding out her hand for me to sniff. Her empty palm carried the smell of her mare, her dogs, the woodsmoke of her breakfast fire, all half-lost under the diesel and tobacco of her journey.

'You be a good boy and get better now, Sullivan,' she told me, 'I don't want my mother to have to give up the travelling just because she hasn't got you!'

A few hours later, as dusk was falling, and Ben and Tom were bringing our evening feeds, the old van rattled and sputtered down the track. I looked up to see Blue waving a hand against the window in the back door.

It was around that time Frankie got a new vehicle to work with. New to him, at least. An old farm-cart on heavy wooden wheels, it had probably never been repainted in its long life, and the red-oxide had faded to the softest of pinks, matching the powder-blue of the body. There were lift-off sides of wooden slats that slotted into holes along the edge of the cart-bed. When they were erected they formed a high-sided box that was the very thing for carrying the hay. The arrival of this new transport meant that Frankie could do his share of the carrying, and take the load off Bumper, who was working hard to keep the camp supplied with all its provisions, firewood and everything.

Liz caught hold of my halter and held me at the gate the first time Ben took Frankie out in the big cart. We watched him trundle steadily over the rocky track across the moor until he rounded the bend and dipped out of sight. The steep sides of the cart rocked and swayed from side to side as the heavy old wheels made light work of the rough ground. Liz stroked my nose when I called after them.

'Would you like to be doing that?' she asked me. 'Pulling the auld tumbril off to the town? It's like something they used to carry people off to their executions in...' she mused.

I gave a low call that carried on the breeze as the cart bobbed into view again near the end of the lane. Frankie replied with his high-pitched cry echoing back from the hills behind us.

'Back to work, then! You don't go following after him, now.'

She left me standing by the rickety gate that was tied with baler-twine to the stone piers on either side of the track. I had no intention of pushing it over to follow Frankie. Instead I sauntered casually back to the camp behind Liz and nibbled around the edges of the field while she filled the air with the scent of fresh bread baked over the bright little fire.

When Frankie returned a few hours later the cart was loaded. They had been to the farm for bales of hay, the shops for groceries. They had also collected Blue from the train-station in the town. She was tired after her journey but jumped down off the high cart and came over to meet me as I was strolling across the field to see if there was anything edible being unpacked. The girl looked more bedraggled than usual in her grubby denim clothes. The smell of the train lingered in her hair despite the buffeting the wind had given her on the way back.

'So how are you now, Sullivan? Getting better?'

'Yes, yes...' I pushed her aside so I could see more clearly what was coming off the back of the cart.

'Hey! Aren't you glad to see me?' she asked indignantly, taking me by the halter, and giving my head a little shake.

'Alright, I'm sorry,' I said. I gave her a nudge on the chest with my nose, and she responded by scratching my face. She no longer wore a bandage on her damaged finger, which looked pink and fleshy, slightly twisted at the tip, but unmistakably healing. New growth of white nail was starting to appear.

'Let him have these cabbage leaves!' Ben called to her, indicating a few bits of greenery that had fallen out of a sack he was unloading. Blue snatched them up from the ground and held them for me while I crunched them noisily.

'That good?' she asked me, smiling. 'You funny horse. You really like cabbage don't you? and the others all turn their noses up at it!'

It was true, the other horses pushed the dark green leaves aside, only eating them when the rest of the food in their buckets was gone. Birch and I would eat ours first, relishing the bitter juicy flavour.

We didn't see much wildlife on the mountain in those first months. A few rabbits in the dusk and dawn hours would venture from their burrows on the ramshackle stone walls to pick what they could of the grazing that the sheep overlooked. The occasional hare might be glimpsed stopping and starting amongst the rocks. As the days shortened their coats became tinged with white, and in the darkest time, they were almost perfectly camouflaged in between the frosted stones and the bare ground. The ubiquitous rats that scavenge every part of this country had also found their way here. Any morsel of grain we were unable to pick off the ground was their after-dark feast. But no vixen gave voice to her haunting moonlight howl, no badger shuffled by on his nocturnal ramblings.

So I was completely taken by surprise one morning to wake in one of the fields that adjoined the moor and see a group of animals the like of which I'd never before encountered.

It was around the time of the Solstice. The sun would barely clear the top of the mountain before it was setting again. Snow had fallen on the high peaks, sparkling in the brief midday but chilling the air all around so that we had to eat more just to keep ourselves warm. These were big animals. Not quite as big as a horse, but considerably bigger than the goat or any dog I'd ever seen. A herd of maybe a dozen were milling around on the other side of the wall, probably attracted by the smell of the hay, or just the greenness of the little fields. Their leader was bigger than the rest, and carried on his head a mighty spread of horns. Unlike a goat or sheep, this magnificent beast had horns that branched off from the main trunk, tree like. A couple of the younger males had slightly smaller sets of horns. The rest of the group seemed to be made up of females, and youngsters who carried no horns. All their coats were a dark red-brown, the big leader being slightly darker than the rest. They talked amongst themselves in voices that sounded guttural and throaty. I didn't understand the noises, but it was clear that they were hungry, no other urge would have brought them down from their high mountain domain.

They were still around, picking over the few stalks of hay that had escaped our notice the previous evening, when Liz arrived shortly after daybreak to bring me out onto the moor for the day.

'See the deer, Sullivan? And you think you're hungry? How'd you like to have to scavenge for yourself all winter?' It didn't sound like a good idea at all, and I watched them out the corner of my eye while I was eating my morning feed. When Liz brought me a bucket of water, the whole family trooped along with her. Maybe they'd never seen the deer before, either.

Ben was carrying half a bale of hay on his shoulder, and after shaking some of it out for me he walked along the track until he was near the herd and scattered the rest of it on the ground for them. They turned and ran a short distance, but the leader of the herd soon stopped and grunted to the rest of them to do the same. No sooner was Ben's back turned but they were making their way over to the pile of hay, pushing to get at it. The big male stood by while the females fussed over the feed, digging their dainty little hooves into the ground, stamping impatiently as though this might enable them to eat faster. When he was convinced that no tricks or traps were involved, he slowly, still watching the retreating man, joined in the feed.

For the next few days, the herd stayed around. They were seen by people driving along the road who slowed their cars for a better look. Some would even get out of their cars and walk across the moor, to get closer, or point cameras at them. Then one early morning, I was woken to the sound of a gunshot. The sharp crack cut the still mist of the frosty morning, and the herd scattered across the moor. The leader roared in anger and confusion as he tried in vain to keep them all together. Another shot caused him to shake his mighty horns, as the bullet pierced a hole through one of the outer branches. With a last howling bellow, he set off in pursuit of his herd. The young female who had taken the first shot in her shoulder staggered around bleating, squealing most piteously. The gunmen hurried over the rocky ground until they were just a few feet away from her. One of them raised the rifle to his shoulder and pulled the trigger again. The top of her head was turned to bright red pulp, and she fell heavily into a shallow pool amongst the stones. The splash as she landed was echoed by the smaller sound of lapping water as her legs twitched and jerked their death-throes.

I was watching in horrified fascination the men uncoiling the rope to bind her legs. They slipped a long pole under her hooves and hoisted it onto their shoulders. Then they began their stumbling progress back to the old pick-up truck they had parked on the track. Throwing the dead animal onto the flat-bed, they hastily covered it with a sheet of dirty green tarpaulin. As they made their noisy getaway, I looked over at the pool where I had often quenched my thirst. Slow patterns still rippled the surface as the fresh blood gradually mingled with the peaty mountain water. Ben noticed it when he was tying Frankie out later that morning. I was following along behind.

'Bastards!' I heard him mumble to himself.

New Arrivals.

With the darkest time of year passed, the days seemed crisper. The peaks still dusted white sparkled against a bright blue sky. Cotton-wool clouds threw shadows over the distant hills, the days still short but somehow sweeter. One dark evening in the early Spring Ben arrived back at the camp with another horse in tow. He had been all the day at a horse fair, and then only managed to get a lift for himself and the horse as far as the town. They had to walk the rest of the way. From what the horse told us it had been a dangerous journey. The road was narrow in places and the fast moving traffic swerving at the last minute to avoid hitting the horse had very nearly caused several accidents. So they arrived in the camp, hungry, weary and footsore in the dark time before the moon had risen.

The horse was a bay colt, barely a two-year old. He'd been raised on a farm, left to run with his mare for the first year of his life, then separated from her to share a field with a couple of donkeys and a flock of sheep. The first night he was put into the small paddock that I was in. The next day he was introduced to Frankie and Bumper. They immediately set about showing him the rules of herd behaviour, Frankie in his usual way saying 'I'm the boss. This is Bumper. I see you've already met Sullivan.' The big horse still treat me somewhat disdainfully, but I thought I might have an ally in the new horse. At least he was younger than me, and smaller. I was no longer the 'new boy'. When Liz brought my morning feed, Blue was with her also carrying a bucket of oats, beetpulp and vegetables, which she offered to him.

'What you gonna call him, Blue?'

'What do you think of 'Sunny'?'

'Yeah, why not?'

Her usual cheerful demeanour was absent from her voice. When she stood up beside me I saw that her face was badly bruised. Dried blood still clung to the creases under her nose. Her eyes were black; one was swollen.

'How are you feeling honey?' Liz put an arm around the girl's shoulder, trying to comfort her.

'My nose is really sore,' she sniffed.

'It's broken, darling. It will be sore for a while.'

'Will I always look like this?'

'No, of course not. You might have a little scar on your cheek there.'

'I still can't believe that woman slammed the door on me when I went to ask for water. She didn't know I'd been kicked by a horse. I could have been attacked or anything. She didn't even ask!'

'There are a lot of strange people in the world, darling. She'll probably be in Mass on Sunday morning, full of her own self-righteousness.'

'I just don't understand how anyone could be like that...' Her voice drifted away as I watched them walk across the field, swinging their empty buckets.

Another newcomer that winter was a donkey who came trotting down the track behind the sidelace one afternoon. Bumper had set out early that day with Ben driving. A young fella who had been camped with us for the previous few weeks was sitting on the seat beside him.

Andy was this man's name, his woman was called Patsy. They often came out to bring us tasty morsels in the daytime, and make a fuss of us. Since I was still left to roam free, I would sometimes visit the little field where they had their tent pitched. There was always a fire going outside the tent-flaps, with Patsy spending her time washing clothes or preparing food and Andy busy cutting wood, sometimes sticks for the fire, sometimes shaping planks for the flat cart he was building. They would stop whatever they were doing when I appeared and come over to stroke me and talk to me.

Seeing the new arrival, I called out to Bumper, then trotted over the moor to join them on the track and pace along with them back to the camp. While Ben was untacking Bumper, Andy led the donkey away. I followed along, curious to get to know all his business. He was by-far the sprightliest donkey I'd ever met. His brisk trot was a match for Bumper's; he surprised me with his fitness as we climbed the steep field and clambered over the tumbledown wall for a short-cut to their camp. Patsy heard us coming and came out of the tent to greet us.

'What do you reckon?' Andy asked her.

'He's lovely.' She put an arm around the donkey's neck and gave him a hug. 'Does he go well?'

'Brilliant!' replied Andy. 'You should have seen him! He kept up with Bumper all the way back!'

'You weren't gone very long,' said Patsy. 'How far was it?'

'Oh, a good few miles, down on the Cork road there. It was a couple of miles down an old farm track then. A real out-of-the-way place. This old couple living there with loads of donkeys. That's what they do. He trains donkeys! They must be about the last people in the country still working donkeys the whole time. Ben reckoned this lad was the best of them, he's got real good feet. And fast! He's amazing! I'm gonna call him Flash Gordon.'

'How much did you pay for him?'

'Twenty-five quid, and they threw in the set of harness!'

'Great!' Turning to me, Patsy asked, 'What do you think, Sullivan? Will he pull our cart as well as you could?' She continued to scratch the donkey's face, rubbing between his ears to make them wobble from side to side. He stood patiently, quietly resting while they fussed over him. After a while, Andy went over to the fire and poured the boiling water from the kettle into the teapot.

Patsy said, 'You look after him, now?' to me, and 'Good boy, Gordon. You go off and meet the others, and don't be wandering off, y'hear?' Then she went to join the man at the fire.

I led the way back down the steep field to where the other horses were grazing beside the river. Bumper had been rolling in the mud on the banks and was splattered brown across his back and up his legs. The woollen blanket that had been wrapped around him lay scrunched in a heap with one corner trailing in the river.

He looked up briefly at our arrival, muttered a greeting to Gordon, then carried on with his feeding. Frankie gave a snort of disdain when the little donkey trotted brightly over to introduce himself. But Gordon just laughed his donkey-guffaw, saying 'Well, aren't you the proud stallion, then?' in his squeaky little high-pitched voice. I sniggered quietly to myself to see the big horse at a loss for words, being gently mocked by the funny-looking little creature, half his size.

Flash Gordon wasn't with us very long. Over the next few days, Andy finished putting the flat-cart together, gave it a coat of paint. He tried the donkey up and down the lane, coming back with a load of firewood on board. The next time we saw them trundling down the track, they had the cart piled up with all their belongings. The tarp they used for a tent was folded to cover all the rest of their goods, ropes crisscrossing to hold it all secure. Two buckets hung off the back of the shafts where they protruded behind the cart. We were out on the moor, watching them leave. The rattle of the buckets and the squeaking of the springs reminded me of the travelling days and the bright morning held the promise of another summer.

Meanwhile, Sunny had settled in with the rest of us. He was a willful and stubborn horse when it came to relating to people, but he got on well enough with me and the other animals. Blue would bring him his feed twice a day, and try to make a fuss of him, but he wasn't used to being handled and didn't care for the attention at all. When she tried to catch hold of his halter, he would spin around, snatching the strap from her hand, and lashing little kicks that stopped short of actually hitting her, but giving warning all the same. Ben could hold him by the head, and make him stand quiet, but as soon as he was free, he'd be away, and the only thing that could entice him back would be the bucket of feed.

'He'll be quieter once he's cut,' Ben assured Blue one day, after Sunny had been giving her the run-around. Not long afterwards, the familiar white van drove up to the camp. The dark-haired man who had visited me every day during my illness opened the door and put on rubber boots.

He spoke to Ben: 'How's Sullivan these days?'

Hearing my name, I called out my own reply: 'Here I am! How do I look?'

The man looked up, and seeing me, he smiled. 'You're looking well, boy!' he called.

'Feeling it too!' I told him.

Turning to Ben again he asked, 'Have you the others brought in?'

'Yes, they're over by the old barn. D'you need a hand to carry anything?' The man lifted a black box from the back of the van, and handed it to Ben. He took a smaller bag, glanced inside it briefly before snapping it shut and gesturing to Ben to show the way.

Some time later the van drove off, and Ben and Tom led Sunny and Bumper into the little field alongside the camp where I was grazing. Blue was following behind with a bucket of water in each hand. The twin girls were skipping along in her wake, hand in hand, singing songs with nonsense words. Bumper and Sunny were both stumbling as they walked, heads down.

'There y'go!' said Ben, giving Sunny a slap on the rump as they came through the open gap in the stone wall. 'Go see if Sullivan has any sympathy for you!'

The young horse tried to give his backwards kick, but found himself swaying and staggering as he lost his balance and almost fell over. Tom let go of Bumper's halter and gave him a friendly pat on the neck.

'How you feeling, boy?' he asked. 'A bit sore, eh? Never mind, you'll be better for it in a week or two!' Bumper muttered something in a groggy voice; he didn't sound too convinced.

'Come on then, the lot of you!' called Ben, 'Leave the poor creatures in peace till they recover from the anaesthetic. You twins! Don't be bouncing around behind them like that! They could still kick you!'

Blue set one of the buckets by the wall and carried the other over to where Sunny was standing. He didn't move when she put the water under his nose, and she put a hand on his neck to stroke him. He tossed his head angrily, indignant at his own helpless lethargy, as well as the pain he was feeling. 'I'm sorry,' she said. 'It had to be done...'. But he wasn't interested.

The days were gradually lengthening, the temperature gently easing upwards. The mornings dawned mist laden, but the overnight frost was gone.

One afternoon saw Bumper bringing the side-lace car along the track piled high with firewood. I watched over the low wall as the timber was offloaded into two great heaps, side by side with a space between them. After the family's evening meal was finished, Ben and Tom lit the two woodstacks, and soon had bright bonfires following white smoke into the night sky. Liz came striding across the dark moor and unclipped the chain from my halter. 'What's happening?' I asked, hearing the other horses being led towards the camp.

'Don't worry,' she reassured me. 'This is Beltaine, and the fires are just for a ceremony. They won't hurt you, I promise!'

I followed the others along the track and into the small enclosed paddock where the fires lit up the darkness. The dry wood crackled and sent sparks high into the starry night.

Ben led Frankie towards the gap between the fires, the big horse obediently following until they were close enough to feel the heat, be hit by flying pinpricks of light. Then he baulked, and tried to back away. Ben walked him round in a full circle until he was facing the fires again and tried once more to lead him through the gap. Frankie was very reluctant to put himself into this obvious danger, and again he stepped backwards, tossing his head from side to side, trying to break free. But

Ben held tight to his halter, and walked him round in tight circles until he quietened down, then half-dizzy, trotted him through the space between the fires before he really knew what was happening.

'Do we really need to do this?' Liz called out. She was clearly reading my thoughts.

'Please yourself!' Ben scoffed back at her. 'But it's your horse needs it more than any of them!'

Muttering something underneath her breath, she strokes my nose, rubbing her cheek against my lips. Strands of her hair tickle my nostrils. She says 'Come on, then, Brave Boy. Let's do this thing together!' and trots me straight towards the fires. Frankie is standing on the other side calling out, but I can't tell if he's encouraging me, or warning me against the action. For a split second it feels as though we are engulfed by the flames, then we are out in the field again, the fire behind us.

Liz is patting my neck, congratulating me even though I've no idea what it is we're doing, or why we're doing it.

We watch as Tom leads Bumper placidly through the gap. Misty just follows him through with no one leading her.

Blue was holding Sunny by the halter, but the moment she started leading him towards the fires, he reared up and tossed his head sideways. She tried to hold him, but he shook her away, and turned-tail and galloped off through the gateway, down the track onto the moor.

'Shall I try to catch him?' the girl asked, a plaintive note in her voice.

'Ah, leave him off,' her mother replied.

'What about your goat?' Ben asks, and Liz leaves me standing with the others while she goes and untethers Birch from the hedgerow. She is very reluctant to approach the fire at all, and it takes all three of them.... Liz at her head, Ben from behind, Tom waving a willow-stick... to get her through the gap.

With all the animals, except Sunny, ritually 'cleansed' the ceremony ended with a cheer and hugs all round. The fires collapsed into glowing heaps of embers, and the young ones stayed up late that night running back and forth between them, round in circles.

During the hours of darkness, while all the people slept, little Misty lay herself down on a patch of mossy ground, and quietly gave birth to a long-legged colt. By the time they came to check on us, he was already up on his feet and wobbling about at his mother's side.

Excited squeals rang out as the young twins scrambled and tumbled over the moor to see the new arrival.

'He's gorgeous!' Blue announced.

'Well, at least he's not a mule!' Ben conceded.

'Love the coat,' Liz remarked. 'What colour would you call that? Skew-pie-bald?'

'A coat of many colours?' Tom observed. 'Wasn't that a Bible story?'

'Jacob,' Liz replied. 'I suppose that's what we'll have to call him, then?'

'Little Jake. He's just gorgeous!' Blue repeated, catching the new-born by his tuft of mane, and hugging him close. Misty looked on, whickering quietly to reassure her foal. She really was the gentlest of creatures.

The Devil's Punchbowl.

Getting me back into training began one day when Liz came to visit me carrying the saddle and bridle over her shoulder. She spread the saddle carefully over a rock while she shifted the loose hairs from my back with the plastic brush. Talking to me all the while, she explained that if we were ever going out on the road again this year, I'd have to start getting fit. My winter of doing nothing had left me weak and flabby, and I needed to start building muscle.

She said 'Easy, boy...' when I shied a little under the weight of leather and the jangle of metal. I had seen Frankie wearing this saddle a few times in the past couple of weeks, Ben sitting up on his back, as they trotted along the track. Now it was my turn. Liz buckled the strap under my belly, then walked around me to the other side to adjust the fastening there. 'You're a good-bit thinner than Frankie!' she observed, pulling the strap tight so that it pinched the loose skin under my front leg. She ran a hand under the strap then, freeing all the trapped hairs, and once I relaxed it wasn't too tight or uncomfortable.

The bit in my mouth felt strangely bulky after its long absence, the metal grating against my teeth cold and unpleasant at first. Next she unclipped the chain from around my neck and slipped the short reins over my neck. Gathering them up firmly so that the bit dug into the soft corners of my mouth, she said 'Stand UP, now!' in a voice that sounded a little shaky, but conveyed a sense of obligation. With one foot in the metal stirrup, Liz gripped the front of the saddle and made a clumsy sort of jump to get herself onto my back. As soon as I felt her weight on the saddle I started to sway from side to side, convinced that the strange contraption was about to pull me over. She managed to get her other foot in the opposite stirrup, and standing up, she joggled the saddle back into a more comfortable position on my back. Then she leaned forward, and fumbling under the leather skirts of the seat, she pulled the girth strap tighter.

I was all the time shifting my weight from one foot to the other, jibbing on the spot. Liz kept talking to me, trying to calm me down, but she sounded really nervous too.

'Alright,' she said, 'Walk on!' And easing my head in the direction of the track she walked me over the rocky moor, letting me pick my own route amongst the boulders and puddles. Once we reached the track, she asked me if I wanted to have a little trot. Responding to the pressure of her heels under my belly, I changed pace, and Liz quickly picked up the new rhythm as we trotted along the deep rut gouged out by the cart-wheels.

By the time we reached the end of the track, I was puffing and blowing.

'You really are out of condition, aren't you?' Liz sounded breathless herself, turning my head to walk me back to the camp.

'How did he go for you?' asked Ben, getting up from the fire to take the saddle from my back.

'Be a while before he's pulling a cart again,' she replied.

For the next few weeks, I was ridden every day. Usually it was Liz who walked me around the moor or up and down the track; occasionally Blue would accompany us riding Misty, with the new foal tagging along at her heels. With each passing day I felt my strength returning. One bright day it was Tom who brought out the saddle.

'Feeling fit for a trot up the mountain?' he asked me as he tightened the girth strap. He sprang lightly onto my back, and turned me towards the river.

'We'll sup at the Devil's Punchbowl,' he whispered in my ear as we splashed through the sparkling mountain water. I didn't know what he was talking about, but the excitement in his voice was contagious and once clear of the water we took off at a canter over the bracken-choked fields, scattering the stupid sheep. Soon the slope of the hill became steeper, and I eased back to a trot, then a walk, as we negotiated gaps in the tumbledown walls. Then we cleared the last of the enclosures and we were half-way up the hill in front of the camp. Tom reined me in for a few minutes, while he turned in the saddle to look back into the valley.

'Good view, eh?' but I was more interested in getting my breath back before we pressed on. From there we followed sheep tracks amongst the bracken and gorse. An occasional wind-beaten tree clung to the slope, the area around its trunk bare earth, the vegetation worn away by sheltering sheep. I was well-sweated-up by the time we reached the summit of the hill. Tom slid off my back, landing lightly at my side, patting me on the neck.

'Good lad, Sullivan!' he congratulated me. 'How d'you feel now?'

I answered with a shake of my mane and a shout that echoed around the hills. I listened for an answering call from the other horses, and sure enough, Frankie's high-pitched whinny was carried back to us on the wind.

'Feels good,' I murmured to Tom, giving him a nudge on the back as he turned away to look back down the hillside.

After a while, he led me along the crooked path that ran the length of the ridge. The view changed as we turned to follow the hill crest. In front of us, the land fell away sharply, sheer sides of bare rock with almost nothing growing on them. The odd crack in the rock sprouting green. At the bottom, a lake of black water spilled over into the valley on the other side.

We skirted the first lake and started the descent. Tom walked ahead of me, sure-footed on the narrow path. In a few places, our feet disturbed the pebbles, sending little cascades that gathered momentum as they plunged to the water below. When we reached the lip that spilled the lake's water, we could see the rest of the valley, far below. The frothing waterfall roared over the edge, a damp mist rising from its face. Hurtling against the rocks, the water instantly gathered itself into a mountain river, pouring into the next lake. From where we stood we could see other lakes linked by waterfalls, a winding thread of them filling the valley.

Tom was intent on returning to the camp by way of the lakes. I knew the other horses were now on the other side of this mass of water, and before we could return we would either have to retrace our steps or cross the water. The string of bright water that stretched before and below us seemed to reach to the distant horizon, making me reluctant to venture further in this direction. However a glance over my shoulder reminded me that we had already slithered and scrambled down the shore of one lake.

'Look, don't even think about it, Sullivan!' Tom was berating me, 'There's no way we're going back up there!'

He gathered up the reins and jerked my head down.

'Now Walk On!'

Leading me to a level-enough patch of ground away from the edge of the waterfall, he quickly mounted into the saddle. With his feet in the stirrups, he leaned back, and directed me away down the steeply sloping bank alongside the waterfall. In places the ground just seemed to fall away under my feet, and I grazed the back of my legs against the rough shrubbery and sharp gravelly soil. Then I would recover my balance, only to be pressed onward by a slap on the rump from the flat of Tom's hand.

Soon we were walking along the shore of the second lake, the waterfall behind us a hiss that pounded my eardrums. When Tom urged me on, I gave a last shake of my head before launching into the fastest trot, only too glad to get as far away as possible. Before us we could see a wide valley, laced with lakes of different sizes, circled around with high jagged peaks. The far distant horizon seemed flat, hazy, the land petering out to the vast expanse of water. As we raced along the edge of the second lake, we changed direction again. This lake spilled its overflow into another valley, off to one side, back towards the camp.

On a smaller scale, but no less spectacular in its own way, this turn in the mountains accommodated its own series of lakes, the one pouring into the next, waterfalls and rapids linking them. Once past the edge of the lake, the river that ran to the next was a loud torrent of white water. Bouncing over great rocks in its path it charged headlong down the ravine it had carved for itself. At last it dropped sheer into the waiting hollow where another lake was formed. By this time the noise of the water was such a constant backdrop that it no longer bothered me, and I trotted easily along the lakeside, or scrambled gingerly down the steeper drops.

Between the second and third lakes, Tom stopped me abruptly.

'Hey, check this out! Whoa, Sullivan!' He reined me in, and jumped from the saddle. Turning me and leading me back a short distance, he pulled the reins over my head and looped them around a branch of a prickly holly bush at the water's edge.

'Stand up!' he told me, and crouching down, he crept towards a place where the water shot over a flat-edged slab the full width of the river. Behind the water, there was room for him to sidle in and pressing himself against the rock wall, he crawled across to the other side, where he re-emerged with a big grin on his face.

'Hey, Sull., look at me!' he called, waving his arms to further attract my attention. 'Come on, see if you can do it!' He laughed.

I just shook my head at him, saying 'Forget it, pal!'

He was only joking, of course, and after a few minutes on the opposite bank, he started to make his way back. Stopping on the wider strip of rock about mid-stream, he squatted down and tentatively reached his hand into the fall of water. His fingers appeared briefly on the outside before being snatched back into invisibility. Then he was back beside me, exhilarated, wet, raring to go.

The last lake was the biggest of all, but somehow it seemed shallower, and lacked the urgency of the previous ones. Its water ran into a river that tumbled more gently down the softer slope. Still there were outcrops of rock to impede its progress, but they were less frequent. We were down from the steep high ground, re-entering sheep land, cropped grass showing amongst the ever-present inedible bracken. The first wall we encountered was a tumbledown affair, which I easily scrambled over. After that we had to seek gaps and gateways to take us from field to track, threading our way back to the camp. It wasn't possible to follow the river all the way back, but we came to the shallow place where we had first crossed and I called to the other horses who were grazing the fields on the other side.

As Tom was taking the saddle off me, Liz stepped down from the wagon.

'How'd he go?'

'Great, you should start working him in harness again.'

'You reckon he's ready?'

'I reckon....'

Serious Miscalculations.

And so the next day, Liz brought me round to the fire after breakfast, and gave me a good brush down. The sweat from the previous day's adventure had dried, causing the hair to mat together in hard bristles. I was still a bit footsore and scuffed around the knees and coronets, but I was feeling full of energy, and having fun catching hold of Liz's clothes, and nudging her with my nose whenever she came within reach. Out came my old harness from under the wagon. Ben, who was sitting at the fire drinking tea, observed, 'That could have done with a clean and oil job...'

'Yeah, yeah,' replied Liz, struggling to get the bit between my teeth as I playfully tossed my head from side to side. 'I don't know if it's even going to fit him.'

She pulled the winkers up my face, the metal digging into the corners of my mouth as the top strap bent my ears before digging in behind them. 'Do you suppose he's grown this winter, or have these winkers shrunk?'

'Of course he's grown!' said Ben. 'They do, at that age. Besides all the feed he's had these past months..'

Liz was tugging and pulling at the cheek-straps, trying to undo buckles that had not been undone for the past year. Eventually, she loosened them and extended the straps so that the bit no longer cut into my mouth, but hung slacker than it used to, jangling against the back of my teeth. She had to make similar adjustments to most of the rest of the harness, so I was getting to be somewhat impatient by the time she finally led me over to where the side-lace was standing in the corner of the field, near the gateway.

In the time Liz had been struggling with me and the harness, Ben had brought Frankie to the camp, and tacked him up. With the traces tied together over his back, the big horse walked patiently along beside the man who was pushing his bicycle with one hand, holding a leading rope in the other. They slowed to pass us, Ben asking, 'Are you sure he'll be alright?'

'What's the problem? Tom's here to help me, Blue's looking after the twins. How long are you going to be gone anyway?'

'Shouldn't be too long, I'll just pick up the cart, and go on into town for the shopping. Shouldn't be more than a couple of hours.'

Tom helped her get me between the shafts, and walked with us as far as the gap that led out onto the moor. The cart was stopped. Then he climbed up onto the seat, and Liz handed him the reins so that she could climb up beside him. I felt the reins move across my back, heard Liz tell me, 'Walk on!'

I leaned into the collar to get the wheels moving, but something was stopping one of them, probably just a stone on the track. I swayed from side to side, the shafts rocking with me, but the wheel was stuck fast. The free wheel was rolling backwards, and with the winkers restricting my vision, I found myself looking out across the moor, the track off to one side, out of sight. A moment of panic. Liz shouting 'Come around!' and pulling hard on one side of my mouth. I jerked my head, seizing the bit between my teeth.

I felt the top strap behind my ears go slack, and in the same moment the winkers fell away from my face to hang under my chin, still clinging to the bit. Liz instinctively tightened her grip on the reins, but the bit just pulled my jaws open, exerting no control. With my head tossing wildly, I could suddenly see all around me. The wide flat expanse of the rocky moor on either side. The winding track before me. Behind me, the big green wheels of the side-lace jumping and jerking as the one that had been stuck mounted the stone and bounced itself free. Then I was gone. Off down the track at my fastest trot, with the wheels in hot pursuit. Liz was shouting

'Whoa, Sullivan. Whoa, whoa, damn your eyes!'

I could hear Tom's voice too, but couldn't make out what he was saying until we came within sight of the quarry where all the old rubbish was dumped. A shout of 'Jump, Liz!' and the cart bounced again coming back lighter as I caught a glimpse of Tom landing on the grassy verge.

When I broke into a canter, the cart started to behave like a wild creature intent on overtaking me. By the time we came to the place where the land fell away, I was at a flat-out gallop, and the wheels of the side-lace where leaping along, hardly touching the ground at all. Liz was still hanging on to the reins, and the bit was still between my teeth. Some instinct kept me on the track as it dipped and rose again, scuffing the banks on the sharper bends. We were almost out to the road, the last turn in the track, when the wheel mounted the verge and collided with an outcrop of rock.

Liz was thrown clear as the cart went over on its side, landing with the boss of the wheel on the grassy aisle between the ruts. I never even hesitated when the girth strap snapped, buckle digging me in the ribs. Galloping on, hit the road with the cart behind me still skidding along on its wheel-boss. A broken shaft clattered along the road, the other one thumped me on the back at every turn of the hooves. Spitting out the bit, the winker-set dangled between my front legs, the reins still threaded through the terrets on my collar and back-pad. The looped end of the reins dragged along the road, under my feet. I must have stood on it, because I suddenly felt the bit digging into my chest, and the back-pad was pulled along my back, over my tail. The crupper caught it as the terrets hit off my legs.

A man loomed up in front of me, closely followed by another who was scrambling over the wall from the roadside forest. I had already stopped my headlong rush, reminding myself of the fiasco of my first day in harness, I realized the pointlessness of causing any further damage to myself, the cart, the harness. The man stepped confidently up to my head, saying 'Easy, boy, easy!' and catching hold of my nose. He had the smell of horses about him, as well as the rich resiny smell of the trees he was working amongst.

Liz came hobbling along the road, sobbing and cursing. She must have hurt herself falling from the cart, but she was also furious at me. 'Stupid! Stupid! Stupid!' she kept repeating. I stood sheepishly head-bowed in the wreckage of splintered wood and tatters of leather.

'He's alright, now, missus,' the man was saying.

'Oh, yeah, he's alright! Too bad about the cart and harness!'

'Ah, sure, ye'll be able to fix them up. So long as the horse is not hurt, that's the main thing...'

I agreed with the man, but Liz was still waving her arms about and berating me. After a few minutes she calmed down a little and started to unhitch the traces which were still attached to the shafts. The braker strap was gone from the shaft which was on the road, but the one over my back was still attached, so she reached up and undid that one, which then released the trace, and the back-pad fell to the road behind me with a clatter.

The two men helped to get the cart back on its wheels, and parked it on the narrow verge. It leaned at a drunken angle, a few strands of wood clinging onto the splintered shaft that buckled inwards. The whole body of the cart was twisted away from the wheels. The bright green paint was scuffed off the wheel that had been dragged along the road, revealing grey undercoat, and bare wood. Its metal boss had lost all the dark red paint from its edge, which was crumpled in over the shiny brass nut at its centre.

Liz retrieved the back-pad from behind me, jerking it unceremoniously clear of my tail. She slammed it down on my back, looking with dismay at the broken girth strap, which she threw over my rump. I flinched when the buckle hit my flank.

'Stand up, you stupid animal!' was all the sympathy I got. Liz was still assessing the damage, and untangling harness when Tom came jogging along the road.

'Will you be alright, now, missus?' one of the men asked. She thanked them, and they climbed back over the wall into the forest, leaving her and Tom to finish sorting the harness. 'We're missing a braker strap...'

'It's at the end of the track, where you turned the cart over by the look of it.'

'Thanks, Tom. Do you think we'll be able to get this lot fixed before Ben gets back?'

'You serious? Come on, let's get him back to the camp and see what we can do with the harness, anyway!'

Tom looped the reins, and threw the remnants of the winkers over his shoulder. Liz took hold of a handful of my mane and pulled me around in the road, leading me back as far as the track. After that, she just let go, stooping to pick up the scrap of leather from the verge, and I followed sheepishly behind them. When we arrived back at the camp, Blue and the twins looked up from the plates of food they were eating, to ask, 'What happened?'

'See if you can guess!' Liz snapped at them, dragging the collar over my ears. She dropped the back-pad on the grass beside me, saying 'Where's his chain? Here, Blue, tie him over there behind the wagon. I don't want him wandering back to Bumper just yet!'

I tried to eat some of the sweet grass that sprouted around the base of the stone wall, but my mouth was still aching, and tender in the corners so that chewing was quite painful. 'Looks like you pulled the mouth out of him,' observed the girl. Liz growled something under her breath, stomping onto the shafts of the wagon and disappearing inside.

She returned to the pile of harness a few minutes later, opening the tin she was carrying and shaking out needles, thread, awls. I watched as she ran lengths of thread through a small block of yellow wax in the palm of her hand. Then she threaded them and started sewing buckles and straps back in place.

By the time Ben drove Frankie into the field, she had mended the winkers and was battling with the girth strap, forcing the awl through the heavy leather skirt of the straddle. Frankie was under the shafts of a vehicle I hadn't seen before. It was a four-wheeled dray, on tyres that looked like they might have belonged to the front wheels of a tractor. A chunky metal casing enclosed heavy planks of wood, a solid floor. The shafts were of bent tubular metal. The big horse leaned into the collar, puffing plumes of steam from his nostrils as he trotted up the slope of the field to the camp.

Ben called 'Stand up!' casually tossing the reins to Tom, who rushed to meet them. The man jumped off the bed of the dray, storming over to the fire. "No problem', eh?' he yelled at Liz. 'So what happened?'

'Work it out for yourself!' she snarled back, 'You're the expert!'

He snatched the straddle from her hands, throwing it across the fire. It landed in the field, upside down, the awl still piercing the strap, threads dangling.

'Don't give me that!' he shouted, taking hold of her wrist and dragging her to her feet. 'I asked you what happened! What am I supposed to say when I see my cart in bits at the end of the track?'

'I'm sorry,' said Liz, tossing her head back to get the hair out of her eyes. 'He bolted. The winkers snapped, he took off down the track, turned the cart over. You've seen it...'

'Too right, I've seen it! It's totally knackered! I was trying to sell that cart, remember? What do you think it's worth in that state?'

'Sorry....' she mumbled again.

'Sorry?! Not half as sorry as I am!' he yelled, shaking her wrist before pushing her away.

Tom and Blue had been untacking Frankie while the row was going on.

'So. Any chance of a cup of tea?' Ben turned to the fire, lifting the lid of the kettle. A puff of steam scalded his hand.

Liz was behind the wagon, emptying the dregs of tea leaves over the wall.

'See the trouble you cause!' she hissed at me. I whickered an apology.

'Is HE alright?' Ben called, looking in my direction.

'Yeah, I think so....'

'Typical!' he grunted, walking over to me, as Liz put fresh tea in the pot and poured on the water from the kettle. He ran a hand along my neck and down my leg.

'Pick it up' he ordered.

I dutifully lifted my hoof. He gave another grunt before dropping my foot and moving alongside of me to check my back legs and hooves. Ben noticed every little scratch and nick on my skin, touching them lightly with his fingertips.

'You haven't put anything on these cuts, have you?' he called to Liz.

'Think he might get tetanus?' she asked, rinsing cups by pouring hot water from one to another.

'Cut the sarcasm!' he shouted. 'Clean up these cuts on your horse before they go septic. You, Child!' he called to one of the twins, standing just behind him. 'Go get a bowl of water and put some Dettol in it!'

The little girl toddled over to her mother, asking for help. They returned a few minutes later with the bowl of white liquid. Liz had a handful of cotton wool, with which she proceeded to dab the scratches on my legs and neck. The astringent smell and sting of the liquid reminded me of that long-ago day when I grazed my knee, climbing the hill for the first time.

'One over here....' Ben was pointing out a little gash behind my ear. 'Y'know, I've had a helluva day myself. Coming back to this, I really could have done without!'

'Why? What happened to you? Was Frankie alright?'

'Well,' he hesitated, then continued, 'Yeah, he was okay. He was grand. We picked up the dray, and I took him into town. Just going past where all the jarveys are parked there's this flash bitch in a brand-new Merc. Not even registered! And she was determined to keep coming, even though there's cars parked and double-parked, you know what they're like... I was on my side of the road, and there was no room, with all the horses parked on my side, but she keeps coming anyway! She must have thought I was going to stop and let her through!'

'Whoops!' Liz smiled. 'Serious miscalculation!'

'Sure was! No way I could have stopped with Frankie amongst all the mares. Next thing, she's rammed the front of her windscreen against the corner of the dray, and she's shunting the whole yoke backwards. All the jarveys are yelling we're going to crash into one of the outfits there, so what could I do? I just had to drive him on! He was great! Just ploughed on, taking the side out of her motor. The full length of it! Side screens, back window, the whole shooting-match just mangled, and yer-woman's sitting behind the wheel screaming with a lap full of broken glass!'

'You're mad!' Liz was saying as she looked me over for any scratches she might have missed.

'Yeah, that's what She said!' he chuckled at the memory.

'So what happened? Did she get the Gards?'

'Sure. By the time I had him untacked in the car-park, there were half a dozen of them around. The first young-fella was demanding to see my insurance, he must have thought I was a jarvey, or something. Yer-woman got out of the back of their car and started screaming abuse at me, but I just laughed at her.

"How am I going to pay for the damage?" she was shouting.

"How did you pay for it in the first place?" I asked her. She didn't like that! Anyway, a bunch of the jarveys came down and told the Gards what had happened and they told her there was nothing they could do, unless she wanted to make a civil case of it. She was furious. When I said she'd scuffed the paint on the front of my cart, she nearly lost her mind!'

'So you had a good day, really?' Liz smiled at him. 'You ready for that cup of tea?'

I heard Frankie calling to Bumper, 'Hey, you wanna hear what happened to me?' and imagined him giving his version of his adventure in the town, but I was kept tied behind the wagon until Ben had finished his cup of tea. Then he picked up the straddle which was still lying in the field, and sewed the strap back in place. Liz was washing vegetables in one of her steel bowls, then transferring them into a pan hanging over the fire. Leaving Blue with instructions not to let the food burn, Ben and Liz brought the newly repaired harness over to me, and tacked me up again.

'You don't think we ought to let Bumper bring it back?' Liz asked tentatively.

'Oh, yeah, let him get away with this and you'll never be able to trust him again!' Ben was adamant, leading me back down the field.

They walked along the track, not talking. Ben was at my head, Liz limping along behind.

When we reached the side-lace, he said, 'Here, take hold of him!' handing the reins to Liz. She talked quietly to me, stroking my nose, imploring me to behave myself this time. Ben had taken a roll of tape from his pocket and was binding up the broken shaft. It wasn't quite straight when he had finished, but he said 'That should get it back...'

Liz walked me around and made me stand still while Ben manoeuvred the shafts into the tugs on either side. He fastened the braker-straps, fed the reins through the terrets on collar and back-pad, saying to Liz, 'Get up, then!' She made a groaning sound, but dutifully scrambled aboard the cart. When I first leaned into the collar, and the big wheels started to wobble on the verge, I had a moment of panic, but Ben was standing beside me and instantly grabbed the reins under my chin.

'Don't even think about it!' his voice hard in my ear. 'Now, walk on!'

I followed him obediently back to the camp, the side-lace pulling to one side all the way down the track.

There was lots happening at the camp over the next couple of weeks. People coming and going, some staying a few days, others just passing through. Different people riding me, mostly with Ben and Frankie, easy trots over the moor; exercise for me. The people reacting differently. Experienced riders urging me into a canter on the home-run. Absolute beginners teetering and wobbling, keeping me at a walk.

One evening a familiar truck meandered along the track, and parked up at the gateway. It was the garishly-painted mobile home of the couple called Dave and Vicky; I remembered seeing it in another part of the country, the year before. When

Liz was bringing me into one of the 'night-fields' after our day on the moor, she stopped beside the truck to ask the woman if she remembered me.

'Is that Sullivan?' Vicky asked. 'Hasn't he grown?'

'He surely has! Bursting out of his harness these days!'

Dave appeared from somewhere behind the truck, and Liz told them the story of my tetanus, and my recovery. She also told them the story of me wrecking the side-lace. Then she invited Dave to take me for 'a spin' just to show how well-behaved I was these days.

'I haven't been on a horse in years.' He hesitated.

'You used to ride Juno over in Wales.' Liz reminded him.

'Yeah, that was the last time!' he admitted.

'Come on, you'll be alright,' she cajoled him. 'He's really quiet! Even I ride him, and I'm no rider!'

'Give us a leg-up, then!' Dave leaned against Liz as he struggled onto my back. 'Where's the reins?' he asked, a break in his voice betraying his nervousness.

'Go on, I'll lead him for you!' Liz laughed. To me she said, 'Walk on, Sullivan...' and started to walk ahead of me, back out onto the moor. I went a few steps before the man gave me a dig in the ribs. He wanted to trot? His hands grabbed my mane, wrenching out stray hairs, as I changed pace.

'Easy!' yelled Liz as I barged past her. She stumbled sideways, dropping the coil of rope and chain that was still attached to my neck. I broke into a canter, the man still desperately clinging onto my back, his voice a croak as he pleaded with me to stop. Then I was jerked to an abrupt standstill by the rope jamming itself between a clump of rocks. I spun around, my shoulders dragged down, back legs kicking out. Dave shot over my neck, landing heavily on his back. He lay there moaning and groaning until Liz arrived, winding the rope around her arm. Thinking she might be angry at me, I shied away, almost stepping on the man as he struggled painfully to his feet.

'Stand up, Sullivan!' she told me. 'Stupid animal! Don't start your tricks with me!'

To Dave she said, 'Are you alright?' the way people always do in those situations. He was still groaning and rolling his shoulders, moving his head this way and that.

'I told you I hadn't been on a horse in years....' he grumbled.

'Sorry about that,' said Liz. 'He must have remembered you from last year!'

'What?' mock indignation. 'What did I ever do to him?'

'I seem to remember you making some disparaging remark about him...'

'Yeah, well I was right, wasn't I?' But to me, he said, 'Quits, now?' and gave me a friendly pat on the neck.

Liz said, 'You better be good to this man, Sullivan. He's come to paint the wagon, and he can't do that with a broken arm. Your hands alright, Dave?' she asked, genuinely concerned at the way they were creaking and cracking as he flexed his fingers.

'Yeah, they seem to be all still working.....'

Dave spent the following three days painting the wagon. On the first evening, there were dark red scrolls in repeating patterns all over the varnished timber of the backboard, the front panels and along the ledges. By the end of the second day the scrolls were highlighted with bright yellow. The black outlines he added on the third day gave the patterns an extra dimension. Vicky was painting rearing horses, one black, one white, on either side of the door when Liz led me down to the river for a drink before staking me out with the others.

Early the next morning, the big truck lumbered away down the track, air-horns blaring a parting farewell from the road as it gathered speed. A few hours later, Ben tacked Frankie under the shafts of the tumbril and set off after it. Tom went along too, which turned out to be just-as-well. That evening Frankie had a story to tell of another encounter with a motor.

It had been a scorching hot day. Bumper and I had spent the day on the moor, glad of the buckets of water that had been delivered to us every few hours. Frankie had taken the big heavy cart into town, stopping on the way, he told us, to pick up a group of musicians from outside one of the big hotels on the way into town. They had piled in with their instruments, laughing and singing as they were jostled from side to side by the swaying of the vehicle on the pot-holed road.

Just before the place where the jarveys parked their horses, Ben had reined Frankie in to allow the passengers off. With Ben holding his head, the big horse had stood still, if not quiet (he never could resist calling to all the pretty mares!) while the musicians clambered over the high sides of the tumbril, making jokes about the Guillotine, and in general good spirits. Tom handed the cases of instruments over to them. While all this was going on, a car which was parked alongside the horse decided to pull out from the kerb. A young woman with white-blonde hair was driving, an older man sat in the passenger seat. Ben put up his hand, shouting to the woman to wait, but she was determined to push her way out. Inching the car forward, she somehow managed to lock the protruding bumper onto the big metal boss of the cart-wheel. Grinding of gears, jerking of wheels, as she tried to back off. The two vehicles were locked together.

With all the newly-disembarked passengers, there was already a small group on the pavement, offering advice and encouragement. The man got out of the car then, bustled around the front to examine the problem for himself. He started shouting and waving his fists around, which soon encouraged a crowd to gather. They consisted mainly of a party of tourists, sporty types dressed in track-suits and peaked caps with matching emblems. Big muscular men. A woman with a note pad on a clip-board seemed to be their tour-guide. They all moved in closer, as the tempers frayed and the voices got more agitated.

The tour-guide woman was standing behind Ben, talking quietly to Frankie when the man from the car took a swing with his fist that was aimed for Ben's face. Of course, he ducked. Yerman's knuckles connected with the woman's nose, blood splattering over Frankie's head causing him to step back. Crump of metal as the wheel of the cart locked harder under the bumper.

Total chaos then, as several of the track-suited team leapt on the man and smashed his face against the bonnet of the car. Blood smeared along the gleaming white paintwork. The young woman at the wheel watching the horrific incident with a look of terror.

And then the Garda arrives on the scene. It's the same young fellow who was first on the scene after the last collision with a motor. Hurrying along the pavement, pushing his way to the front of the crowd. Seeing the man slumped over the car, streaming blood, he must have jumped to all the wrong conclusions.

'Move that horse!' he ordered Ben.

'But, but, hang on a min.....'

'Did you hear me? I said "move that horse!"'

'Whatever you say, boss...' Ben mumbled to himself before 'Walk on, Frankie! Hupp, boy!'

The big horse obediently leaned into the collar, ignoring the drag as the car was pulled along behind him for a few feet before the bumper parted from the chassis with a loud rending sound. It clattered off the road a couple of times before Tom reined the horse to a standstill and Ben walked back to kick it free.

'Satisfied?' Ben asked the uniformed man, booting the mangled strip of metal in his direction.

'You're under arrest!' the constable shouted.

'Me?' protested Ben. 'What did I do?'

At that moment the dark blue van arrived and Ben was hurriedly bundled into the back of it. Tom was left holding the reins of the horse and cart, Frankie protesting at all this stopping and starting, as well as calling to a sweet little bay filly who was paying attention to his antics. Another car arrived, two uniformed men helping the injured man into the back seat.

'Hey, what am I supposed to do?' Tom called to them.

'Do you know where the Barracks is?'

'Yes, but....'

'Right, get yourself down there!' said the man before getting in behind the wheel and driving off.

'Hang on there, boyo!' called one of the crowd, 'We'll come along with you!' and the track-suited men started to scramble up the wheel of the cart, throwing their legs over, landing lightly between the wooden sides. Four or five of them climbed aboard, one of them calling to the rest of their party,

'See ya down there!'

'Righto! We'll bring Mary along.' Two of the men stood either side of the woman who had blood all over her face.

Tom gave Frankie slack rein, driving him away through the town at a steady trot. When they reached the Barracks, he pulled in behind the empty car and van outside. The men jumped off the cart and went in through the door under the curious blue lamp-shade. It wasn't long before the other two men and the injured woman followed them in. Then Ben re-emerged with a big grin on his face, saying, 'Turn him round, son!'

Ready for the road.

Great activity over the next few days. Ben and Liz were rebuilding the wagons. The top of the big wagon was taken off and moved onto the new dray that had been given a coat of dark red paint to match the scrollwork Dave had done. The bright yellow wooden wheels that had originally been under the wagon had a new flat-bed built on them. Tom's little wagon was re-covered. The harness spent its days spread around the camp field in the sun, being taken to pieces, repaired, oiled and polished until it gleamed like new.

We were no longer tied on the moor during the day or in the fields at night. We were all left to wander wherever we wanted to go. The days were hot and long, the mornings misty. Up here on the side of the mountain the grass was still sparse, and we were still getting an evening feed to supplement our grazing.

A pick-up truck with a low-loader made its way to the camp one day and left a few hours later with the twisted remains of the side-lace on the back of the truck and the tumbril aboard the trailer. The same afternoon, Bumper and Misty had new shoes put on. Like me, and Sunny, they had been left barefoot for the past few months. Frankie had been doing almost all the road work, so he had been kept shod.

I hadn't been in harness since the day I wrecked the side-lace. Liz still brought me my food and water, and sometimes talked to me about what was happening. The first time I met a friend of hers, she introduced us saying, 'Sullivan, this is Susie, who is going to be travelling with us tomorrow.'

Susie said, 'Hi, there, Sullivan. Aren't you a handsome boy!'

'Don't tell him!' said Liz. 'He has too high an opinion of himself as it is!'

'But he is lovely!' the woman insisted.

'Yeah, I think so too.' Liz admitted.

'This whole place is like something out of a dream,' Susie was enthusing. 'I couldn't have picked a better location for a movie about horse-drawn travellers!'

'I'm afraid your romantic visions might get a few hard knocks over the next couple of weeks,' Liz told her. 'For one thing, we try to avoid being on the road at sunset. It might look good on camera, but in real life, well... you'll find out!'

'I'm just so looking forward to it!' The woman grinned. 'Y'know, some friends of mine were over here last year and the high-spot of their holiday was taking a jarvey-ride through the Gap of Dunloo....'

'Dunloe,' Liz corrected her pronunciation.

'Dunlow? Okay, well I just can't wait to get back and tell them about you all. Sullivan, you'll be the star of my movie!' She stroked my nose with her bright red fingertips.

I watched Bumper pulling the newly built four-wheeler off down the track next morning. Ben was driving, Tom sitting beside him. On the flat-bed behind them was one of the big rubber tyred wheels off the new dray. After they left I wandered on down to the river, where Sunny and Frankie had found a patch of grass that the sheep had overlooked.

'Leaving tomorrow?' I ventured.

'Not before time!' Frankie grumbled. 'You haven't seen the new grass at the side of the road, but believe me, it's nothing like this!' He took a last mouthful of the riverside grass before lifting his head, curling his lip to taste the air.

'Can't you just smell it?'

Chapter Seven

On the Road Again.

So there we were the following morning. The sky heavy, clouds obscuring the sun. Ben already had Frankie under the metal shafts of the big wagon when Liz led me into the field. Tom and his sister were sorting harness, picking up bits and pieces of equipment from all over the field which they loaded onto the little wagon and the flat-bed on the yellow wooden wheels.

'Will you be alright?' Ben asked, as he fed the long driving reins through the terrets, and looped them over the straddle. He was talking to everyone, but only Liz bothered to reply.

'What if we're not?'

'Don't be facetious!' he told her. 'Look, do you want me to hang on here and help you, or what?'

The twins were clambering up the step behind the big horse, and tumbling into the wagon.

'No, no,' said Liz, wrapping my rope loosely around the branch of an ash tree. 'Go on ahead, we'll see you at the bottom of the hill. Go on, Susie is out on the track waiting to film you.'

Frankie rolled the wagon steadily down the slope with Ben walking at his head. The bright scroll work danced in the morning light as the wagon swayed, the iron wheels on their thick tyres rolling over the rocks and humps. I watched as they negotiated the narrow gateway, and turned back up the stony track that led out to the moor. Tom was busy getting Bumper into his harness. Blue went off to catch Sunny, who was nibbling grass from the wall in a far corner of the field.

Liz brought my collar over to where I was tied, and saying, 'Good boy, Sullivan. Easy now, just get this over your ears and lets get this show on the road!' she slid the oiled leather along my nose. Stopping at my throat to turn it the right way up, she pushed the collar down to rest against my shoulders. She soon had the rest of the harness on me, the winkers coming last. The bit carried the unpleasant flavour of metal polish, and soap. I turned my head away when she tried to slip the winkers over my ears, refusing to open my mouth for the bit.

'Come on, now!' she pleaded, pushing her fingers and thumb into opposite corners of my mouth to force it open. The shiny bit scraped my teeth, then slid into place as she pulled my ears through the top-strap and buckled the cheek-pieces.

Blue had tied Sunny on a short tether to the gatepost. She walked back to help her mother, lifting the rough-hewn wooden shafts of the new four-wheeler, while Liz tried to persuade me to back between them. I was still unhappy about backing, especially when the winkers excluded all rear-vision. I jibbed and side-stepped and grumbled about being asked to do this. Tom left Bumper standing under the shafts of the little wagon and hurried down the field to help.

'Push his nose back,' he suggested.

'That might work on Bumper,' said Liz, 'But this lad has had too many bad experiences going backwards!'

'Ah, you're too soft on him Liz,' replied the boy, sounding a lot like his father. 'He's never going to learn if you keep letting him get away with it!'

'Alright, spare me the lecture, just give a shove on the back of that cart, will you?' Tom must have tried his best. I could hear him groaning and straining, trying to move the laden cart over the rough ground. After a few minutes, he panted, 'It's no good, Liz, you're going to have to back him into those shafts.'

'Right, then, drop the shafts, Blue, and I'll walk him round again.'

She gathered up the reins under my chin, and led me a few steps forward before turning me again, so that I had a clear view of the cart. The shafts lay on the ground, the girl still standing beside them. Over the top of the dark green tarpaulin that covered most of the load, I could see Tom leaning against the back of the cart. Still keeping the vehicle in my line of sight, she walked me slowly towards it. 'Help her lift the shafts right up!' Liz called to Tom, and he ran round the far side and helped his sister push the rough wood poles into an almost upright position. Liz walked me steadily forward, under the shafts, then turned me abruptly.

'Good boy,' she said, 'Stand up, now!' as the youngsters lowered the shafts over my back. There was still a bit of stepping forward and being pushed one step back as they juggled the tugs into place and secured the traces and braker straps, but I tried not to let my nervousness at this new experience bother me too much.

Tom ran back up the field and led Bumper past me towards the gate. Sunny was still tied there, but Blue reached him just ahead of her brother and pulled the rope end to release the knot. Bumper obeyed Tom's 'Whoa', stopping just beyond the gateposts so that Blue could tie Sunny's rope to the spring-hanger on the back of the little wagon.

Birch, who had been quietly browsing the hedgerows while all this was going on, suddenly had a panic attack at the sight of little wagon leaving, and she came belting across the open space where the camp had been, bleating at the top of her voice.

'You're alright!' Tom told her, as she almost collided with the horses' legs going through the gateway, 'You can walk to the end of the track, can't you?'

'Okay, lovely boy,' Liz muttered in my ear, 'Walk on!'

I put my shoulder to the collar, and the traces tightened. The wheels didn't budge.

'Go on!'

I see Bumper's little wagon bounce ahead, off up the track and with a mighty heave, (and maybe a shove from Blue...) we're rolling through the mud and under the trees, through the gap, and up and away. When we reached the entrance to the moor, I could see the back of the wagon tipping and tilting as it hopped and jumped along the boulder-strewn track.

Susie was waiting for us just outside the gateway, pointing the camera she carried around her neck. 'Sssh-click', in my face as we pulled clear of the trees. At that moment, the rain started. A few drops spattered my back, flicked my ears. It very quickly grew into a torrential downpour.

'Talk about the "nick of time", eh?' Liz said to her friend, as they walked at my head. 'We had a hard-enough job getting out of there as it was, any more mud and we'd have been stuck there!'

Turning around, she called back, 'Are you alright, Blue?' but the girl's answer was lost under a crack of thunder, that rolled around the surrounding mountains to echo away in the distance. A sheet of lightening dazzled against the backdrop of dark cloud, followed by another explosion of thunder. Misty gave a low call to reassure her foal as they overtook us. Blue in the saddle struggling to tie the strings of her raincoat hood under her chin with one hand. Head down, I plodded steadily along the track, on the heels of the frantically bleating Birch.

When we reached the road, Tom stopped Bumper, and shoved the poor drenched goat up into the little wagon. Then he hopped up onto the ledge at the front and drove Bumper on at the trot. Blue fell in place behind, perhaps hoping for a bit of shelter. The foal was tucked in between her and Sunny who was still struggling to find a pace that matched Bumper's. Liz made me stop too, so that she and Susie could climb aboard. She allowed me a gentle trot along the road beside the forest, but when we came to the top of the hill, she reined me in, making me walk. A car pushed past us on the first bend, spraying me with water from the road. A short distance further on we met a huge truck making its way up the hill. On the low-loader it carried a monstrous yellow earth-shovelling machine. Liz pulled me over as far as possible, and the great vehicle rumbled past us, shaking the road. The vibration under my bare feet was scary, and Liz kept a firm grip on the reins to stop me bolting. My feet jittered on the spot, and I felt the breeching tighten and the trolley started to sway from side to side as I inadvertently pushed it back up the hill.

'Easy, Sullivan! You're going to have us in the ditch!'

'Will it jack-knife?' her friend asked.

'Looks like we're about to find out!' Liz answered her. She slackened the reins, slapping me on the rump with the wet leather to drive me forward. I walked on and the trolley straightened up in my wake.

Ribbon of houses starting at the last bend of the hill. Some of the people standing in the shelter of their doorways, calling out greetings and good wishes as we pass. Liz answering with a smile on her voice, and a wave of her hand that sends a ripple along the reins. I toss my head, asking permission to trot when I hear Frankie calling from not far away.

'Go on, then!' She gives me slack rein, and I roll into an easy trot on the gentle downhill slope. Tom walking Bumper along the verge, looking for a good place to tie him.

'We camping here?' Liz asks.

'Don't you want to?' his reply.

'What do you think? I've had enough for this day!'

We're already past them, so she directs her next question to the sky,

'Is this rain ever going to let up?'

Susie answers with some proverb about the Irish weather.

Frankie is tied behind the wagons. Liz slows me to a walk and directs me onto the verge. The front wheels follow me onto the grass with a loud clunking noise. The bed of the trolley twists and creaks as the back wheels slowly roll forward. I'm up against the rough stone wall before she turns me to straighten the shafts and line up the wheels.

Then its 'Good boy, Sullivan. Well done!' from Susie, and 'Well, at least he managed to get it here without wrecking it!' from Ben.

'Did you get out before the rain started?' he asked.

'Just!' replied Liz, walking around me to undo the traces and braker straps. Susie was standing in the road, under a bright green umbrella, taking more photographs.

'The thunder was something else, wasn't it? We were just coming out onto the moor when it started. I thought, "oh, no! here we go again!", but he was great, he just ignored it!' Liz slipped the tugs from the shafts, giving me a pat on the rump to signal me to walk on. I stepped forward, and she lowered the shafts to the ground.

'Who's my clever boy?' She came to my head and unbuckled the winkers.

As the bit fell from my mouth I shook the rain from my forelock, showering her face with warm droplets.

'He's a horse, Liz. A pretty stupid one at that..'

'Don't mind him, lovely boy,' she whispered in my ear as she pulled the collar over my head.

'When you've quite finished...' Ben was saying, '...we're not going to be able to get a fire going until this rain lets up, so I'll go into town and get something for dinner, while you get the wagon sorted. Alright?'

'Sure. Where shall I tie this lad?'

'There's plenty of grass back up the road where Bumper is....'

'Great. See you later then!'

Frankie was right about the grass. It was like being turned into a hay-meadow. The seed-heads were sweet and ripe, like fresh grain. The flowers and blades of succulent grass were delicious. After our months on the mountain, coming down to the lakeshore was like entering another country. We had travelled only a few miles, but the difference in the vegetation was unbelievable. Bumper and I were packing it into ourselves when Blue came walking along leading Sunny. She let him go when he called to us, and he trotted the last stretch of road to join us on the lush verge.

'Alright!' the girl sighed, 'Don't go wandering off!' She carried on down to the roadside camp, leaving Sunny with a leading rope still dangling around his neck. Misty was also left untethered, and had crossed the quiet road to find grazing for herself and Little Jake on the narrow verge.

Frankie was on a long running line that stretched along the hedgerow from behind the wagon, almost to the wider section of verge where Bumper and I were tied, and Sunny and Birch were grazing free. He spent the whole wet afternoon working his way gradually along, taking only the choicest feed. The rest of us had slowed down after a couple of hours. Bumper had hollowed out a place for himself under a thorn bush and was lying down to snooze in the relative shelter. Birch was rubbing her horns along his back, making him grunt with pleasure in his half-dream state. I was standing with my back to the road, nose in the bushes enjoying the summer scents. Sunny trotted along to the camp, only to be brought back by Blue, who tied him further down the road. I wasn't at all hungry that evening when Liz brought me a half a bucket of feed. I was glad of the water; in spite of all the wet grass, I was thirsty.

Ben called, 'Did you see this fella, Liz?'

He was offering Frankie a bucket of feed, but any of us could have told him that the big horse had been seriously overdoing the feeding that afternoon.

'What?' she asked, looking over her shoulder. 'What's wrong with him?'

'What do you think?'

Frankie was standing stiffly, with his legs stretched out behind him. He was curling his top lip and making grunting sounds in his throat.

'Ooh-oh, not colic!'

'Looks like it, doesn't it?'

'Send Tom to phone the vet. I'll see how much olive oil we've got...'

She hurried back to the camp, returning a few minutes later with a square sided plastic bottle about half-full of thick green liquid. Tom raced off on his bike. Ben bit the cap off the bottle and spat it into the road. He took the length of clear tube that Liz handed him and gradually inserted it into Frankie's nostril. The pipe disappeared until only the end with the little funnel attached was protruding. Ben began to pour the contents of the bottle slowly into the funnel. Frankie snorted at first, but with Ben's fist holding the other nostril, he had no choice but to submit to this indignity. The man dropped the empty bottle onto the road, and quickly retrieved his length of hose.

'That should help,' he said, pressing his ear against the horse's belly. 'Nothing! Stupid animal must have been packing himself all day!'

'Hey, "he's just a horse...", remember?'

'Oh, don't remind me! This is all I need right now!'

'At least it's stopped raining.' Liz must have been trying to think of something to cheer him up.

'Big deal! At the very least this is going to cost our last twenty quid!'

'Sorry.'

'Yeah, look, you go back to the camp and get a good fire going. I'll have to stay with him, walk him about to stop him rolling till the vet gets here.'

As dusk gathered, sparks flew from the bright fire between the wagons. The vet arrived, not in his familiar white van, but in a big dark car. He was wearing a black suit, a dazzling white shirt, fastened at the neck by a black bow, which he untied as he stepped from the car.

'I'm sorry,' Ben apologised, 'Did we call you away from something important?'

'Ah, don't worry about it, it was some boring "do" up at the Gleneagles!'

'Well, here's the horse. Did the lad tell you on the phone, it looks like colic.'

'I got some message alright. Did you give him anything?'

'He's had half a bottle of virgin olive oil.'

'How big a bottle?' Ben stooped and picked the bottle out of the gutter, showing it to the other man, before handing it to Liz. She took the empty bottle back to the camp with her.

'Half a litre,' said the vet. 'That will have helped a lot. Now I'll just give him the Pethadine shots and he should be alright by morning.'

'Will he be able to work?'

'You'll know yourself. Look I'll leave you another shot, you can give it him first thing if he's not improved. But I shouldn't think he'll need it. Call me in the morning if you're worried.'

'Great. Thanks a lot. Come on back to the camp and I'll settle up with you. Do you want a cup of coffee before you head back?'

'That sounds like an offer I can't refuse.' The vet smiled. 'Do you still have that lovely coffee I had with you last year?'

Frankie had a restless night, moaning and groaning and tossing and turning. Ben was out to visit him at dawn, clearly relieved to see the mound of droppings that Frankie had deposited in the early hours.

'You feeling better for that, big fella?' grinned the man.

'Too right!' replied Frankie, shaking excess rain from his back and tail.

Tom was first out of the wagons, a few hours after daybreak. He coaxed the wet wood into a little fire and went to the house beyond where we were tethered to fill a white plastic water container. On his way up the hill he was swinging the empty barrel over his head, letting it fall behind him on his outstretched arm. Returning, he was leaning to one side to counter-balance the weight of the water, and stop the container dragging along the road. He stopped at Bumper, and poured about a quarter of the water into his bucket. Bumper scrambled to his feet and came out of his hollow in the ditch to wet his lips. Tom put the water container down in the road and carried the bucket over to me. I drank about half of it, then let him take the rest to Frankie, who finished it off. Retrieving the barrel of water, Tom filled the bucket and left Frankie drinking from it, saying, 'This is for our breakfast! If you want any more, tell Ben about it when he gets up!'

The rain still hadn't let up by midday, but we were tacked up anyway, and getting ready to leave when the man from the house along the road arrived at the camp saying, 'We thought you might like these, the weather being so bad, an' all...'

He handed Liz three carrier bags, which she took with a grateful smile. Looking into them briefly before putting them in the wagon, she said. 'Thanks very much, John. I hope that chicken is still hot when we get to the next camp. We'll be ready for it then.'

'My wife baked the soda bread,' the man explained.

'Tell her we appreciate it,' said Liz.

'Well, good luck on your travels!' The man shook hands with Liz, and then with Ben.

'If we had more neighbours like you, that's all the luck we'd need!' Ben told him. 'Luck, yourself, now!'

The man waved to the children as he turned to go back to his house. Blue wore a trinket made of twisted horseshoe nails on a leather thong around her neck, and as the man was leaving Tom snatched it over her head and handed to him, saying 'That's for all the water!'

'But what about your sister?' the man protested.

'That's alright!' Tom assured him. 'I'll make her another one!'

The man dangled the necklace from his hand asking Blue if she minded him having it. She shrugged and waved it away saying, 'You can have it if you want it.' The man slipped it into his pocket, thanking her with a little bow of his head. While all this was going on, Ben had Frankie tacked under the shafts of the big wagon and was ready to roll.

'If you twins are travelling with me, you'd better climb aboard!' he called. 'I'm leaving!'

The two little girls abruptly stopped their waving after the man, and ran down the road. Ben swung them both-at-once into the wagon, shouting to Liz, 'You know how to get to Lissyvigeen?'

'We'll find it!' she replied.

'Take the road off to the right before you get to the town, otherwise...'

'Yeah, yeah, we'll be fine.' She didn't look up from the job of adjusting my crupper. The big wagon bounced onto the road with a clatter and creak of metal and wood. Ben jumped onto the step behind the horse and shook the reins to re-enforce his 'Trot on!' Frankie lumbered into his lollapy trot and the wagon rolled away out of sight round the bend.

Trouble with Sunny.

'Come on, now, Sullivan. No messing about today!' Liz had Blue holding the shafts of the trolley upright, and leading me off the road, she walked me under them, then pushed my rump sideways as the girl lowered them over my back.

'Good boy. You're getting the idea!'

To her daughter she said 'Thanks Blue. I can manage now if you want to help Tom catch Birch, and go get your own horse.'

We set off shortly afterwards, Bumper leading the way. Susie sat on the opposite ledge of the little wagon, talking to Tom. Blue was up on Misty, waving her arms at the foal to try and get him between her and Sunny, who was again tied to the back of the wagon. Even as I was walking the cart onto the road, he was getting under the wheels! Dancing round in circles and generally making a nuisance of himself, I soon realized we were going to have a difficult time of it. In response to Liz's command, I broke into a steady trot, and soon caught up with them.

As we stopped at the first road junction, where the narrow little mountain road joined the lakeshore thoroughfare, Sunny twisted his head free of the halter. Leaving it dangling on the end of the leading rope, he gave a sideways kick and cantered off into the main road traffic. Blue shouted after him, but sensibly didn't pursue him. Bumper moved off the junction, and I followed close behind. All the traffic had ground to a halt anyway, with Sunny dodging in and out amongst them.

'Whoa!'

We pulled over onto the hard shoulder, and Blue dismounted and untied the pony's halter and lead-rope from the spring-hanger. He had somehow got himself trapped in the middle of the road, completely surrounded by stationary vehicles. Still he tried to rear away from her when she approached, his hind legs colliding with the bonnet of a car full of people. Screams from the women in the back seat.

'Sorry!' Blue shouted, slipping the halter back over Sunny's ears. She led him back, and re-mounting Misty she decided to hold onto the rope rather than re-tie it to the wagon.

We carried on a bit further, the cars revving away in both directions. When we passed the car-park opposite the imposing gateway, he saw all the other horses patiently standing under the shafts of their traps and gigs. A grey mare was waiting to pull her laden jaunting-car across the road. The huge continental coach turning in to the car-park held up the oncoming traffic, and her driver used the opportunity to cut across in front of us. Bumper called to her as she moved her load towards the ornate entrance to the parklands. The mare said something back to him before disappearing through the gates.

Tom drove Bumper on to stop him following her. Blue jerked on the lead rope to stop Sunny doing the same, but he was determined to break free again. This time, he spun around and catching her by surprise, he ran behind her, snatching the rope from her hand as she tumbled into the road. A car that was overtaking us sounded his horn as he swerved out to avoid running over the girl. Sunny was away down the drive in pursuit of the mare. Blue picked herself up and ran after him. Liz jumped down from the trolley, holding my reins in one hand and catching hold of Misty's reins with the other. She steered us both in to the wide entrance to the gate, the foal staying close to his mare. Once off the road, she pulled me to a halt.

Blue went running after the pony, but a man in a grey suit hurried from his little wooden hut inside the gate and grabbed her by the arm.

'You can't come in here...' he was saying.

'But that's my horse!' she wailed, pointing after the fast-retreating Sunny. Still the man kept his grip on her, determined not to allow her into the park. Tom and Bumper were rolling on down the main road, oblivious to all this. I called to Bumper, 'Hey, wait for us!' and he heard me over the traffic noise and answered. His reply must have alerted Tom, who looked back to see us parked in the gateway. Adding to the confusion, he stopped the cars and coaches in both directions while he did a U-turn in the road to come back and help his sister. Parking his little wagon alongside the trolley, he effectively blocked all access to the gateway, so that horses wanting to come out or go in had to wait, causing a three-horse queue on the inside of the gate. Out on the road, a trap-full of tourists found themselves stuck across the white line. A few cars managed to inch past them, but the first coach that came along was forced to stop. It wasn't long before the stationary traffic started to make impatient honking noises.

Liz shouted at the man on the gate,

'Are you going to let her get the horse back, or what?'

Looking around at the confusion, he eventually released the girl's arm, and she ran off along the drive. The grey mare had stopped when Sunny had galloped in front of her, and she was standing quietly while her driver attempted to drive the silly young horse off with his whip. Sunny was enjoying his freedom, running around on the mown grass, kicking his heels and shouting. Blue reached him and made a grab for his rope, but he reared up and lashed out at her, his front hoof connecting with the middle of her face. Her hands went instinctively to her nose, and she fell on the grass. A woman climbed down from the jaunting-car and bent over the girl, offering her white tissues from her handbag, which turned instantly red with the blood now gushing from Blue's nose.

Tom was off the step of his wagon in an instant. Tossing the reins to Susie, he said 'Stand up!' to Bumper and went running along the drive after his sister. The grey-suit shouted something after him, but his words were lost under the cacophony of motor horns. The boy raced up to the horse, snatching the rope from the air and jerking his head down. He landed a punch clean on the end of the horse's nose, shaking his hand from the wrist afterwards. Sunny swayed backwards, rolling his head. The shocked onlookers murmured amongst themselves.

Still holding the lead-rope, Tom walked over to his sister, who was being helped to her feet by the woman. They exchanged a few words before he led her away. The woman climbed back aboard the car, and the driver started the grey mare at a walk. The eyes of all the passengers were fixed on the two young people leading the subdued horse back to the gate.

'Do you want me to tie him on the back of the wagon?' Tom asked Liz.

'You could try, I suppose...'

With his lead rope fastened to the inside spring of the wagon, Sunny was obliged to stay close to the back wall. Swerving sideways, he mounted the pavement, but was pulled back by the short tether. Still groggy from his punch of the nose, he started off obediently enough.

'Are you alright?' Liz gave the girl a hug, and helped her back into the saddle.

'It feels like he broke my nose again,' she replied, more sad than complaining.

Bumper moved the wagon back onto the road, the cart which had been causing the traffic jam pulled forward, and I turned the shafts of the four-wheeler to pull out after the wagon. The coach rolled forward, the cars quietened down as they started to move again.

Our side of the road was empty at first, but it wasn't long before we were past the back-log of vehicles on the other side, and the overtaking started. Sunny had been trotting along as though he knew what he was doing, but when the cars started cutting in behind him, he started to panic, and kept trying to get onto the pavement to avoid them. Stepping sideways, he managed to slip the top-strap of his halter over one ear. With a shake of his head he was free again, tossing his mane and laughing his squeaky little whinny. He was up on the empty pavement, leaving his halter trailing in the gutter. At first he just kept pace with me, prancing along, proud of himself.

'Just leave him!' Liz said to her daughter. 'He'll be alright!'

Apart from scattering a group of back-packers walking along the footpath, he was keeping up well.

The big two-horse bus was a grand sight coming down the road towards us. Full of passengers enjoying their ride in a bit of shelter from the incessant drizzle, the big bay horses were making light work of pulling the vehicle along the level stretch of road. Sunny heard the double click of their hooves ringing on the wet road, and was instantly alert. He squealed at the horses, who were far too busy about their work to even acknowledge him. This only made him more insistent, and he stopped in his tracks to watch as they passed me on the other side of the road. Then he was over the road and jogging along with them in the opposite direction.

'Stop! stop!' I heard Blue shouting, as Liz 'whoa-d' me to a standstill again. The girl jumped into the road and went running back after him again. She must have been quite a sight herself with the drying blood all over her face.

Bumper was stopped again, and Tom stepped into the road, ready to help again if necessary.

This time, the girl managed to catch the pony and slip a noose of rope over his neck. Tom went round the back of the wagon and untied the rope with the halter still attached.

'When did he do this?' he asked Liz.

'A while back. He was trotting along alright till just now.'

We waited till Blue got back, walking along the middle of the road, annoying the motorists, who sounded their horns at her. Tom put the halter back on Sunny, asking her what she wanted to do now.

'I'll hold him again,' she replied.

So we set off again. Sunny was on the inside, trotting along the pavement, with Blue holding his rope, dragging him on, jerking him back. I realized after a while that he really wasn't able to keep our steady pace. He hadn't learnt to trot properly. He could keep it up for a while, then he'd lose it, and fall back to a walk, or break into a canter.

Nearer the town, the footpath was being used by more people, so Blue pulled Sunny into the gutter. This was fine until we came to the start of the parked cars. Although Liz had steered me out to the middle of the road and there was room for him to trot along beside the cars, he took fright again, and once more we were obliged to stop. Blue dismounted again, and slid the stirrups under the skirts of the saddle. Giving Misty a pat on the neck, she murmured something in the little mare's ear before looping the reins through the spring hanger of the wagon. She scrambled up beside Liz, and clambered over the load to sit on the back of the trolley, so that she could still hold the horse while he followed behind. I was really getting the hang of stopping and starting the new four wheeler by this time. The momentary lag between leaning into the collar and the wheels starting to roll was a bit disconcerting at first, but I had the feel of it now, and moving off was a much smoother operation.

We turned off to the right just before we reached the town. On the narrower road, with less traffic, we kept up a steady pace. Coming to a narrow bridge over a wide river, Liz held me back until Bumper and Misty reached the other side. Apart from Little Jake stopping in the middle of the bridge to poke his head through the metal railings, they crossed the river without incident. While we were waiting, she called back to her daughter, 'You'd better get off and lead him across, Blue!'

'Alright.'

The trolley gave a creak as she jumped off the back. Then it was 'Walk on, Sullivan. Easy, now!' Liz kept a tight rein on my mouth at the start of the bridge. It was barely wide enough for the wheels of the trolley. The wooden planks vibrated under my bare feet, sending shivers up my legs. The hard rubber tyres thrummed over the bridge, making the whole structure shudder. At the far side, Bumper stood patiently waiting for us. Liz breathed a sigh of relief when the wheels were back on the solid tarmac.

She shouted back, 'Come on, then!' and I could hear Blue's voice over the babble of the shallow water.

After a few minutes her plaintive cry, 'He won't go!' Tom was down from the wagon again, his shoes making a hollow sound as he ran back over the bridge. I could hear him shouting at the horse, slapping him, trying to drive him over the bridge, but I didn't hear the sound of hooves on wood. Instead, a splash and Blue's squeal as they drove him through the water. Scrambling up the gravel bank alongside the bridge, Tom pulled the horse after him. Turning to look at his sister dragging her feet clear of the water he said 'You know your face is covered in blood?'

'Shut up!' she snapped. 'So would yours be if you'd been kicked in the nose by a horse.'

But she bent down and splashed the river water over her face, rinsing away some of the dried blood.

'Is that better?' she directed her question at Liz.

'Your nose looks pretty swollen. How does it feel?'

'Feels like it's broken. What do you think it feels like!'

'Sorry,' said her mother. 'Come on, get back on the cart. It can't be much further to this camp. I hope Ben has a good fire going, to get you dried out.'

Lissyvigeen

We could see the blaze as we rounded a bend in the wide road and started to climb the steady incline. Frankie called to us from a verge elevated above road-level. Bumper answered enthusiastically, but I was feeling too footsore and weary after all the stopping and starting, and just mumbled how glad I felt to be nearing the end of this day's work. The rain had finally eased off after we crossed the bridge, and late afternoon sun filtered through the branches of overhanging trees as we made our steady progress along the quiet road. We had passed a string of cottages coming up to a T-junction where we turned left, joining a main road. We stepped out into bright sunshine, a light mist rising from the black surface, while rivulets of rainwater still gurgled along the gutters.

'What took you so long?' Ben greeted us.

Then, noticing his daughter's blood-smeared face and hands, 'What happened to you, Bluebird?'

'What do you think?' She climbed off the back of the cart and Liz walked me off the road into the lay-by tucked behind a crescent of grass.

'I don't know, tell me!' her father persisted.

'Oh, it's a long story, I'll tell you after,' the girl called back from the other side of the road where she was scrambling up the raised verge to tie Sunny to the concrete fence alongside Frankie. Tom had Bumper out of harness, standing patiently, shaking dust and moisture from his mane and tail, while he untied the mare and took off the saddle. Blue took it from him, offering to take Misty, but Tom led them away from the camp to find grazing.

Liz started to untack me, asking Ben, 'Are you ready to shoe him straight away?'

'I'd like to know what happened to Blue!'

'Is the kettle on?' Liz evaded his question, 'I'll tell you over a cup of tea!'

'I'll make it!' Susie volunteered, opening the wooden box Liz had been using as a seat, and taking out a tin which rattled when she shook it. 'This tea?'

'Nice one, Missy!' Liz smiled at her friend, leading me over to the patch of cut grass beside the road.

'Now you just stay here till we've had a cuppa, melad, and then Ben's gonna sort your feet out.'

She uncoiled my tether chain and rope back across the lay-by, behind the wagons and tied the end to a thorn tree growing out of the old stone wall. I was left to pick at the sweet new growth while the family all sat around Ben's roaring fire to recount the adventures of our day's travelling.

When they dispersed to go about the various camp-jobs, I noticed that the fire was also heating a set of shoes. Ben strapped on his leather apron, and while Blue had a hot wash from a bucket of water behind the big wagon, I lifted my weary feet one at a time, and let Ben burn the glowing irons onto my hooves. Then the nailing-on, and the final rasp-over with the file. Tom painted the resiny brown liquid over my hooves before hopping up onto my back and trotting me along the length of the lay-by, and back.

'He's picking them up, lovely!' Ben pronounced his satisfaction with the job. 'Take him over and tie him with the others, son!'

'Bring his rope, Blue?' Tom asked his sister, who was sitting by the fire rubbing her long yellow hair with a towel.

'Aww...' she began, but Liz said, 'It's alright, you dry your hair, I'll get it for him.' And she left Susie scrubbing the vegetables to bring my tether across the road.

Another hazy start to the day, after a dry night. Ben took his bike and headed back towards the town, leaving the women and children to clean up the camp after breakfast. When the wagons were packed and the trolley loaded, they all came across the road. Tom and Blue were carrying short lengths of rope, which they attached to mine and Bumpers' halters. Tom threw himself across my back, leg over, ready to go.

'Who's gonna ride with me?' he asked, and both the little twins shouted, 'Me! Me!' and jumped up and down on the spot, waving their arms in the air.

'Okay, Ellie-May, you ride with Blue. Eve, give me your hand, here.'

He reached down and pulled his little sister up to sit in front of him. I could feel her skinny legs on either side of my neck, her heels kicking excitedly.

'Don't kick him, Eve!' Tom was saying. 'We're not ready to go yet!'

He looked over his shoulder, resting a hand on my rump.

'You alright, now?' he called to the other girls. Liz was lifting the other twin up and putting her in front of Blue on Bumper's back. The girl was talking to her little sister as they settled themselves.

'Doing anything with you folks is like NATO troop manoeuvres!' Smiled Susie.

'Tell me about it...' replied Liz. 'You all set? Come on then, these stones have been waiting a few thousand years for us to visit them; let's not keep them waiting much longer!'

Tom gave me a light dig in the ribs, and I followed behind the two women who had set off walking along the verge. Birch, who had been tied overnight on her chain, bleated that she wanted to come with us. Pip, who was also put on a chain and left under the big wagon, also gave a high pitched whine that said he'd like to join the expedition.

'Lie down!' Liz shouted at him. 'On guard!'

To Susie she smiled, 'One of these days!'

We turned right and found ourselves twisting along a narrow lane which soon became a steep uphill climb.

'Lean forward...' I heard Tom instruct his sister. Her hot little hands tightened their grip on my mane. The protruding nails of my new shoes gave good grip on the hill, I didn't slip at all. Another right turn brought us to a rocky track, snaking up between overgrown hedges. A tall iron gate, with a cottage gable-end facing the track. Liz pushed it open, flattening the long grass on the other side. We followed her through into the yard, and round the back of the cottage. A farm-gate with its top bar wound around with barbed wire blocked our access out of the yard, but Liz untied the baler-twine and lifted it out of the way.

A short distance over a sloping field brought us to a thicket of old trees, gnarled and wind beaten. Two sentinel stones stood watch at the outer edge. Liz and Susie walked between them, and Bumper and I followed, although we could as easily have walked on either side of them. The space between them was just wide enough for us to pass through without our riders' legs hitting the stones.

Beyond, a rough circle of smaller stones nestled amongst the trees. The grass was dark, and rich with flowers and aromatic wild herbs. I took a mouthful as Liz reached up to lift the little girl from my neck. Tom threw his leg over my head and slid to the ground with a light jump. Susie took her camera out of its case and started to click the shutter, persuading everyone to sit on the stones. The heavy mist became a light drizzle, then a few heavier drops started to find their way through the trees.

'We'd better head back.' Liz suggested.

A dark green van was parked beside the wagon. We could see it as we walked back down the hill.

'Great!' Liz tutted, 'Some guard dog that Pip! Here, Eve, jump down, and let Tom go see what they want.'

She lifted the girl off my back, and Tom gave me a dig to hurry me back to the camp. We cantered along the lay-by, scattering gravel when he pulled me up short in front of the fire.

Ben grinned at him, 'Alright, son? I got a lift back with these lads. Tea or coffee?' he asked the three men sitting on the far side of the fire. I was still standing where Tom had left me when the others arrived back a few minutes later.

'Good news!' Ben called to Liz, before she reached the fire. 'Tim and Becket left Cork yesterday, pulling for Caramee. These fellas saw them heading out of town. And there's a card from Becket I got in the post office. Here. It's for you.'

'What does it say?'

'Here, read it yourself!' He handed her the square of bright coloured paper.

'What does it say?' echoed all the children.

Liz read the card to them, 'It says, "See you at Caramee fair 12th of July. See you there. You better had be there". We'll be there, honey!' she finished.

The men drank their tea and left in their van. Then we were tacked up and walked out of the lay-by. Trotting along the main road, Sunny was keeping up well, he really seemed to be getting the hang of it. Half an hour down the road, Ben was resting Frankie, so we pulled in behind to get our breath back too. Liz realized that she had forgotten to collect my tether chain from verge at the last camp and Tom was dispatched on his bike to go back for it.

'See if you can find my pen-knife, too!' Blue called after him. He disappeared with a wave of his hand, and I relaxed in the shafts to await his return. The rain had let up, and only occasional scudding clouds marred the bright blue sky. The hedgerow smelt delicious with the warmth of the afternoon evaporating the moisture from the grass. I nibbled at the seed-heads, not really hungry. Tom arrived back with a skid of brakes, a spray of loose chippings. He tossed the chain onto the back of the trolley, handed Blue her knife. She gave him a quick kiss on the cheek, almost pulling him off the bike.

'Thanks!' she put the knife into her jacket pocket and climbed back into the saddle.

'All set?' Ben called, leaning around the side of the big wagon to see if Tom had managed to load his bike. The boy called back, 'Roll!' and we set off again. Sunny started to stumble just before we reached the next town. We all stopped, Ben lifted the horse's feet, conferring with Blue. When we set off this time, we left Susie and the girl to walk along the verge with Sunny, who was too footsore to keep up his trot. We stopped in the town, parking amongst the cars at the kerb side. Ben got his bike out of the wagon, saying to Liz, 'I'll go see if I can get a field to put him in.'

'Any luck?' she asked when he got back.

'No chance, Kerry Buffers!' he sneered. 'Anyway, I managed to tie some leather boots on him, should get him to the next camp.'

The next camp was a few miles beyond the town, a high meadow of roadside verge perched above road level and reached by a narrow path. From here we looked down on the wagons parked beside the wide bend in the road. A neat white cottage with a tidy garden sat at one end of the camp. I saw Liz and Tom trundle the metal water churns along the road, and clang them through the narrow gate. The old man in his garden greeted them warmly, indicating the tap on the wall of the cottage where they could get water. By the time the churns were full he had picked two carrier bags full of vegetables which he handed to Tom as they were leaving.

Ben shod Sunny the next morning. It was another wet start to the day, so he didn't bother to heat the shoes in the fire and burn them on, just nailed them on cold. Still raining when we started off, but after a few miles it passed over and we did most of our travelling in the glorious afternoon sun. The heat of it drying my back felt good. Sunny in his new shoes ringing the tarmac in time to my own trot.

That evening we pulled off the road, to make camp on a half-circle verge opposite a big old farm-house. The dogs came out snapping at our heels until the woman called them in. She seemed very friendly, showing Liz and Ben where they could get water and wood. We were all tied along the concrete fence that separated the weedy rough grass of the verge from the new-cut field. It wasn't the best of grazing, but the road was quiet, and it was only for one night.

The last few miles.

Early start next morning. Sun already beating down by mid-morning, we were soaked in our own sweat after a few miles, but it was better than the rain. After a couple of hours of steady pulling, we stopped off at a cross-roads. Parking the vehicles in a pot-holed lay-by, we were untacked and tied in a boggy patch of roadside scrub to cool off and pick what grazing we could. Liz lit a stick fire beside the trolley and filled her kettle from the plastic water barrel she had brought along with her. Ben went off on his bike. As soon as he'd gone a car stopped, and a woman and a young man got out. She started by asking Liz how long she was intending to stay here. Liz replied that she was just making a cup of tea and waiting for her husband to get back from the village, but the woman interrupted her saying the wagons would have to be moved as she had 'a permit' to sell strawberries there. Liz offers to move the trolley forward so that the woman will have room to park her car. Not good enough. The woman wants to know,

'When, exactly, are you moving from here?'

'What?' Liz is starting to get angry at this. 'Exactly! It might be a couple of hours, depending on how far we have to travel from here,' she explains.

'Two hours! That's too much!'

'Tell that to the horses, missis!'

'I'll tell the gards...'

'Tell it to the Cruelty as well!' Tom chimes in, and she looks at him as though he had given her a mouthful of abuse. Slamming of car doors, revving off down the road. The kettle was just coming to the boil when Ben arrived back, a smile on his face.

'Great camp just down the road!' he called.

'Nice one,' Liz replied, seriously, 'We'll probably have the gards here in a few minutes. Are you ready for this cup of tea. I know I am.'

'Why? What happened?'

She told him while they drank their tea. Then they quickly packed everything away into the box, and we were tacked up again.

The camp was outside a big modern factory. Great swathes of lawn for the children to run barefoot over. On the roadside the uncut grass was rich with clover and mustard. In the evening, a damping of rain washes the day's dust and sweat from our backs. A narrow little overgrown path runs alongside the factory fence and we are turned loose to forage for the night. Tom and Ben push the little wagon across the entrance to stop us wandering onto the road.

A long pull next morning, up and down. Frankie was resting on a triangle of grass at a junction when we rounded a bend in the road. We parked up and were taken out of the shafts for a lunch break. Ben was talking to an old man from one of the nearby houses when we were ready to leave, so he suggested that Liz and Tom drive on ahead and he would catch up.

Bumper went ahead, setting the steady pace that Sunny, Misty and I could keep up with. We turned right at a crossroads. A big blue statue set in a kind of paved garden, hemmed in by a low wire fence, looked out over the road. Narrower then, the hill became steep for a while, slowing us to a walk. We rested for a few minutes at the top, then pushed on down the other side. Some bad bends on the way down. Bumper was trotting on; the breeching was digging into my rump, propelling me forward. Liz was holding firm on the reins, but letting me trot, sweat streaming, heart pounding as we twisted and turned between the high hedges.

Long grass hid the deep ditches on either side. Tom's little wagon swayed and bounced in and out of the pot-holes. I heard Liz shout, at the same time as she pulled hard on my mouth, steering me out to the right, trying to stop me. The little wagon had left the road on the bend, rolling almost in slow-motion it seemed, onto its side. Bumper was foundering in the water-filled ditch as we overtook him before I managed to stop the trolley. I caught a glimpse of Susie tumbling off the inside ledge, landing behind him in the water. A few minutes later she was standing at my head, trying to calm me down. Pond-weed dripped from her bedraggled blonde curls, her hands were caked with brown mud. Liz ran back to help Tom get Bumper out of the shafts.

'You hurt, pal?' I called to him, as Tom led him past me and left him to forage in the hedgerow. He was soaked in ditch-water up to his chest. His harness seemed to have survived more-or-less intact. He wasn't wearing his winkers. Brave little horse, he just shook his mane, and laughed off the potential disaster, 'Could have been worse!' Tom echoed the sentiment to Susie on his way back.

'Will you be able to fix the shaft?' she asked him.

'No way!' he replied. 'Have to get a new one.'

'Where from?'

Tom looked up at the hedgerows on both sides of the narrow lane. Shrugging his shoulders, he grinned at Liz, 'Do you have the bow-saw, or are we going to have to wait for Ben?'

He set off down the road with the saw over his shoulder, just as we heard Frankie coming over the top of the hill. The big horse called out to us, and Bumper answered. Ben's voice yelling, 'What happened? Is the horse alright? Where's Tom?'

Liz calling back, as he reined Frankie in alongside me, 'He's broken a shaft, Tom's gone to get another one! Bumper's alright, just snapped a buckle on his winkers. Have you got the sewing gear handy?'

A car coming up the hill had to stop to allow Frankie to pull in front of me. A man leaned out of his window to ask, 'Do you need a hand?'

He got out of the car, and helped Ben pull the little wagon back onto the road. Liz and the girls must have been pushing, I could hear Ben shouting instructions and encouragement to them. The man drove off as Tom was walking back up the hill with the trunk of a young ash tree balanced on his shoulder. He had already cut off all the branches. Bumper, Birch and Sunny were grazing up and down the hedgerow while the new shaft was being fitted, but Frankie and I were left standing in the shafts, tormented by horse-flies in the heat of the afternoon. Misty swished her heavy tail around her foal as he took the opportunity to suckle, disregarding the saddle.

When we set off again Frankie took the lead, walking us steadily down the rest of the hill. About half a mile along the road, near the bottom of the hill, we pulled into the concrete yard of a derelict warehouse. It was good to get out of the harness. We were all turned into a weedy overgrown plot round the back of the building, while Liz filled the water barrel from a rusty tap on the wall. A fire was soon lit, and a meal prepared. We were given buckets of water once we'd cooled down. It tasted really sweet, none of the chemical aftertaste that some of the water in the towns carried. I drank a bucket and a half straight down.

The children found an old plastic bath in the corner of the yard, and soon had it filled with water. They took off all their clothes and jumped in the water, paddling and splashing to cool themselves down. Liz called 'Come on, you lot! Have a proper wash and come get something to eat!' The squeals and shrieks of pleasure turned to protests as Blue poured buckets of water over the heads of her little sisters.

After their meal, Ben and Tom filled more buckets and gave Bumper and Frankie a wash down. Bumper needed it after going into the ditch. Ben said he just wanted Frankie looking his best before they pulled onto the fair. Blue scrubbed the mud from Bumper's harness and left it spread along the low wall to dry. Liz and Susie were busy washing dishes and tidying up the camp while all this was going on.

'Are you going to wash your lad?' Ben asked her, when he'd finished brushing the excess water from Frankie's hairy legs.

'You can if you like!' she called back.

He carried a bucket of water over to me and quickly drenched my back with it. The cold shock made me jump, and spin around to lash a kick with my back legs. Ben side-stepped to avoid getting hit, but he got the message. 'Sod this!' he shouted to Liz. 'He's your horse. If you want him washed, you do it!'

She just laughed and finished stacking the plates in the box.

While Ben was washing himself, she climbed over the wall with the brushes and ran them through the water, washing away the sweat marks from my back. She spent some time tugging at my mane and tail, and trying to get the tangles out of the hair on my legs, but to little effect.

'I'm glad I'm not trying to sell you, Sullivan,' she told me.

'So am I,' I replied.

The sun was at our backs when we trotted the last few miles to the town that evening. Coming over the last rise, we could see the steeples and rooftops nestling in the valley below. The road in front of us was blocked by a crowd of people making their slow procession out of the town. They were still a fair distance off when I felt the reverberation under my feet. It was like the road was being pounded with a lump hammer. Only each strike felt much nearer than the one before. Frankie gave a call of alarm, a split-second before a metal ball bounced past his head. It barely missed the wheels of the big wagon before the camber of the road pulled it into the ditch. I side-stepped, unnecessarily, but taken by surprise.

Liz said, 'Easy, boy, don't mind 'em,' but she whipped me on with the rein-ends to get me past the fright. Soon we were forced to stop by the crush of people blocking the road. We were surrounded by men of all ages, some of them clearly knew Ben, calling him by name, reaching up to slap his hand as he bent from his standing position on the shafts of the wagon.

'Ye made it, boy!' one of them saluted him.

'We surely did!' he agreed. 'Tell me, are Tim and Becket here yet?'

'Just pulled onto the field about an hour ago! Are ye pulling on tonight?'

'We might just camp under the auld railway bridge tonight, and pull onto the field for the fair tomorrow,' Ben told him.

To another man he called, 'Good game?'

'Are ye betting?' The man wanted to know.

'I've no money!' claimed Ben.

'Would you bet the horse?' shouted another.

'If you'd give me a grand against him!' countered Ben.

'See Johnny Riley, he's taking the bets!' someone pointed to the back of the crowd. They milled about us, some reaching out to touch me as they passed.

After the men came a mixed group of young people, with a few older women and the occasional baby in a push-chair. The women chatted amongst themselves, obviously enjoying the walk, regardless of the outcome of the game with the ball that was being played along the road.

They stopped to watch us pass, encouraging the children to look at us, to wave their little hands.

As soon as we were untacked and tied on the wide verge under the railway embankment, Liz and Ben left Susie and the children to light a fire and cook their meal. They sauntered off arm in arm, disappearing from sight under the iron bridge that spanned the road. It was almost dark when they returned.

Liz brought me a bucket of water before, saying, 'Well, we made it, Sullivan. Caramee Fair tomorrow. You did well, my lovely boy.' She patted me on the nose, then as I straightened up from drinking she slipped her arms around my neck so that my chin rested on her shoulder. She hugged me tight, and I rubbed my jaw up and down her arm.

'I love you,' she whispered in my ear. 'Thank you!'

Caramee Fair

Smell was the first sense to be assailed.

The smell of horses reached us as we crested the rise and began our steady descent to the town. The side-street was already crowded with parked vehicles. Horses stood with their heads hung low over the gutters. Men loitered in doorways, seeking what shelter they could find. Low-loaders with gigs and traps still tied down. Some horses still in the boxes, resigned to the rain by this time.

We had trotted the short distance from the railway bridge to the town, which was readying itself for the fair-day trading. Stalls set up along the pavements were being stacked from the backs of vans. The rain continued to pour down. At the end of the street of bright shops, beyond the garages, a field where caravans clustered around the muddy gateway. Liz turned me in, following the others. Frankie was tossing his head, and doing his best to prance through the mud behind the trailers, calling to the horses in the field.

Horses. More than I'd ever seen in one place. Horses of every shape and size. Every imaginable type and colour. Piebalds and Skewbalds, mares and foals. Colts and stallions strutting and shouting, fighting and calling for the attention of the fillies. The sight and sound of them confirmed everything the smell had conveyed. Here were horses from all over the country, all together here, an unlikely herd. Young horses terrified by the stallions, foals under the constant protection of the mares. Colts having to prove themselves amongst strangers. Fillies lashing kicks at all and sundry.

The mud dragged my feet, but I kept up a semblance of a trot until we pulled clear, then I was high-stepping across the rough grass towards a circle of wagons that had their backs turned to the gate, and the rest of the field. Ben steered Frankie round the edge of them, and brought him to a standstill facing a clearing with a big fire smouldering in its centre. Liz stopped me alongside. Men were at my head before she was off the cart.

'Are ye selling, Missus, ye are?'

'Not this one!' she was replying, but it didn't stop them grabbing my nose, forcing my lips apart and looking at my teeth.

Becket was helping Ben get his wagon into a good position in the wagon circle, but she strode over to give Liz a hug, while the men stood around, puffing on their damp cigarettes, and discussing my age.

'You made it!' said the girl.

'At last! Where's my new grandson?'

'He's asleep in the wagon. Come on, get this horse untacked and we'll have a drink!'

Liz carried my harness into the big wagon, and gave me a slap on the rump.

'Enjoy the fair, boy!' she said to me.

I shifted my weight uneasily in the mud, wondering if I dared venture into another part of the field. Frankie was tied behind the wagon, on a long rope that reached to the bank of the river. I stayed close to him at first, watching the men and boys riding their horses through the water, soaping manes and tails, and rinsing away the suds with buckets of water ladled from the river.

Tom and Blue were standing on the bank with a group of other kids. They were throwing sticks into the river for Pip to retrieve. He was leaping into the water with a splash of no regrets and swimming around collecting as many sticks as he could hold in his mouth. He'd let them all float away when his mouth got too full, and go chasing after a new one. Every so often, he'd find one that he considered worth returning and he'd swim ashore and drop it at Tom's feet, barking and bouncing towards the river, asking to have it thrown again.

The rain had eased off and patches of blue began to appear amongst the clouds. Bumper suggested we go and meet the other horses. Sunny had already disappeared, so we decided to go look for him.

Away from the caravans, the different groups of horses were playing out their parts. Herd affinities were changing the whole time, as new horses were being introduced, and leaders being taken away. Foals newly-separated from mares were suffering the pain and indignity of rejection. Stroppy colts were making life miserable for all the others. Most of the stallions were tied on secure ropes and chains, but the colts that were running free constantly challenged them, taunting from a safe distance. Men with sticks would run down the field to drive some colt away from their mares or fillies. I stayed close to Bumper, as we made our round.

We found Sunny, ingratiating himself to a very self-contained little group of about twenty animals who had found a small paddock adjoining the main field. A big spotted mare seemed to be the matriarch of the herd. There were two stallions; a stocky little piebald cob, and a long-legged black trotter. I recognised his voice. It was Lightning, the horse I'd met on the bog-lane last year. Relieved to see that he was securely tied, we ventured through the gap in the fence and introduced ourselves to some of the others.

We were still there later when Liz came looking for me. The sun was trying bravely to put on a show for the afternoon. Dark clouds still hung over the river, but the rooftops were glistening as the weak shafts of sunlight filtered through.

With Becket walking beside her, Liz was carrying a bundle in her arms. I strolled over to meet her, see what she was carrying. In amongst the soft wrappings of loosely knitted blanket was a tiny baby. She let me sniff the bundle, sweet and milky, saying, 'This is Erik. Careful with him, he's a bit fragile! You'll have to get used to a baby, Sullivan, there's gonna be a new one in our camp before next year.'

Then she handed the bundle to Becket, and catching hold of my halter, said, 'Come on then, let's show you to the town!'

Liz slipped a riding bridle off her shoulder and put the bit in my mouth. She led me to the gap in the fence and used a concrete post to help herself scramble up onto my back.

'Be a good boy, now!' she implored me.

'Or I'll be riding you next!' threatened Becket.

'You look after me then,' I said, glancing sideways at the big black horse, who was shouting as we walked by. Becket was amongst the horses, collecting empty water buckets.

'Can you manage?' Liz called.

The girl just grinned at her. 'I'm only watering Patches, the rest of them can do their own!'

'See you later, then!'

Liz walked me back past the chrome and white caravans, towards the muddy main entrance to the field. Out on the road, the traffic was at a standstill. Vehicles parked on both sides of the narrow street were adding to the congestion, but what was really holding up the flow of traffic was the almost solid mass of horses and people milling up and down. Apart from the ranks of animals lining the pavements, everything from the proudest hunter to the lowliest ass, there were other riders pushing a way through the crowd. Horses in harness, some just standing, showing off a newly-painted trap, others under the spindly shafts of a trotting-sulkie, high-spirited, looking for a gap in the traffic to show a burst of speed.

Working our way slowly through the throng, we eventually reached the big grey church. Cars and lorries were inching their way by, fewer horses at this end of the town. Men and women spilling out of pub doorways, or trying to argue their way in. A clear plastic box almost the size of a small trailer was parked on the pavement in front of the church. It was lit all around with different coloured light-bulbs. Inside, a jumble of fluffy teddy-bears. People stood on all four sides. They seemed to be manipulating some kind of mechanical arms inside the machine which grabbed the little toys and dropped them into chutes at each corner. A woman or child was there to catch the prize before it tumbled onto the road.

Liz walked me around the machine, onto the pavement, just as one man started to punch the clear plastic wall with his fist. The woman with him was tugging at his arm, begging him to stop. The lights flickered, but didn't go out when the man gave the box a kick on one corner. Two men in dark blue uniforms pulled their peaked caps down and rushed along the pavement. They pushed people out of the way in their hurry to reach the man who by this time was shaking the teddy-bear machine, trying to tip it over.

With a grip on each arm, they pulled him away, out into the street, scattering the crowd. Traffic once again ground to a complete standstill while the gards did their best to restrain the man. He was struggling to get his arms free, kicking the air and shouting at the top of his voice. His woman was wailing and moaning. Hearing the commotion, other men pushed their way through the crowd. Banging on pub windows brought yet more of them out onto the street. The man was still putting up a fight when his friends and relations arrived to 'rescue' him.

A big hefty man swung a punch at one of the gards, catching him full-face and knocking him to the ground. With his newly-freed arm, the man hit out at the gard still clinging to his other side. The gard ducked to avoid the flying fist, but lost his grip on the man. The other uniform was picking himself up off the road, talking all the time into a small black box clipped to his lapel. The crowd watching the fracas let the first man slip amongst them, and he made straight for the door of the pub across the street.

The gards pushed after him, and once again were trying to arrest him. He was shouting at the top of his voice, calling to someone in the pub. The big man who had hit the gard was behind them again, kicking shins and punching wildly. The first man was on the ground with one of the gards securing his wrists behind his back with a strip of white tape. The other gard, a bloody gash under his eye, turned on the big man, pointing an accusing finger and defending himself from further blows. We stood alongside the church railings, watching all this. We see a knot of dark blue pushing its way through the crowd on the street.

A shout of 'Shades!' and men tumbling out of the pub doorway. The man who had started all the commotion was being steered through the crowd by his arresting officer when the main fight broke out. Men with quantities of drink taken spilled out across the pavement and tried to stop the man being hauled off. They were stopped in turn by the newly-arrived contingent of gards. Tempers flaring, fists flying. A bottle sailed past my head and smashed against the railings.

Liz turned me around saying, 'Let's get out of here!'

She headed me back along the almost deserted path behind the stalls, until we were well-clear of the fight. We met a friend of Liz's just before we got back to the camp-field. He was leading a sturdy black cob under the shafts of a roughly-built two-wheeled flat cart.

'New horse, Chris?' she called.

'Just dealt him for my old mare,' the man replied.

'The mare you wanted to swap my trolley for?'

'Yeah.'

'Carol won't be best pleased!'

'Tell me about it....' Then, 'What do you think of him, then? Would you take this outfit for your trolley?'

'Don't know about that,' she sighed, 'What's he like?'

'He's sound-out. Look, I just got him, okay, I haven't even tried him yet. You want to come with me and see how he goes?'

'Yeah, why not? I'll just take this lad back to the camp...'

'Alright. I'll wait for you at the bridge.'

Liz trotted me back through the mud, shouted her intentions to Ben and passed the reins over to Tom who leapt onto my back. One of the lads he'd been talking to made a grab for my tail but Tom gave me a dig in the ribs and had me galloping away down the field leaving them to run after us. Having the boy on my back gave me the confidence to gallop amongst the other horses. They cleared a way for us, foals scattering back to their mothers' side. Puffing from the exertion of galloping across the mud, we arrived back at the little paddock and Tom jumped off my back and took the bridle from me. I stepped lightly through the other horses to where Bumper and Sunny were grazing quietly.

'I'm having a great time!' I called. 'How about yous?'

Sunny had been kicked in the chest by a filly he'd been pestering, so he wasn't too happy. Bumper had been grooming with one of the old mares, so he was feeling well-content. Misty and her foal were in amongst the herd, already accepted.

A colt from another herd had been around chasing the mares all day, and he put in another appearance just after I got back. Lightning was furious to be tethered, rearing and screaming on the end of his chain. The man Tim arrived to bring water to his horses, and seeing the colt pestering his spotty mare, put the buckets down and went to wave his arms at it. The colt turned on him, tossing mane and jeering at the man. Barging him out of the way and turning his attention to Lightning, the young horse was shouting

'What you gonna do about it?'

Tim was at the end of his horse's rope, untying it from the concrete post. Lightning was still prancing to and fro, but not at the end of his chain. He knew what was happening, and was biding his time. When Tim finally had the knots undone and was starting to gather the rope into loose coils, the big black horse went trotting proudly towards the colt who was chasing a foal terrified at being separated from its mare.

Tim looked up, calling 'Stand up, Lightning!' but the horse ignored him. The man made no attempt to grab the rope as it snaked away from him. The colt never knew what hit him. The big horse reared and kicked out with his front legs, landing two mighty blows on the colt's rump. He rolled over sideways as the back legs buckled under him. Lightning trampled him on the ribs as he lay on the wet ground, groaning and yelling. The black horse spun around and lashed a backwards kick that bowled the colt over again when he tried to get up.

Tim caught hold of the chain around Lightning's neck, pulling him around, saying, 'Enough! Easy now!' and leading him away, to tie him further along the fence. Still shrieking his stallion-cry, the big horse pranced along with the man. The colt picked himself up, painfully, and limped away, glancing over his shoulder.

A steady stream of vehicles making their way out of town, horse-boxes towed behind every kind of car and van. Cattle boxes on the backs of lorries. Horses going back where they came from, horses going to new places.

Liz brought the little black cob over to meet me.

'Here ya go, Sullivan. Another new boy in the family. This lad's your half-brother, so the man tells me. We'll call him the Boy for now, what do you think?'

I thought he seemed like a quiet and sensible animal. When Liz had gone we got to know each other through a mutual grooming session. He carried the smell of other horses, the herd he had recently left. He had spent most of the day in harness and was tired and hungry, but he was an uncomplaining sort of horse.

As evening closed in, the rain moved back. Dark clouds carried the first few heavy drops of a shower that had us all drenched again, and the hollows in the mud were soon brimful. We moved in to the shelter of a high wall that skirted one edge of the little paddock, and hung our heads between our legs.

Late on, Ben and Liz came around to check us before settling down for the night. They were stumbling through the mud, falling against each other. He was singing and saluting everyone they passed as they made their way across the field. She was laughing, clinging on to his arm. The entrance to the paddock was chewed-up even worse than the rest of the field. The rain which had been falling steadily for the past few hours had reduced the gap to a quagmire. Liz was refusing to cross the knee-deep mud, saying she'd climb the fence further along, but Ben was saying, 'Come on, get on my back, I'll carry you!'

She squealed and resisted at first, tumbling sideways almost dragging both of them down. He caught her and pulled her to her feet before lifting her clumsily onto his back. Ben made a rush through the mud, hoping to get through quickly, but the squelchy ground caught his boots and after the first few steps, he was bogged down with Liz's weight. The two of them were laughing and shouting. A group of men making their way back to their caravans slowed down to watch and shout encouragement to Ben. A few more strides and they were on wet grass again. He tilted sideways, dropping Liz unsteadily on her feet beside him. Arm in arm, they did their round of the horses.

In the early hours of the next morning, one of the mares gave birth to her foal. With the rain still beating down, she lay on the cold ground and the foal emerged feet-first into the grey dawn. He lay still for a while, a broken string of flesh hanging limp from his belly. The mare got to her feet and nuzzled him all over, pushing at him with her nose, even giving him gentle prods with her hoof to get him to stand. After a couple of attempts, he eventually staggered to his feet, legs splayed out to balance himself. He was an almost-white foal, with skewbald patches. A distinctive brown blaze crossed his face diagonally.

The first people to see him that morning were Blue and Becket. Coming to check us first thing, the girls rushed over to make sure the foal was alright. He was still smeared with blood from his birthing. Blue tried to catch hold of him, but he had been on his feet for over an hour by that time, and knew that he must stay close to his mare. The little bay cob was determined to keep herself between her foal and any danger, real or imagined. The sisters circled around for a closer look at the new-born.

'Is it a filly?' asked Blue.

'Nah! Just an aul' colt!' replied Becket. 'He's nice though....'

Full light dawned with no sign of a sunrise. The rain continued.

Susie looked over the fence on her way out to the road. She was carrying a backpack in addition to her usual camera-bag. She gave a little wave of her hand, calling out,

'See you all again one of these days!'

We were the first horses to leave the wagon circle that day. Frankie stampeded through the mud, the big wagon on its new rubber tyres floating along behind him. He made it look effortless. I followed, under the shafts of the two-wheeler I'd seen behind the Boy the day before. He and Sunny were both tied on the back, flanking Misty and her foal. Bumper followed, the little wagon bouncing over the ruts. The street of the little town looked deserted, after the fair. A few skeletal stalls were being dismantled. The gutters were awash with litter of all kinds. In the middle of town we turned right again and made our way back to the railway bridge. After leaving the wagons at the roadside, we were led up a narrow path to a level stretch of embankment alongside the track. The grazing was varied, scrubby inedible ragweed vying for space with delicious cow-parsley, and every kind of meadow flower and grass.

'Make the most of it, Sullivan,' Liz said. 'There'll be lots of others here in the next day or so!'

I watched her scramble down the bank, slipping on the wet grass. Bumper was rolling over and over, kicking his legs in the air. Beyond the hedgerow where the others were feeding, the landscape of patchwork farmland flowed to the foothills of the distant mountains. Light and shadow alternated over the land as clouds raced across the sun.

Behind the wagons on the wide verge, the sky was illuminated by the full arc of a brilliant rainbow.

Epilogue

In case you're wondering 'What Sullivan Did Next', his story has a happy ending.

After travelling with the family for over three years (during which time some of the adventures recorded here occurred, along with many more...) he was sold to a jarvey in Killarney who worked him for over twenty years. If you visited that town during the 90s or 'noughties' you may well have been lucky enough to ride the four-wheeled carriage he proudly pulled along the lakeshore.

When he grew too old to work, he lived out his days in retirement, no doubt enjoying the easy life under many a rainbow.

Lightning Source UK Ltd.
Milton Keynes UK
UKOW03f0747070317
296007UK00002B/202/P

9 781524 67771